Rib of Atom:
C18H10N2O4

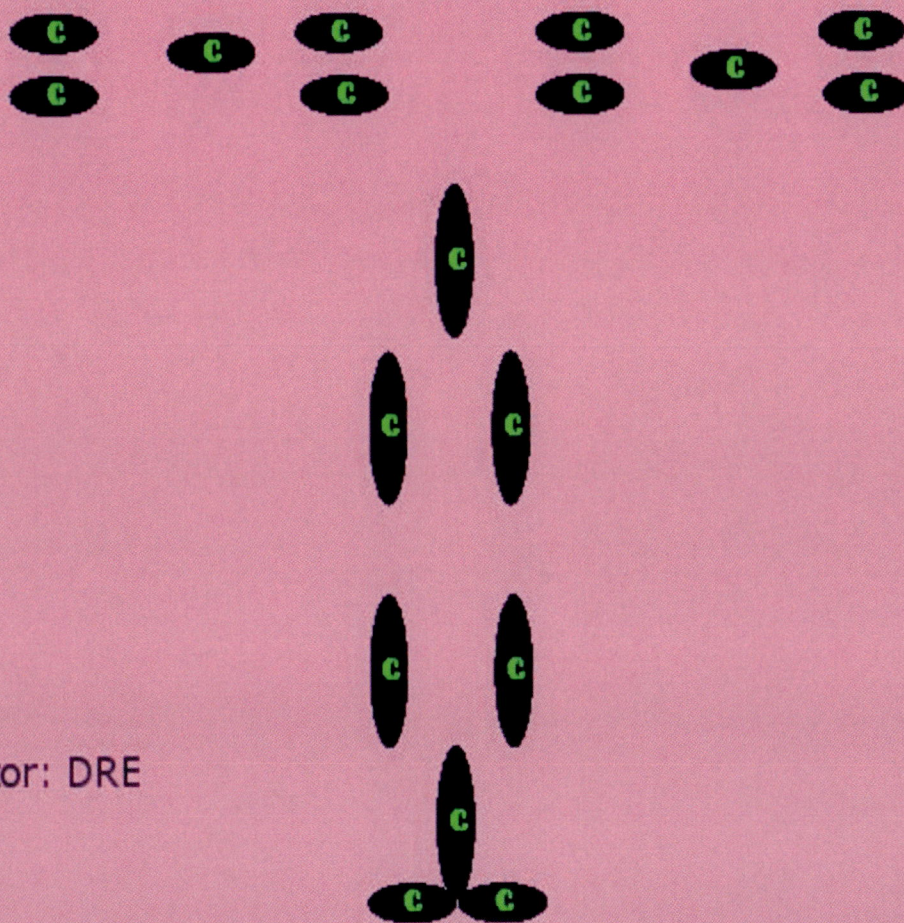

Auctor: DRE

1

This unique art-work was made using the melanin molecule:

Carbon 18

Hydrogen 10

Nitrogen 2

Oxygen 4

Rib of Atom:

Melanin

Molecule

C18H10N2O4

Ribd = de Rib©

Adam and Eve

C18H10N2O4

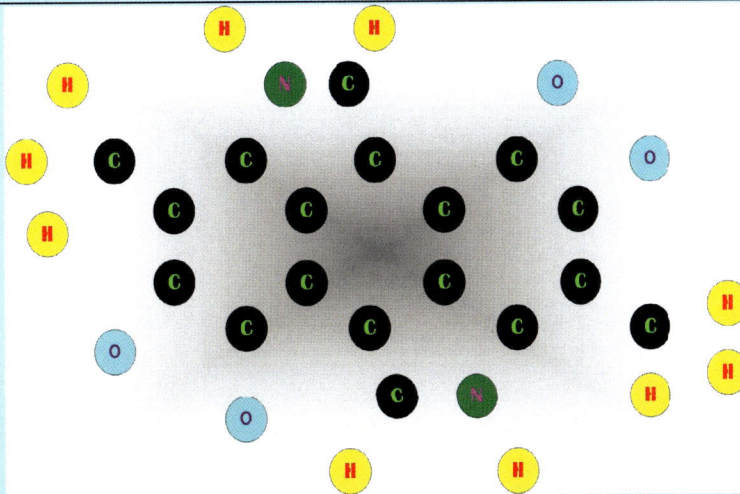

Rjbd = O Rib

C18H10N2O4

C18H10N2O4

18=R, 10=i, 2=b, 4=de

RIB of ATOM

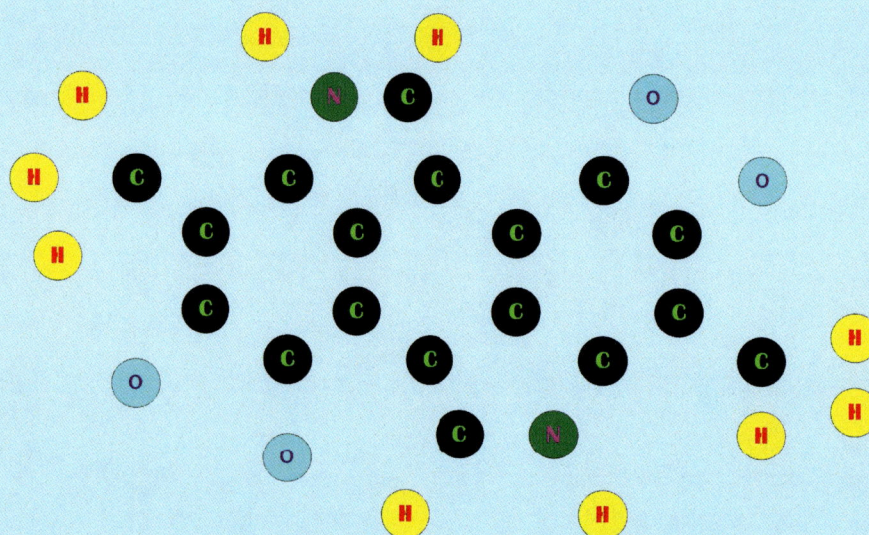

Ri(j)bd = of or from Rib

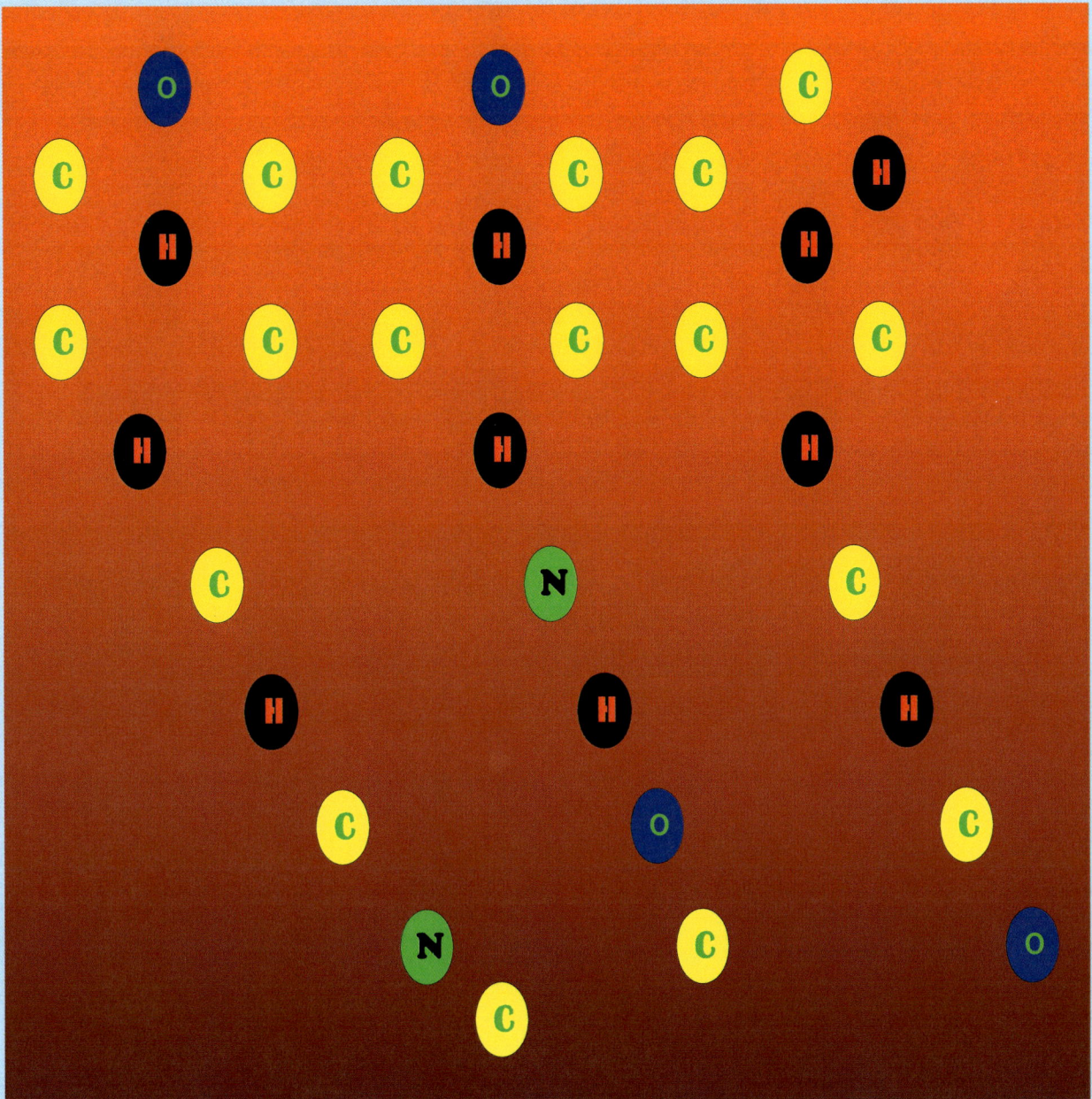

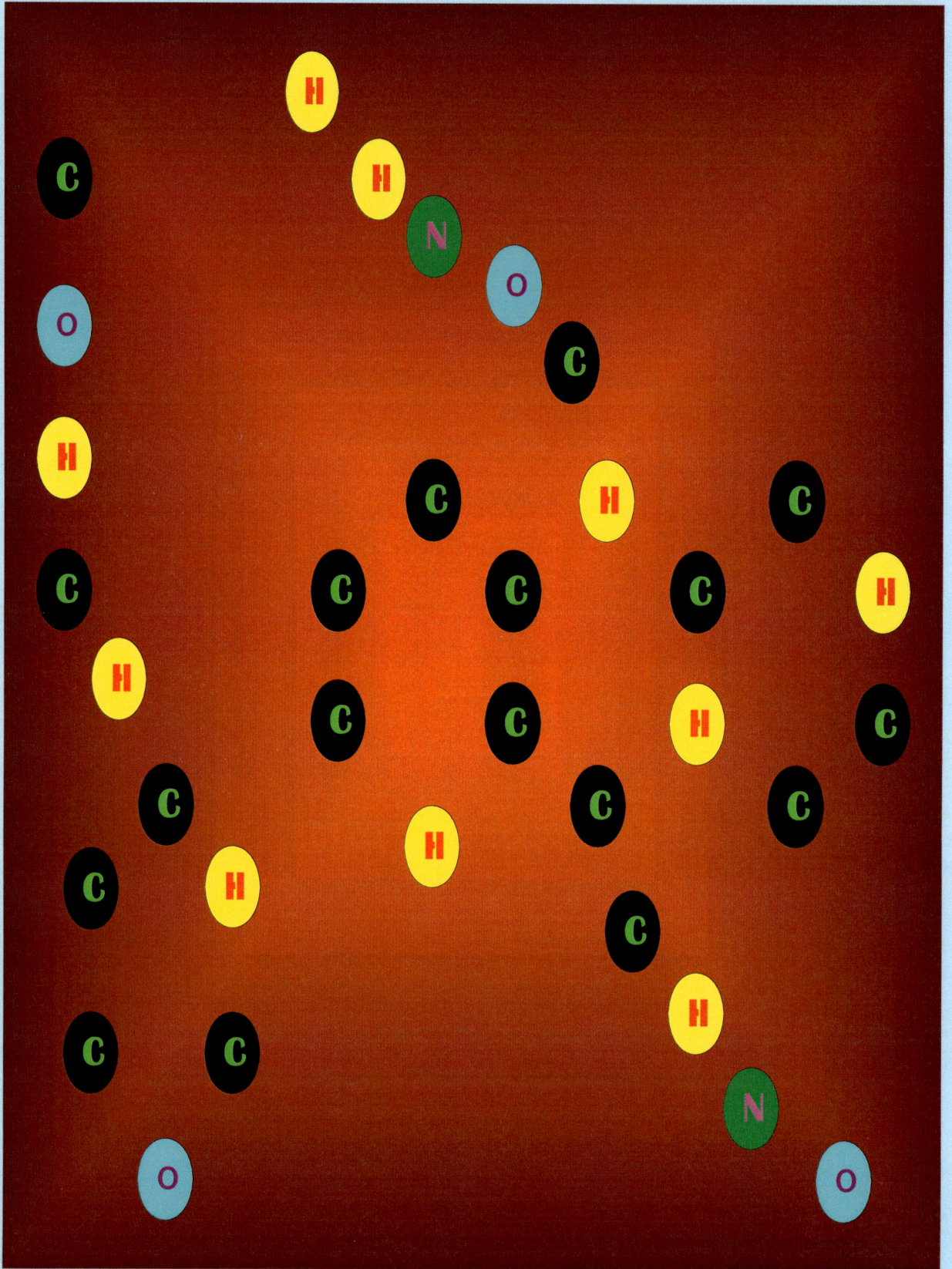

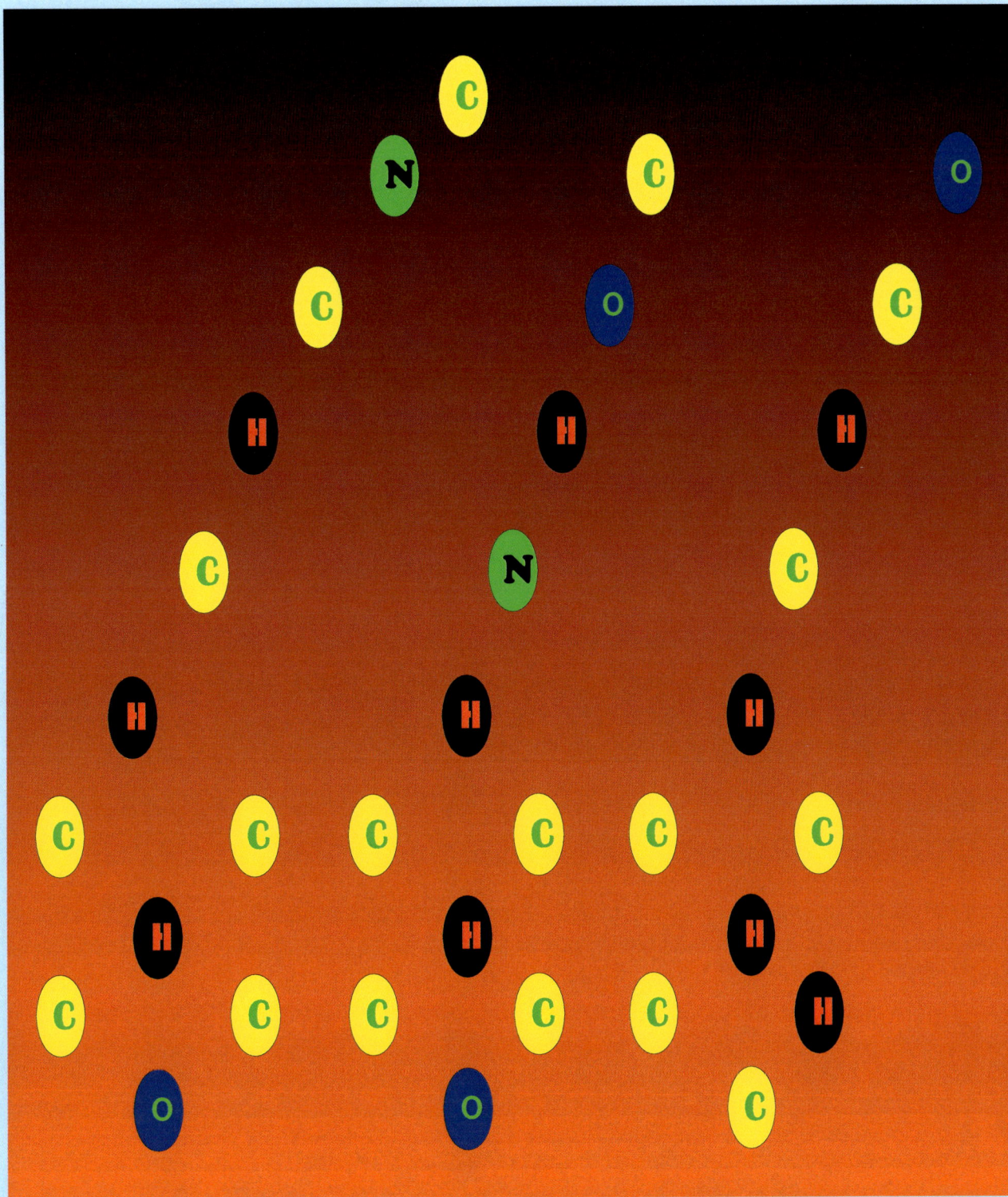

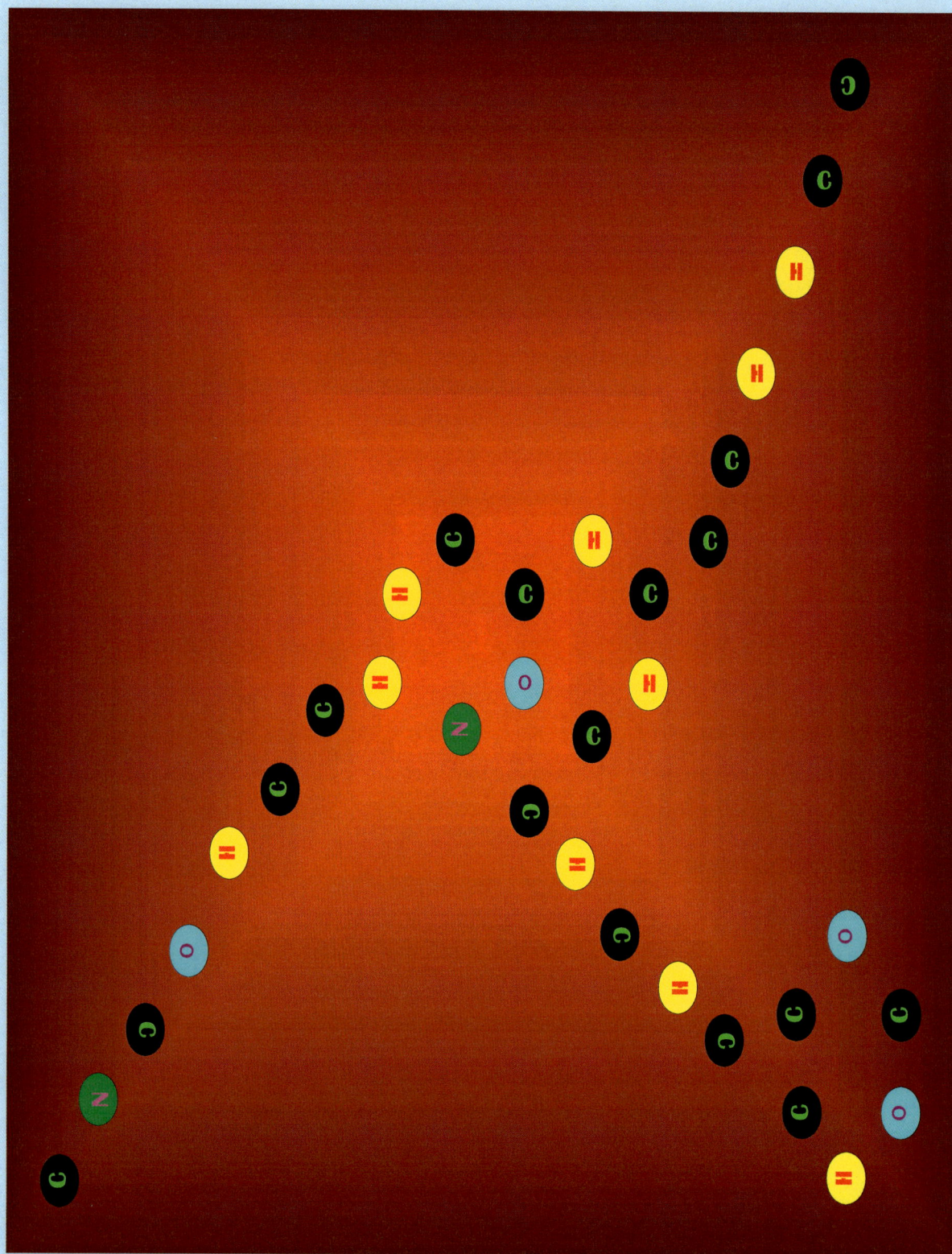

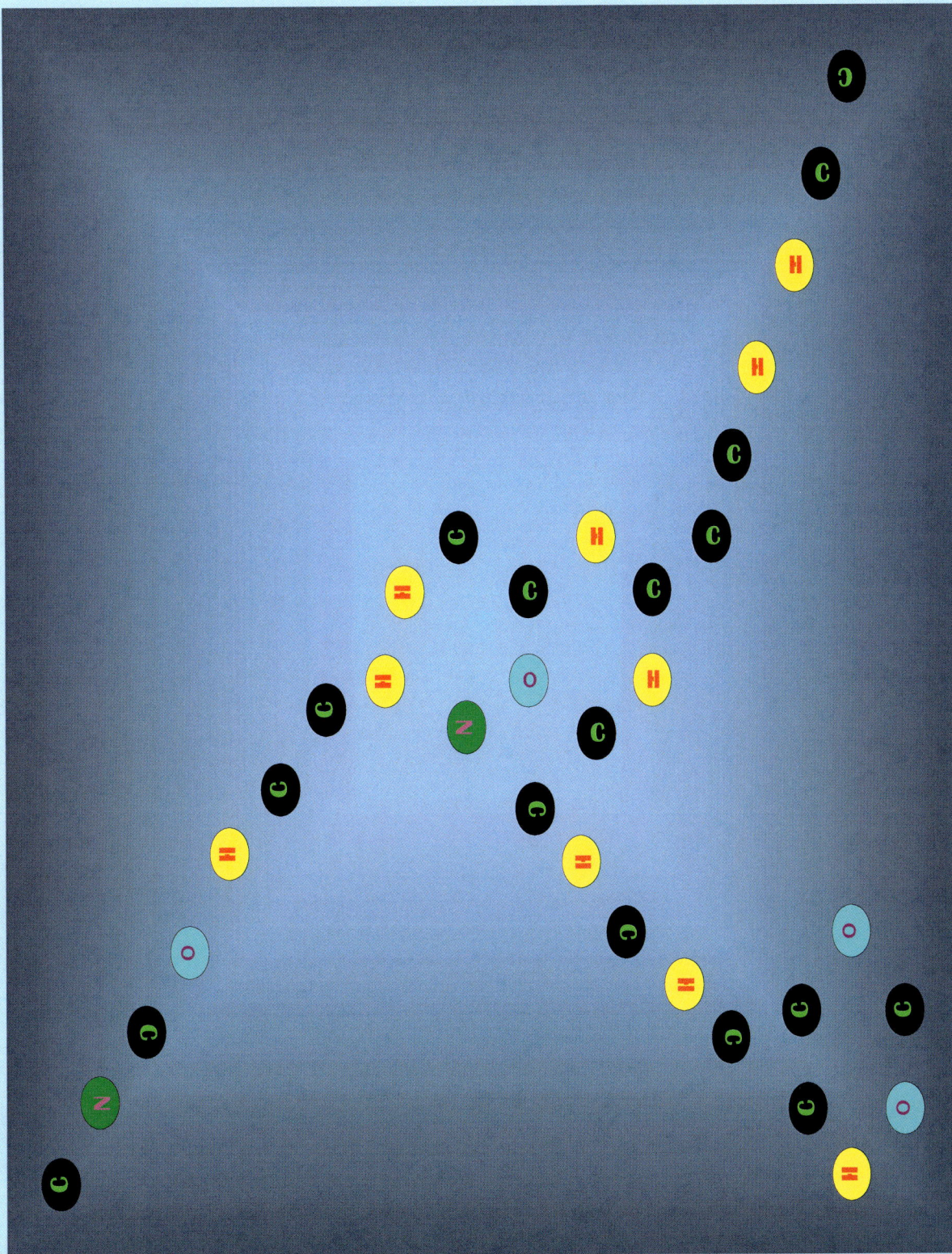

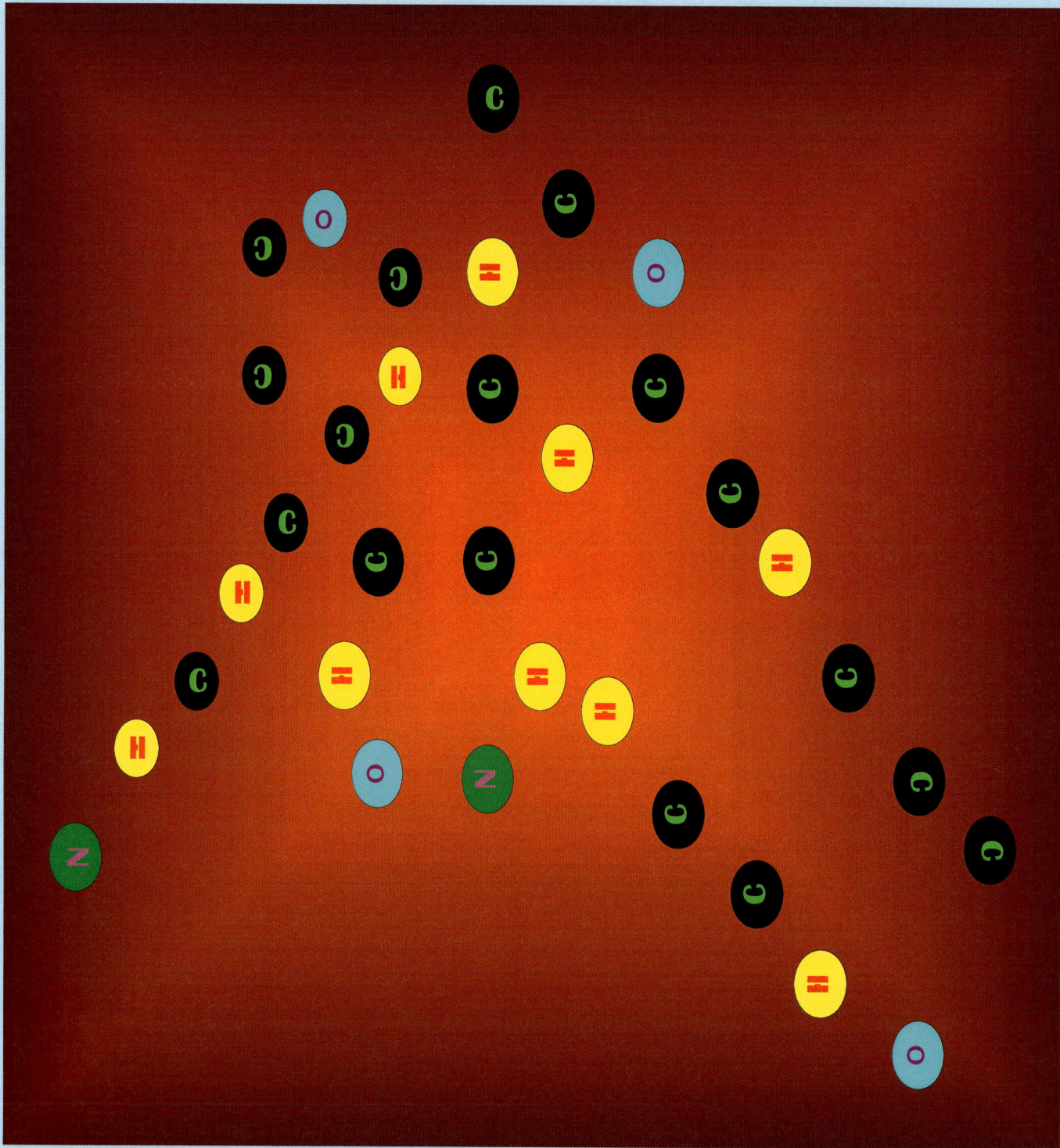

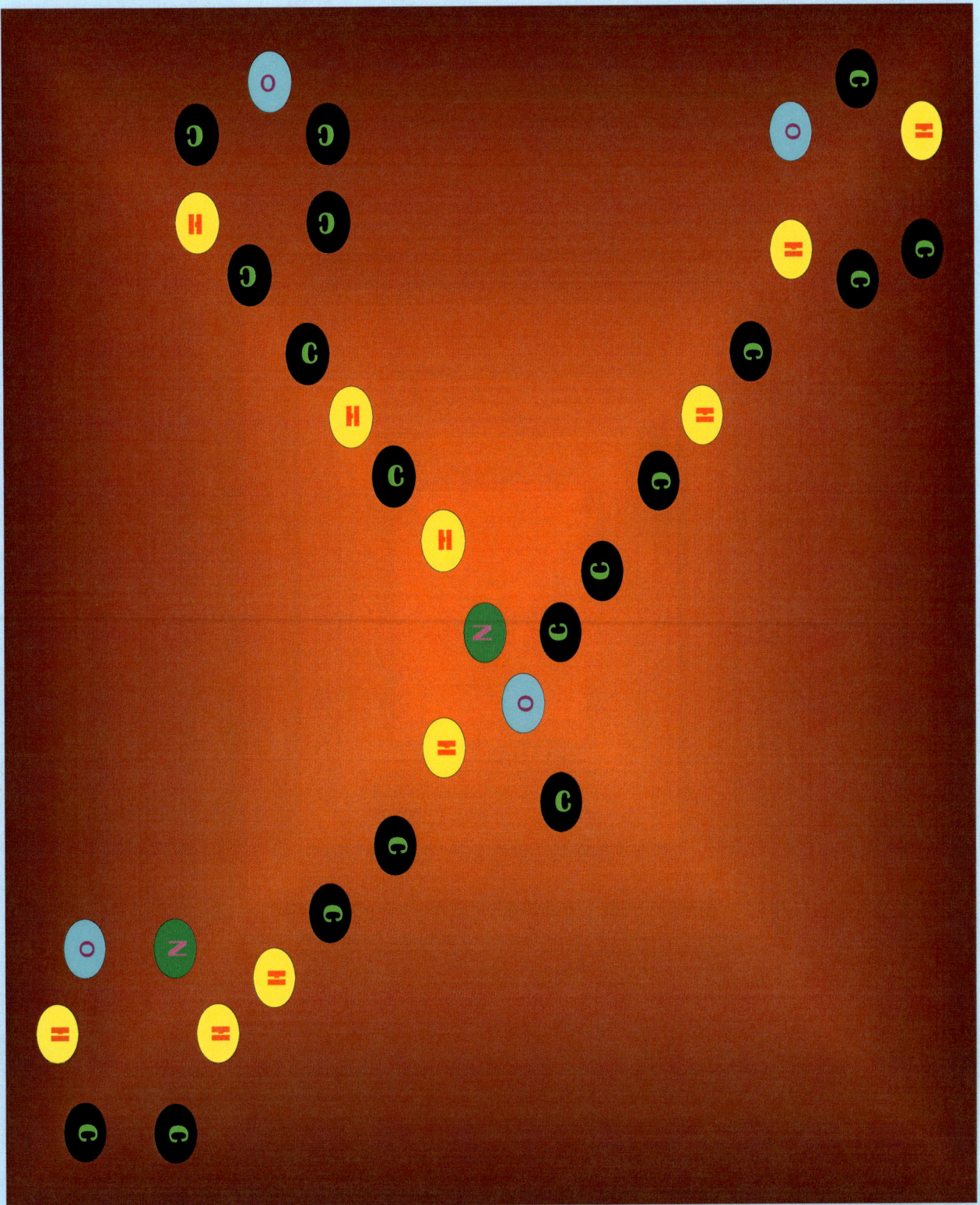

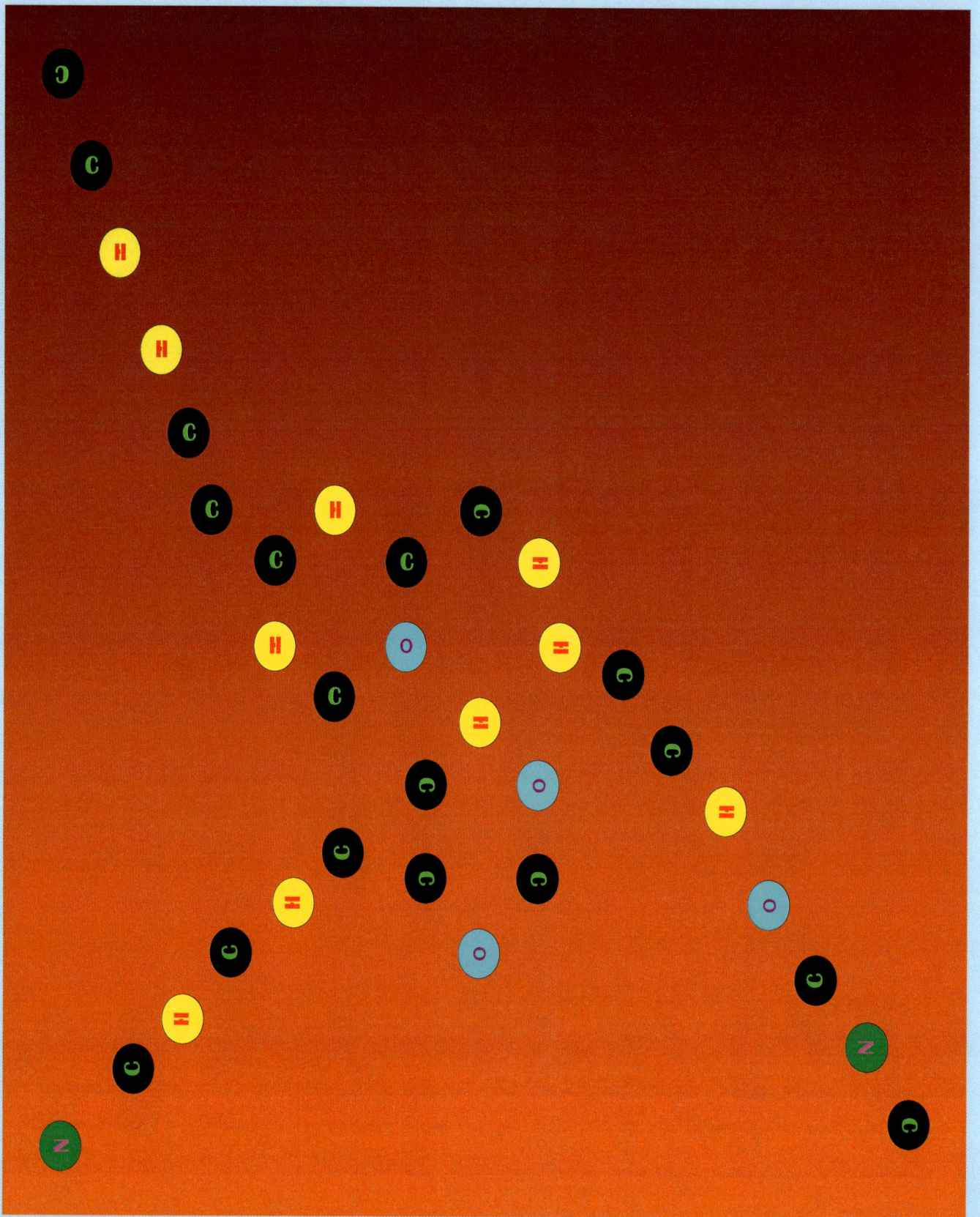

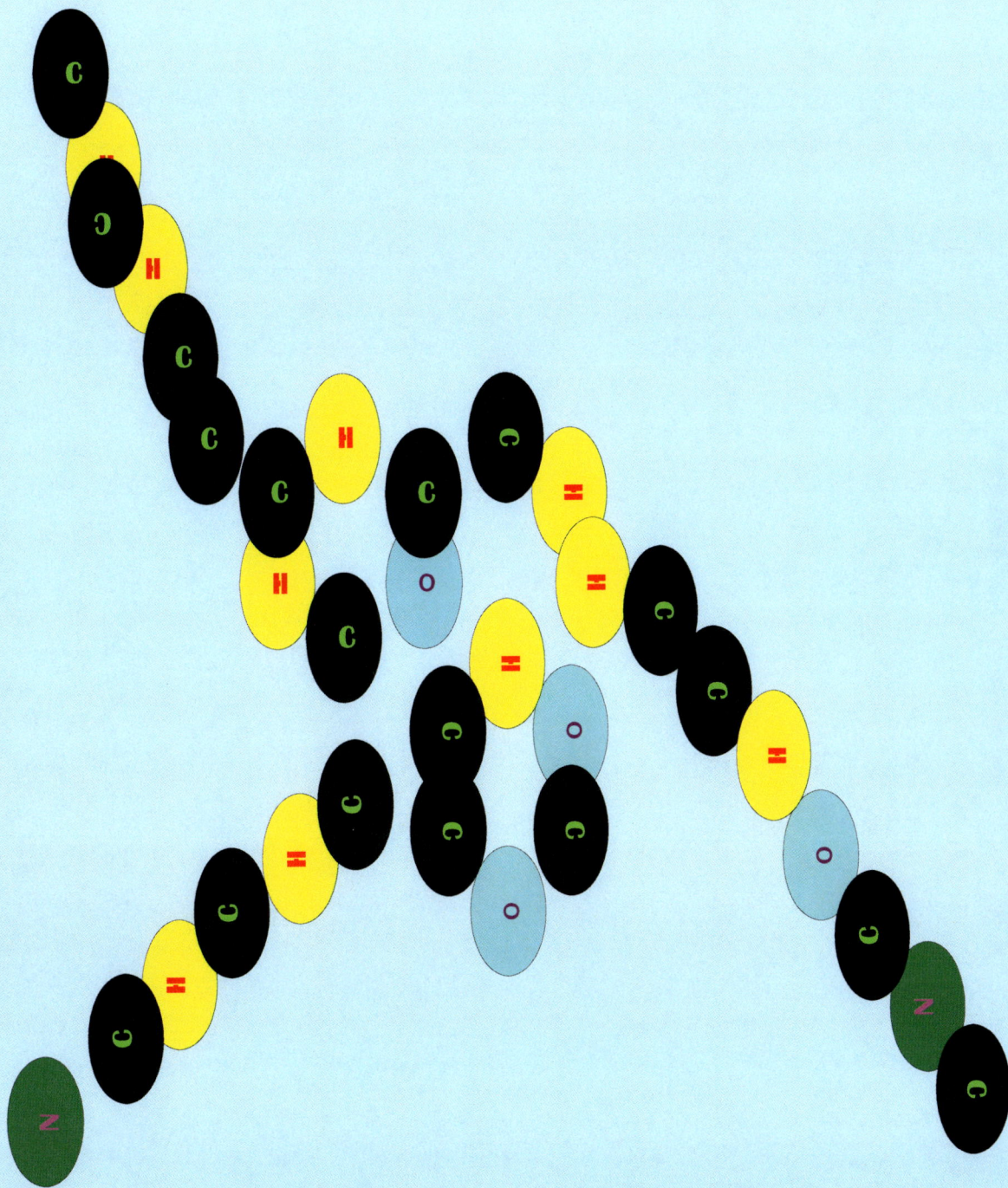

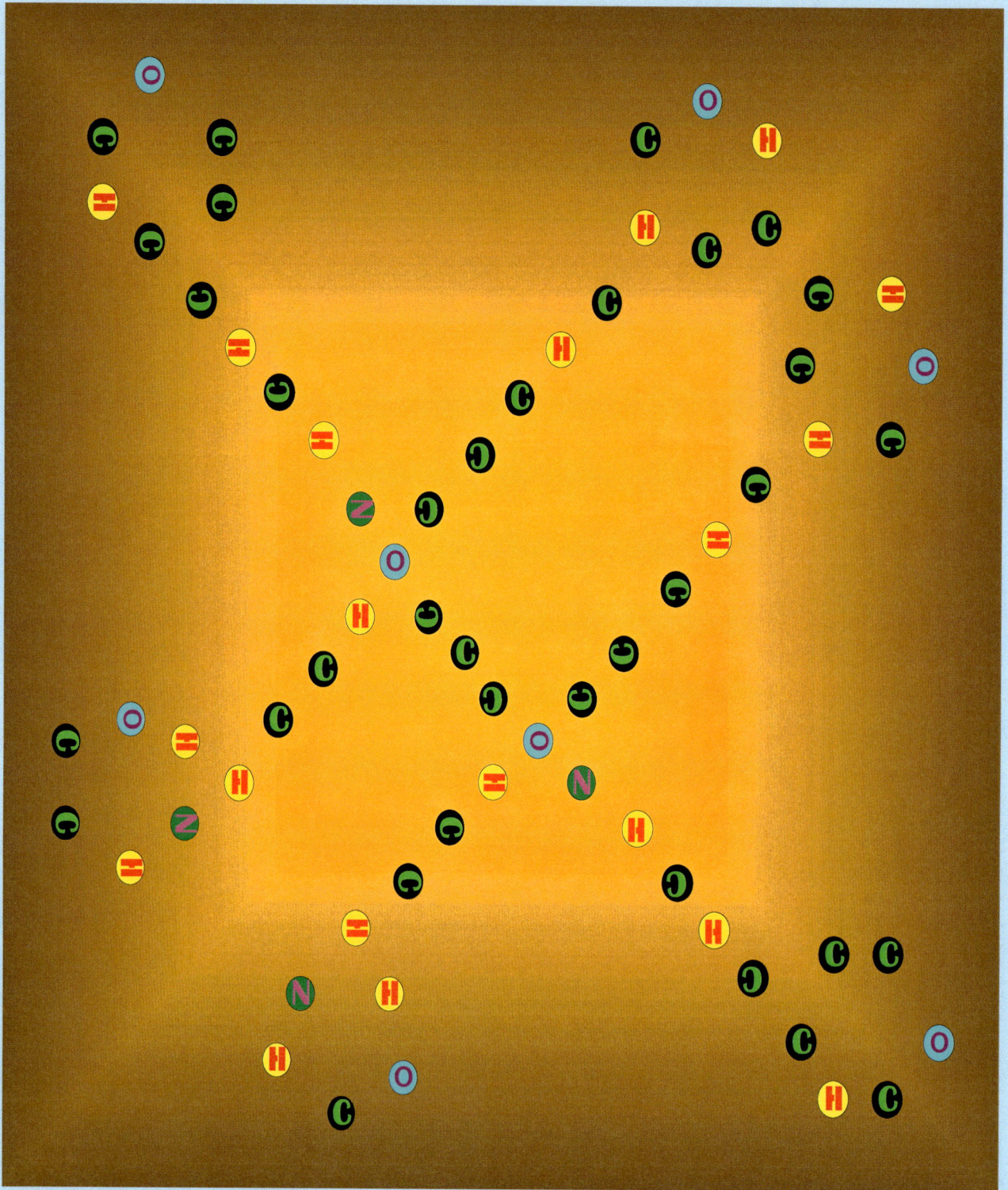

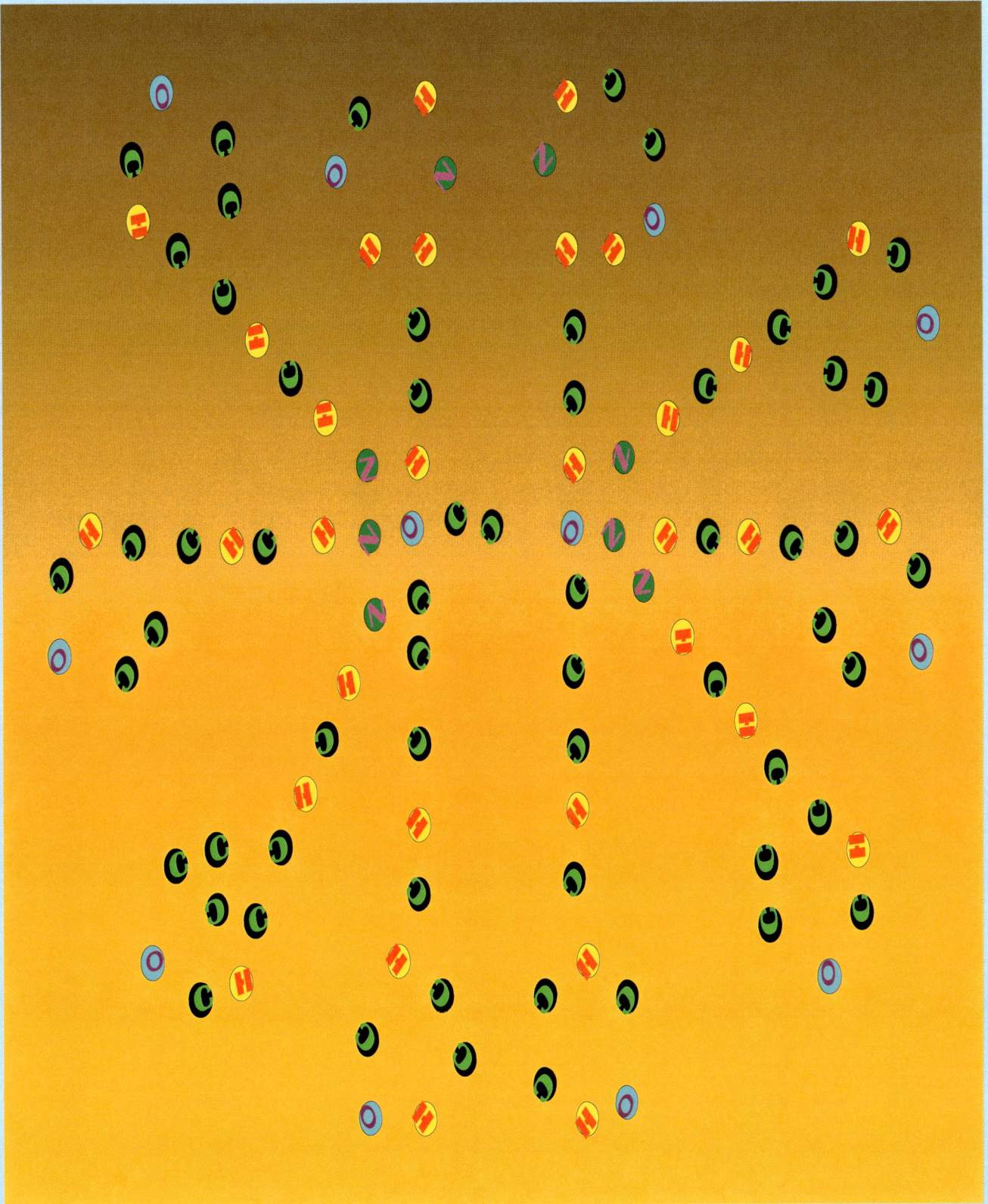

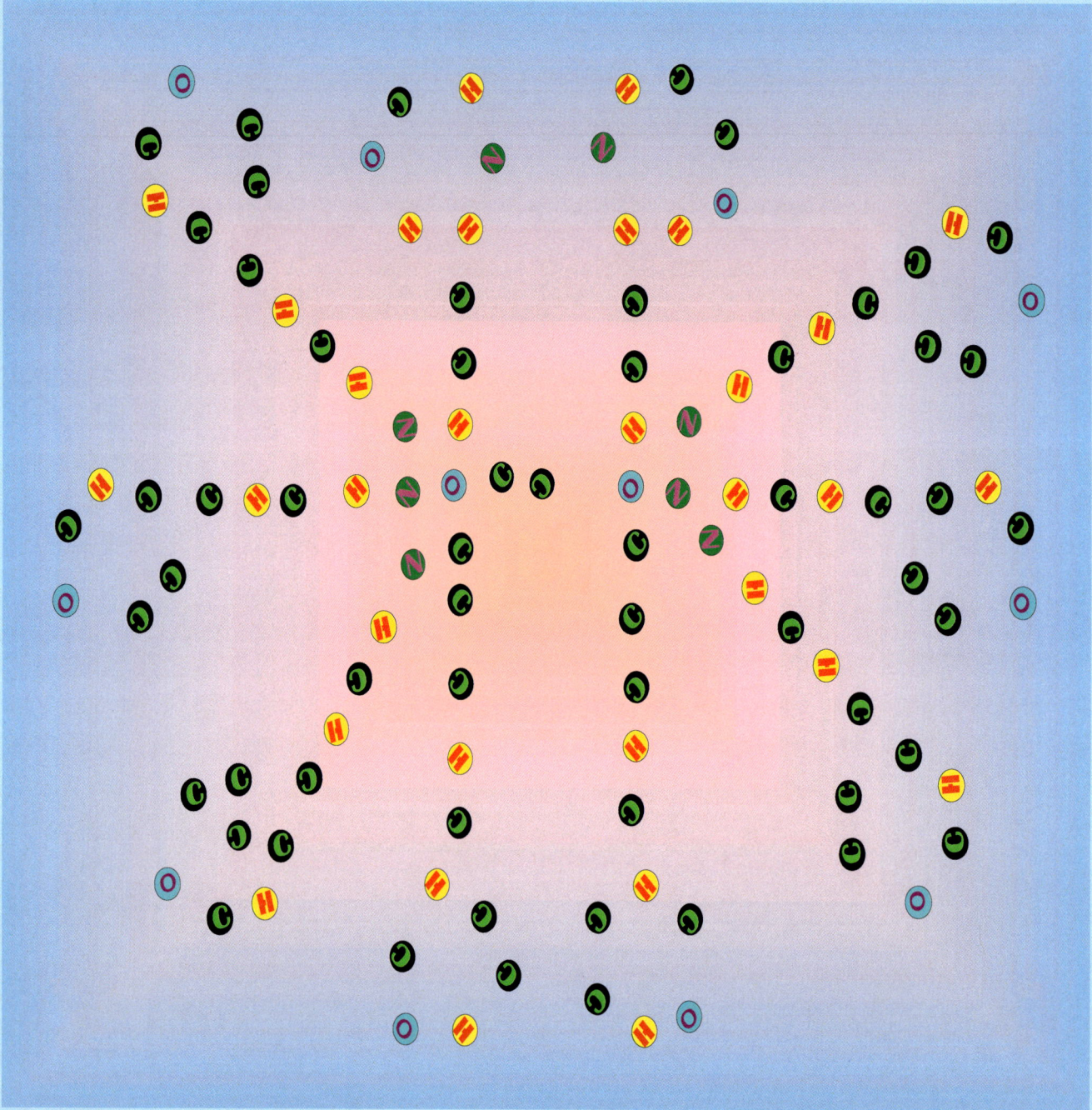

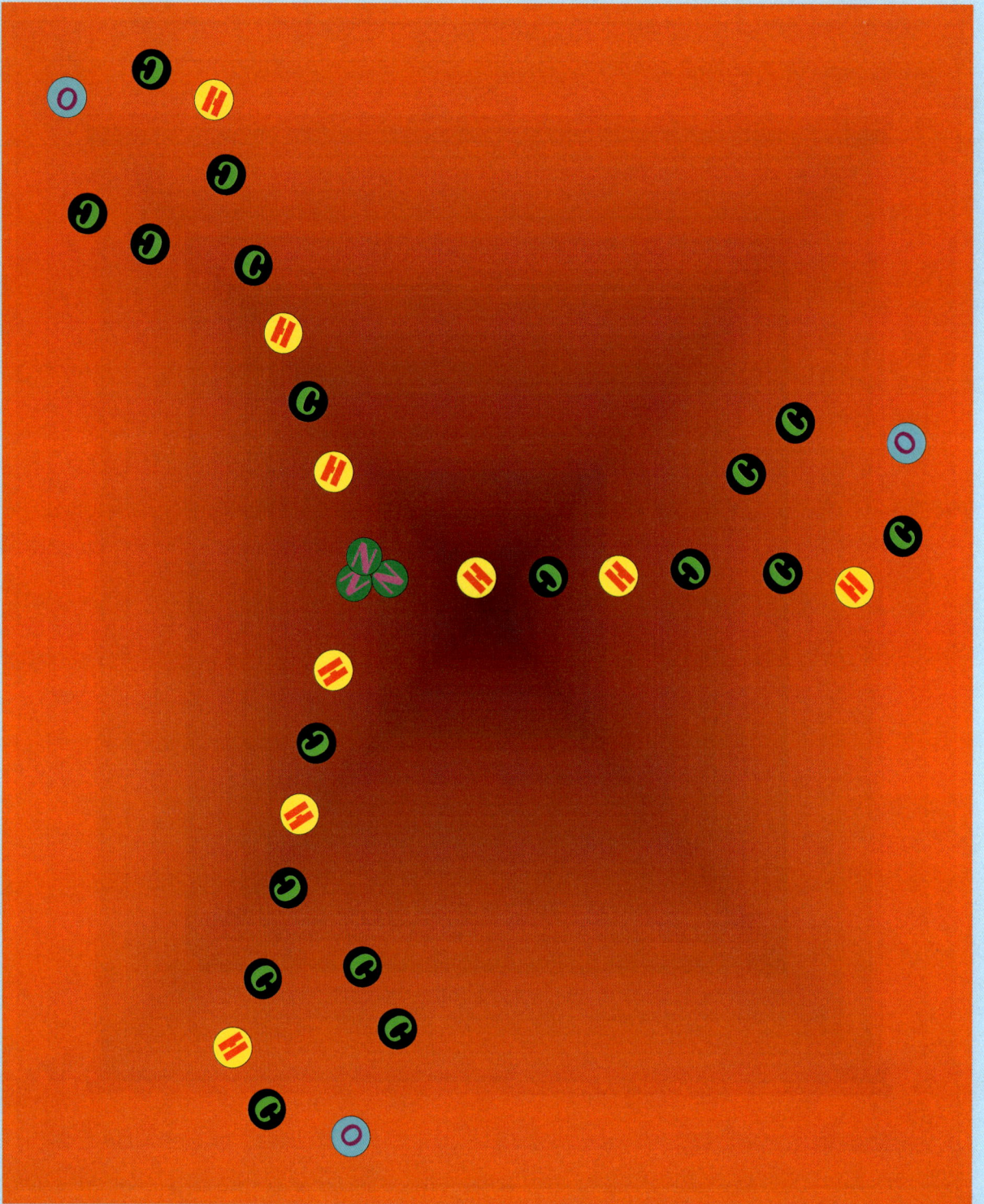

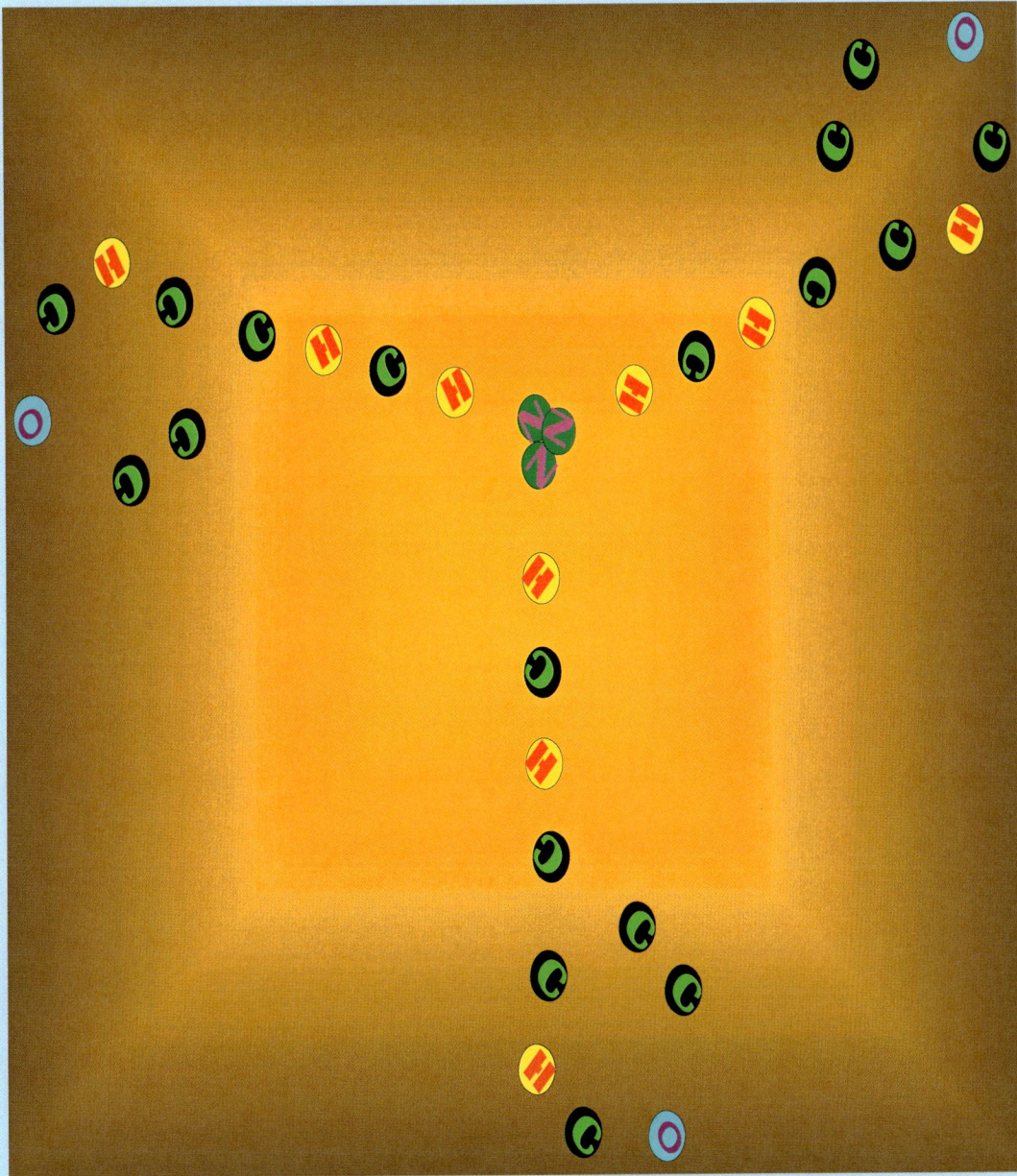

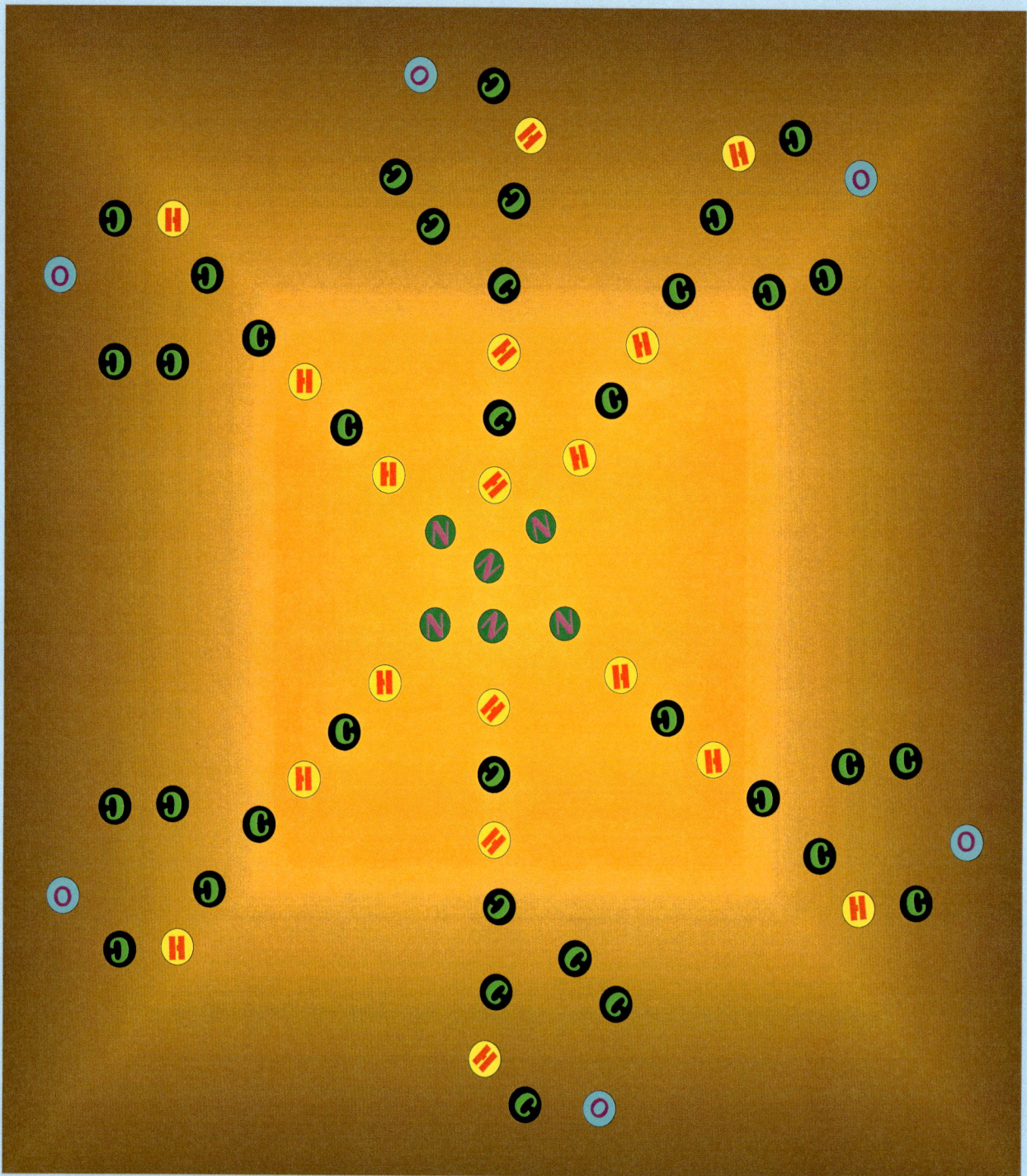

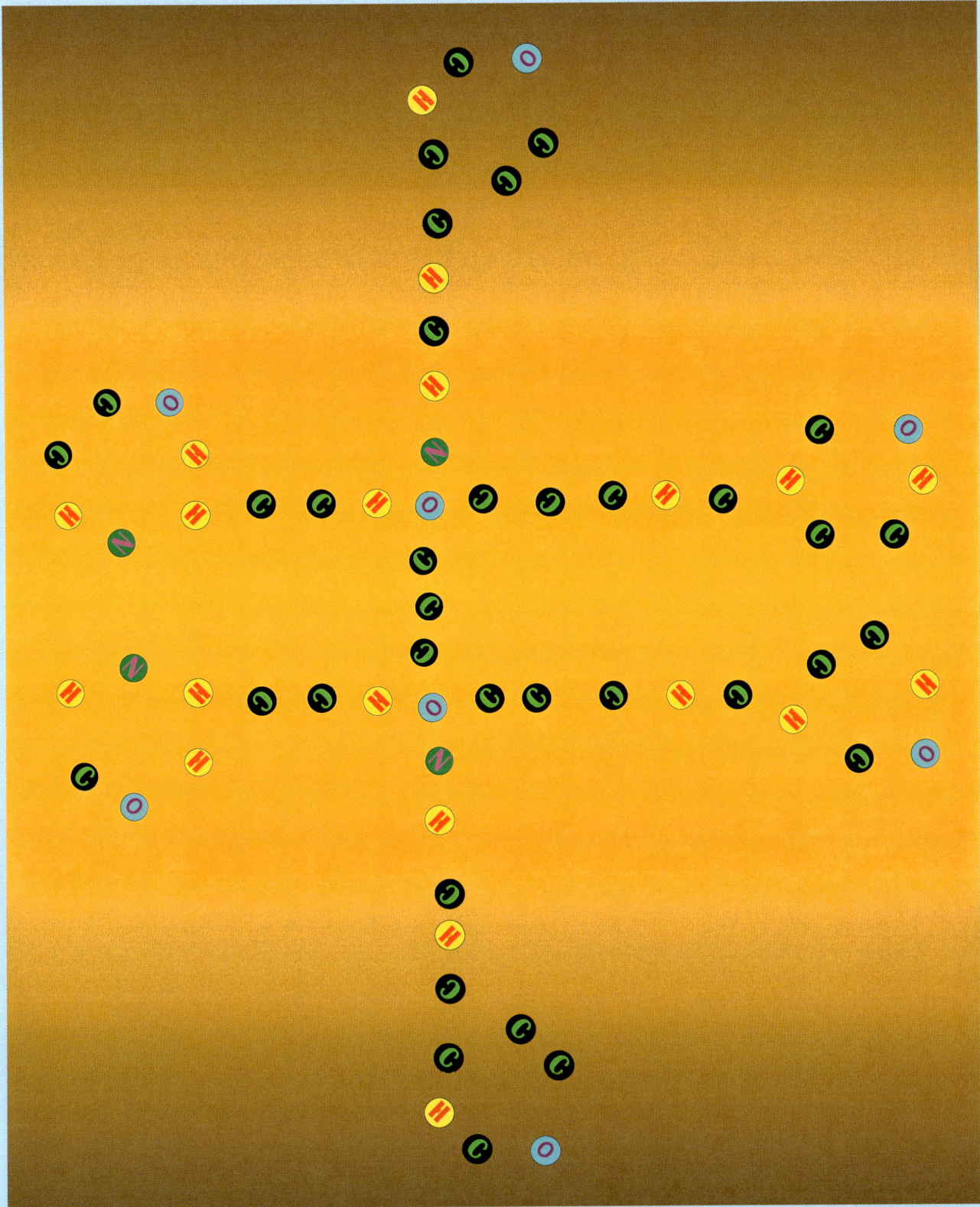

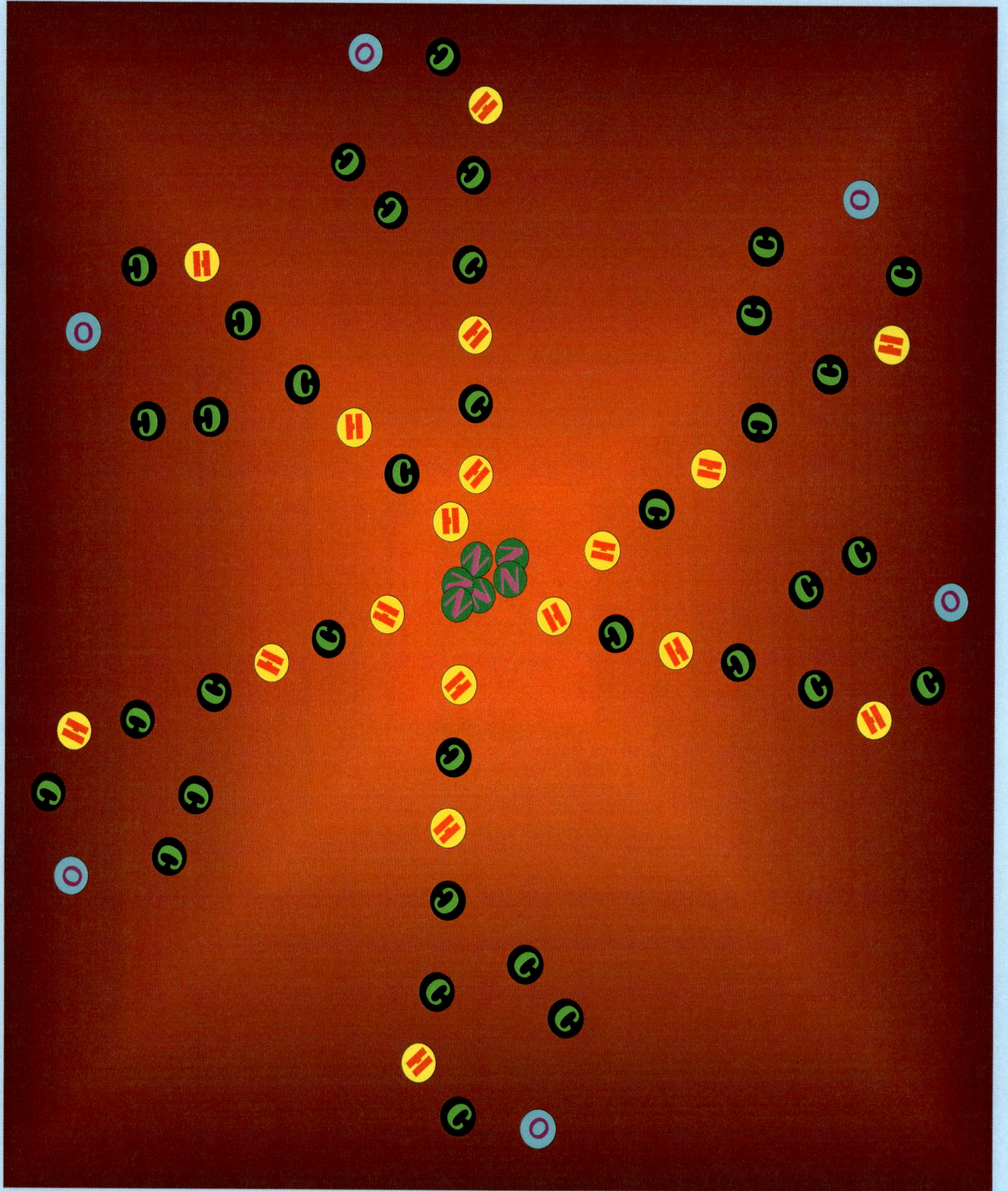

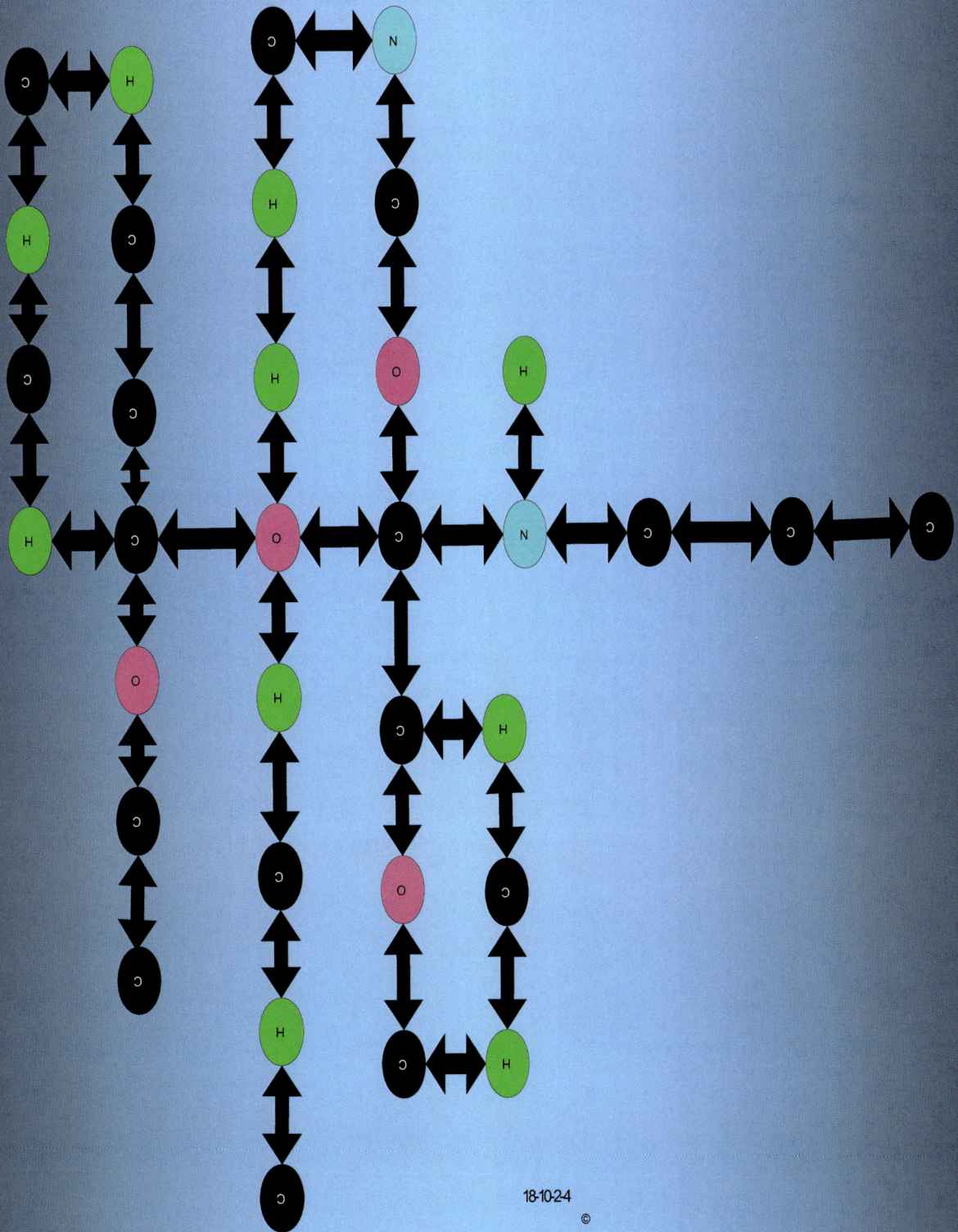

18-10-2-4

RIB

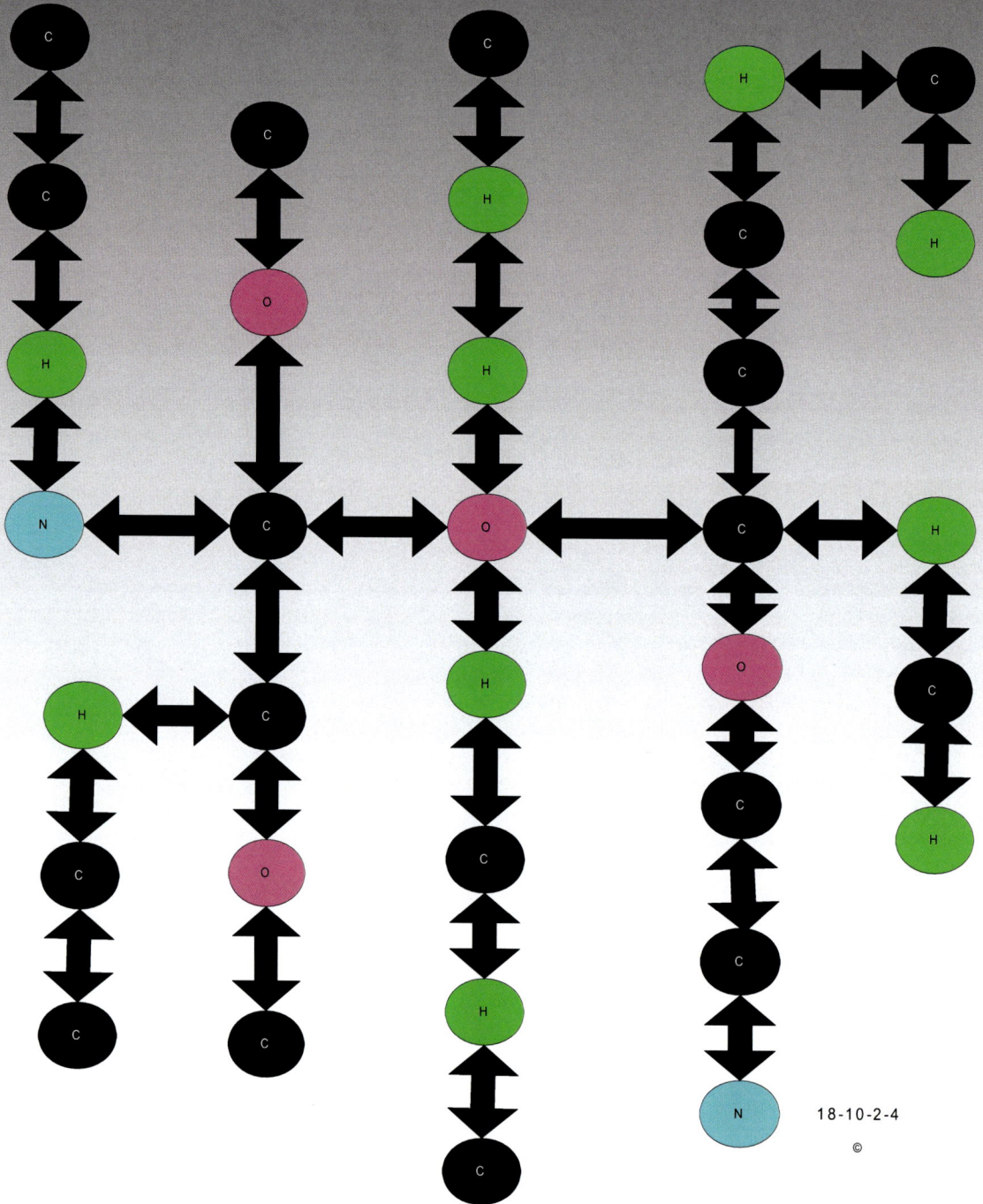

18-10-2-4

©

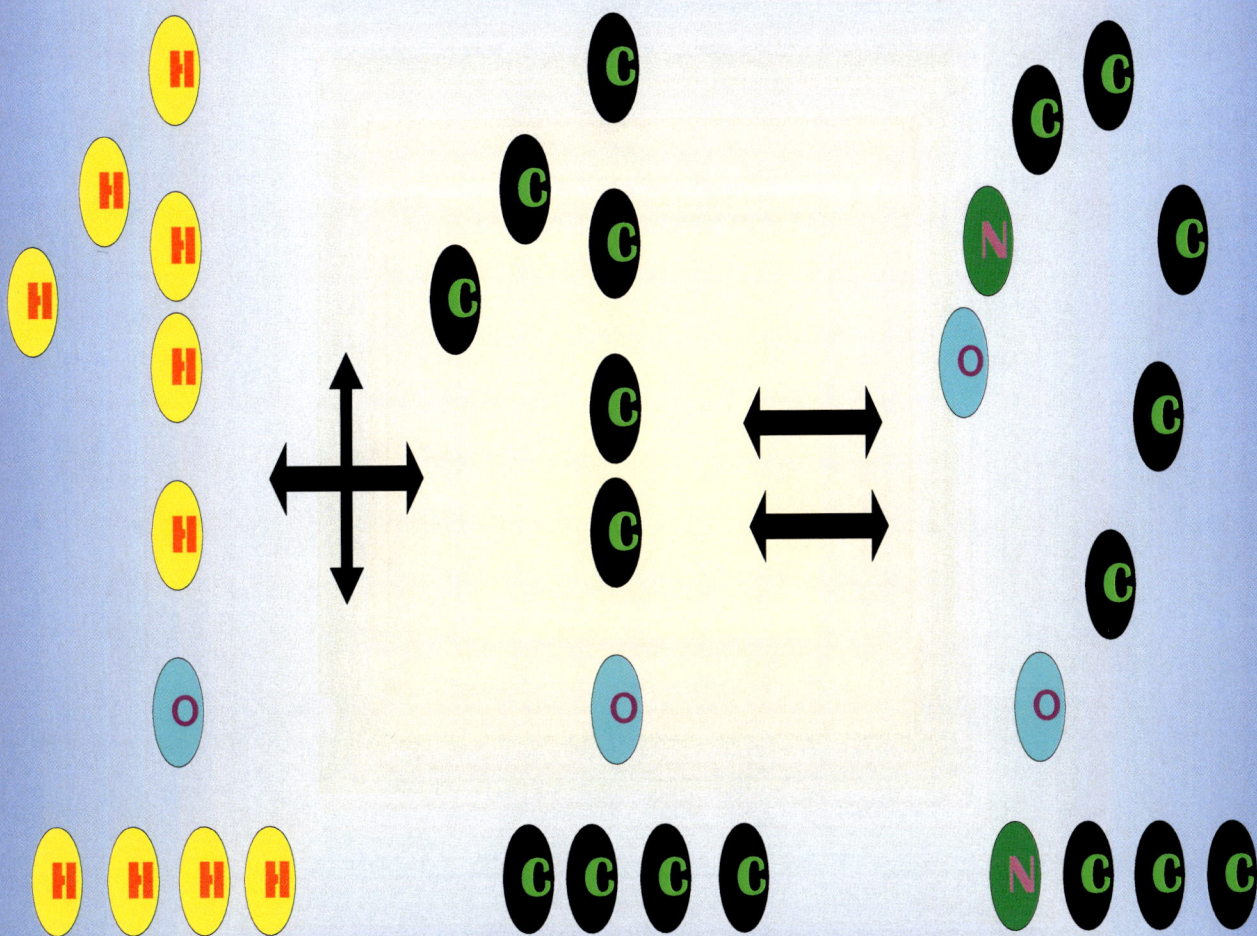

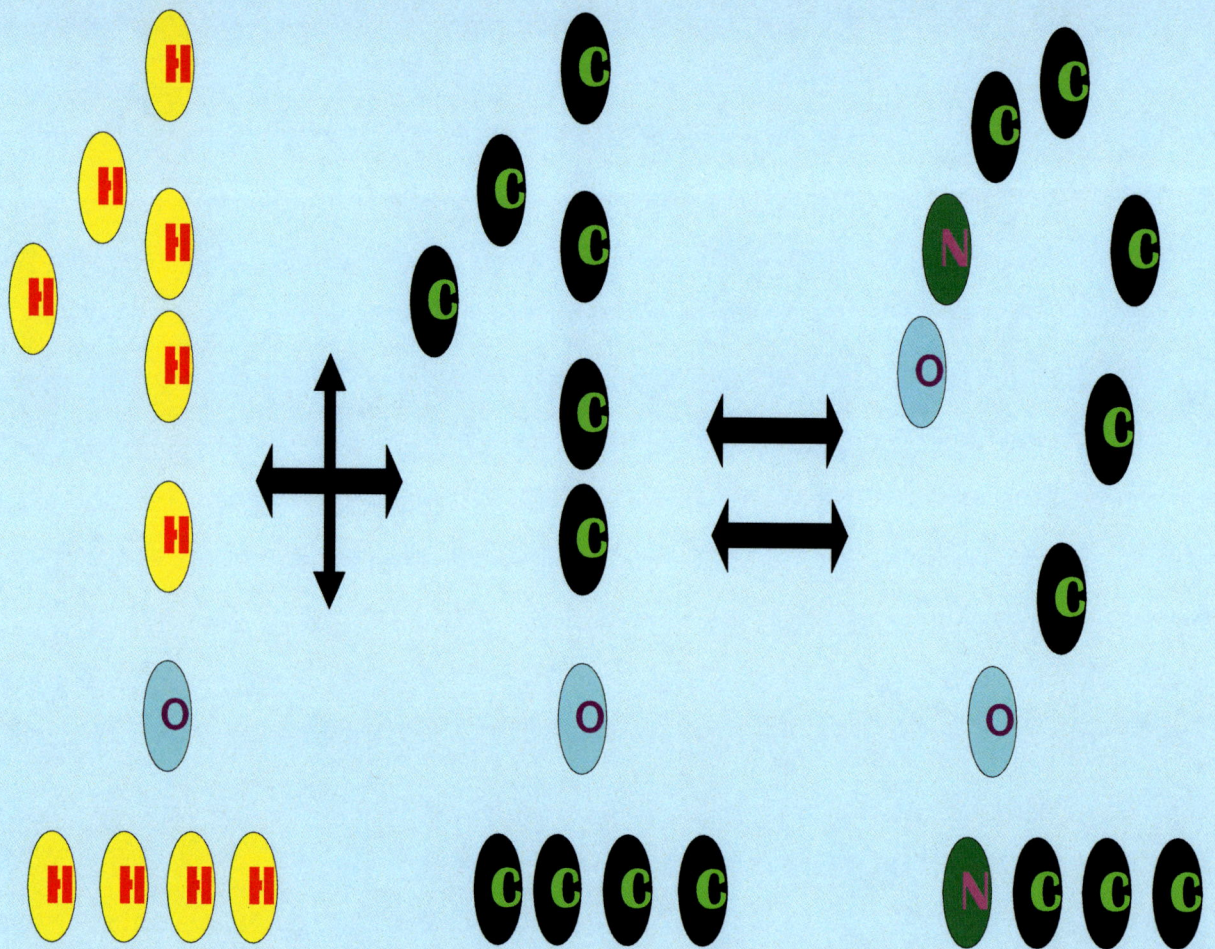

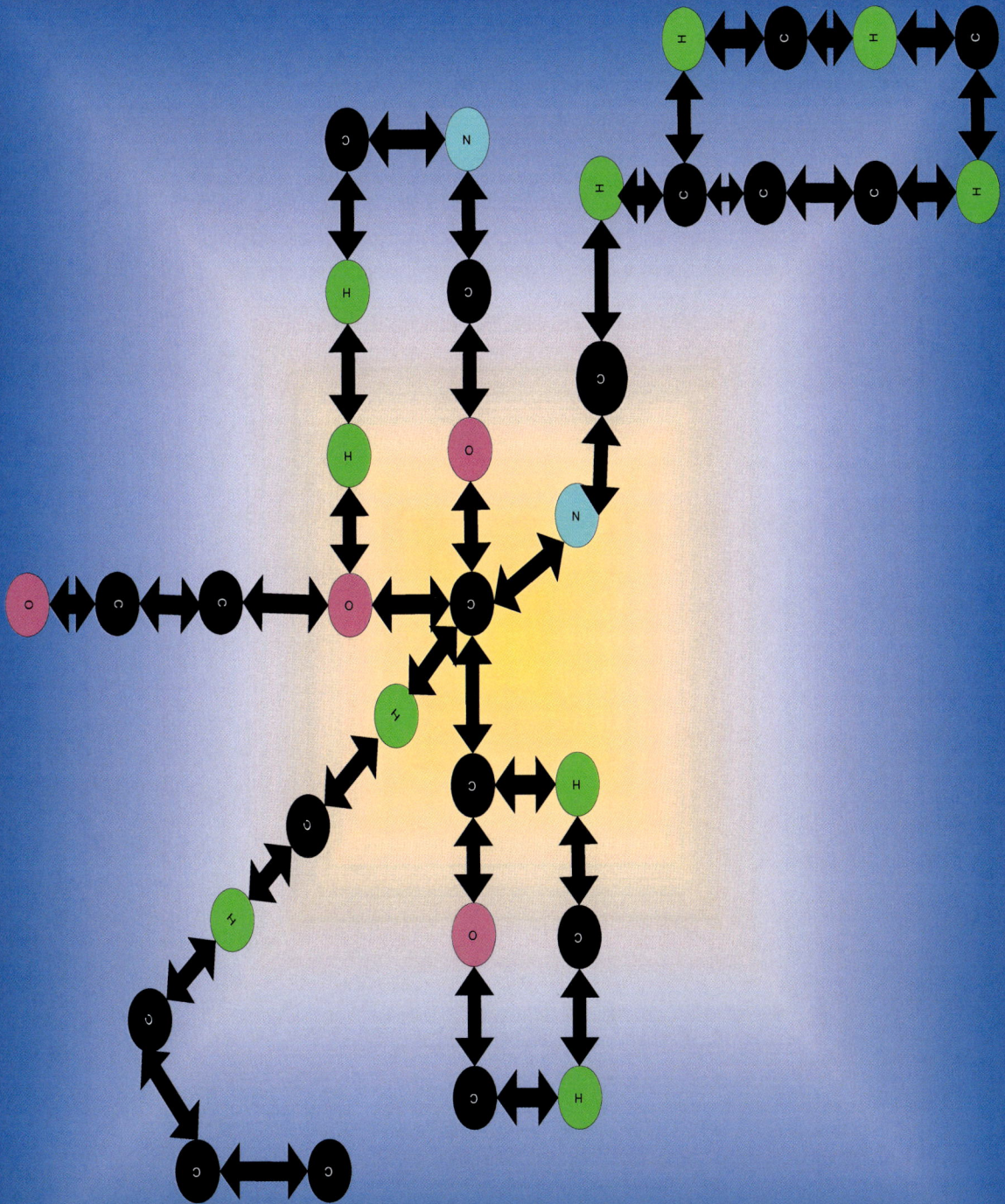

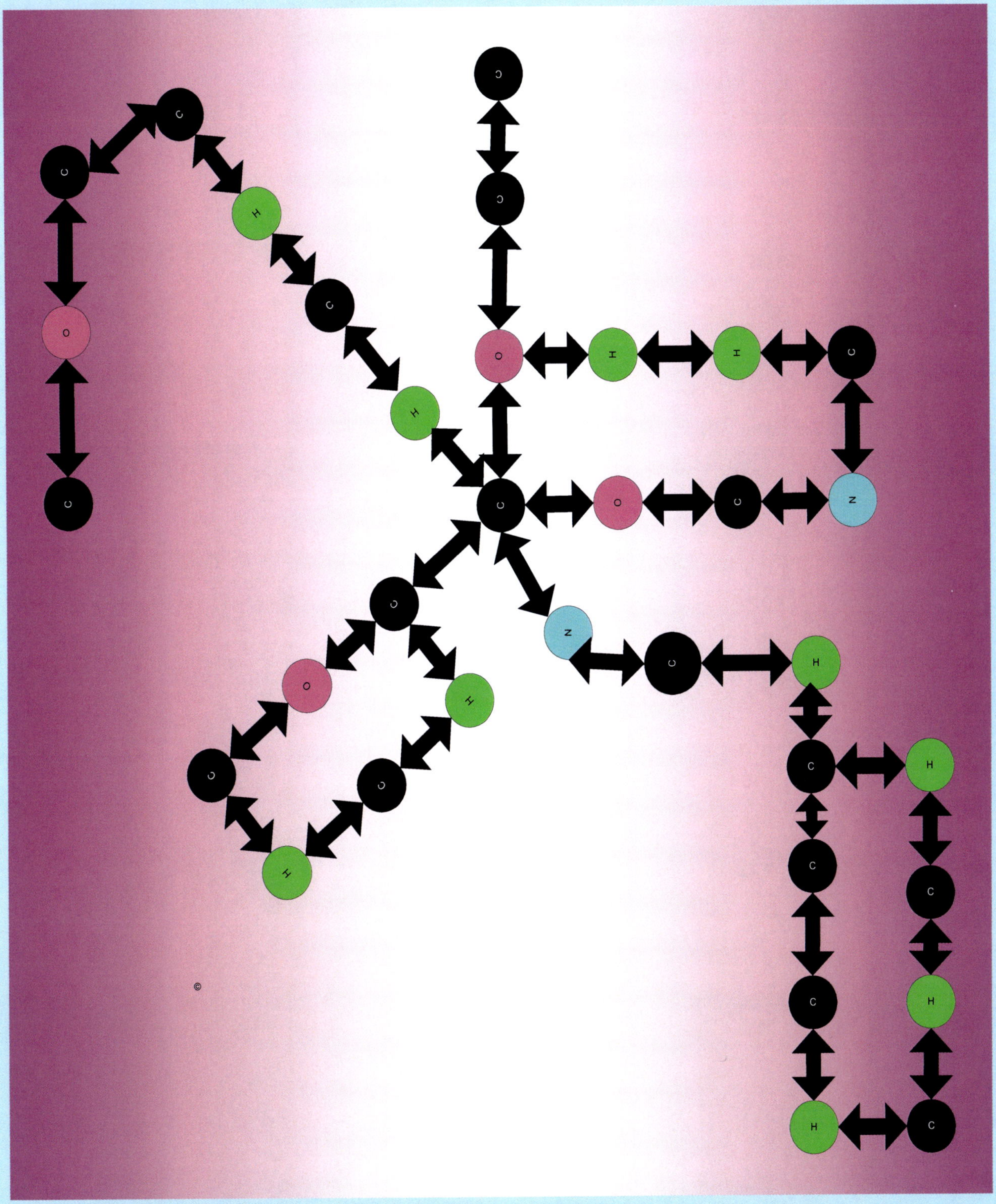
C
C
H
C
O
H
C
C
C
O
H
H
C
C
O
C
N
C
O
H
N
C
H
C
H
C
H
C
C
C
H
H
C
©

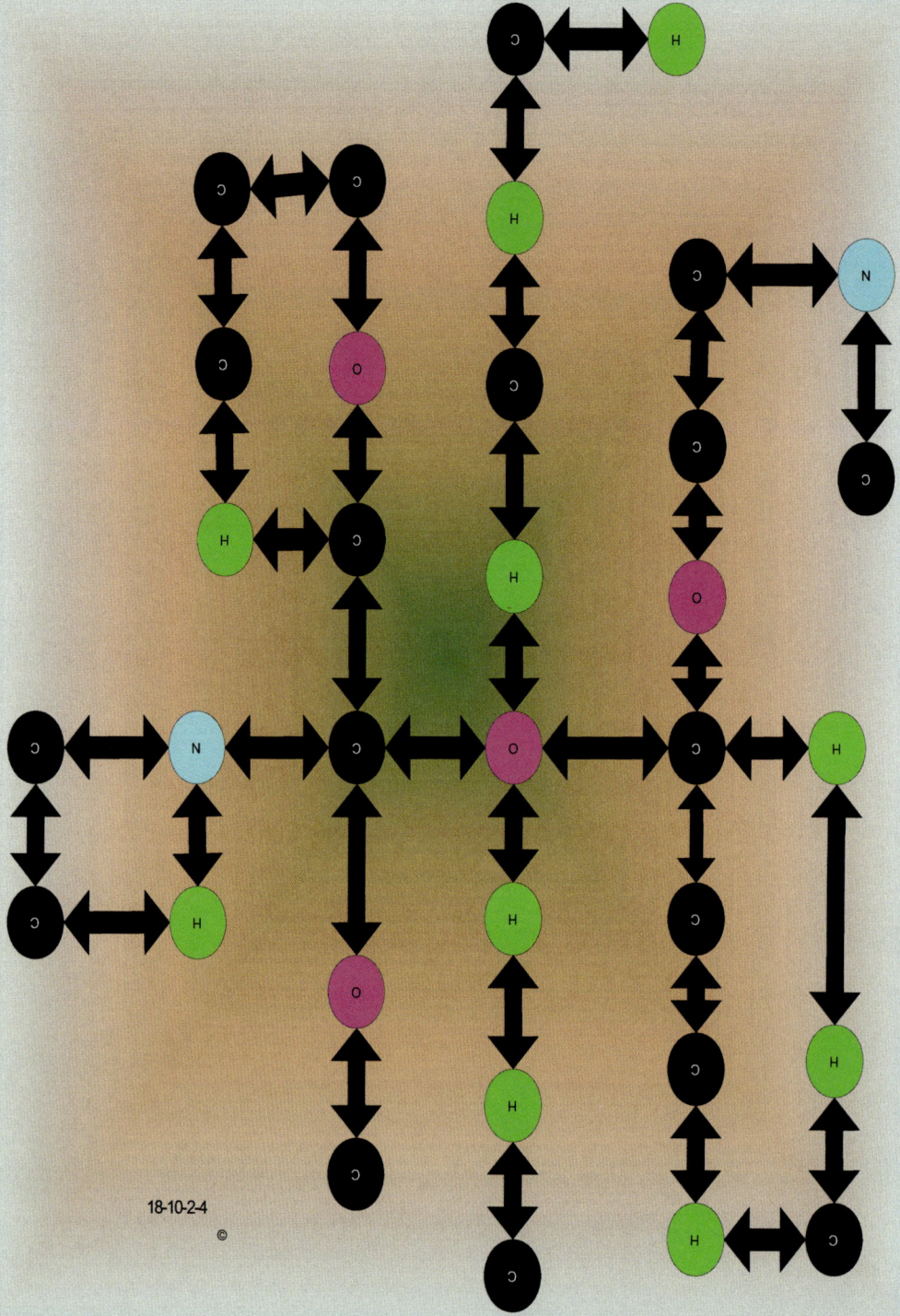

18-10-2-4

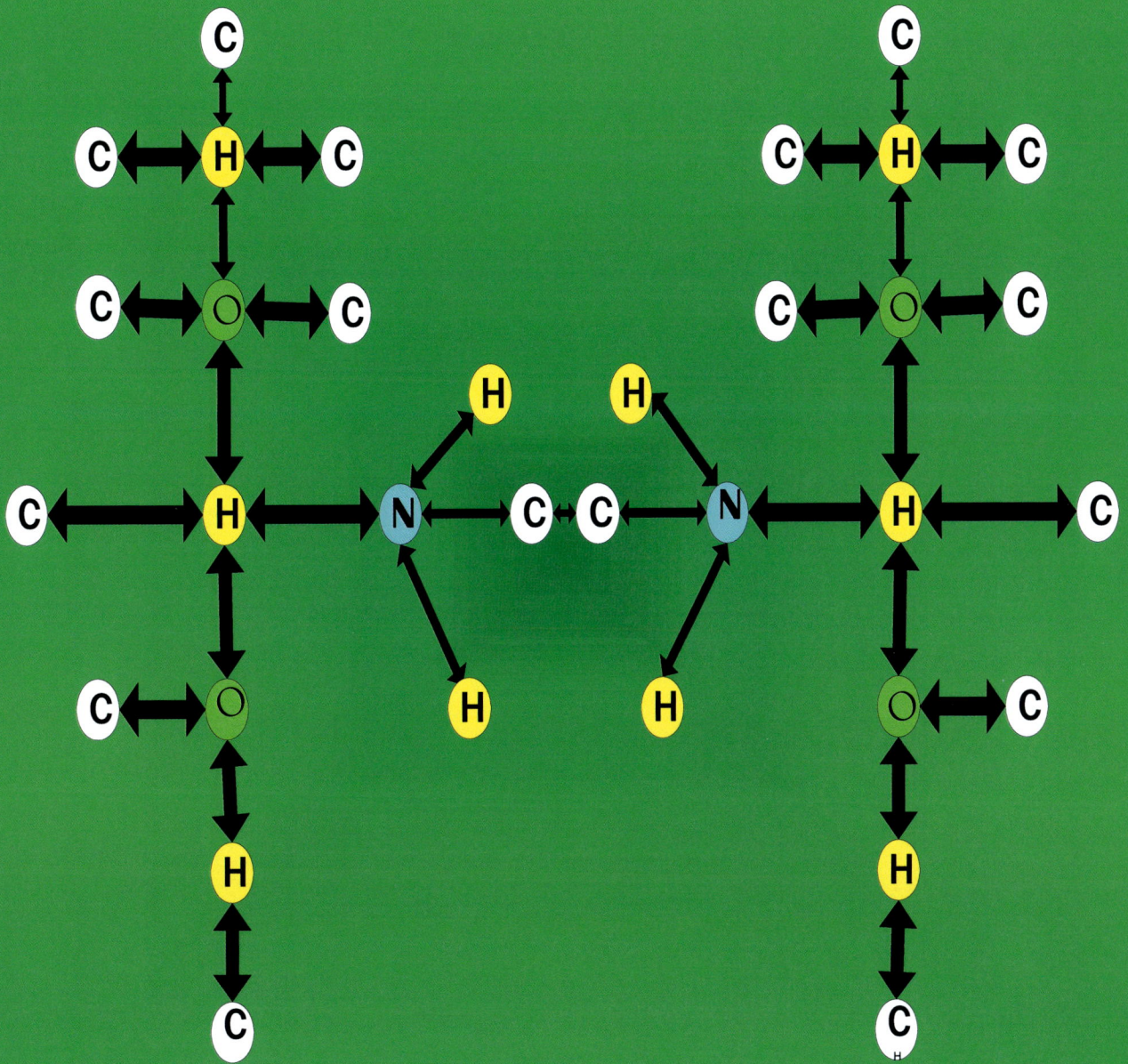

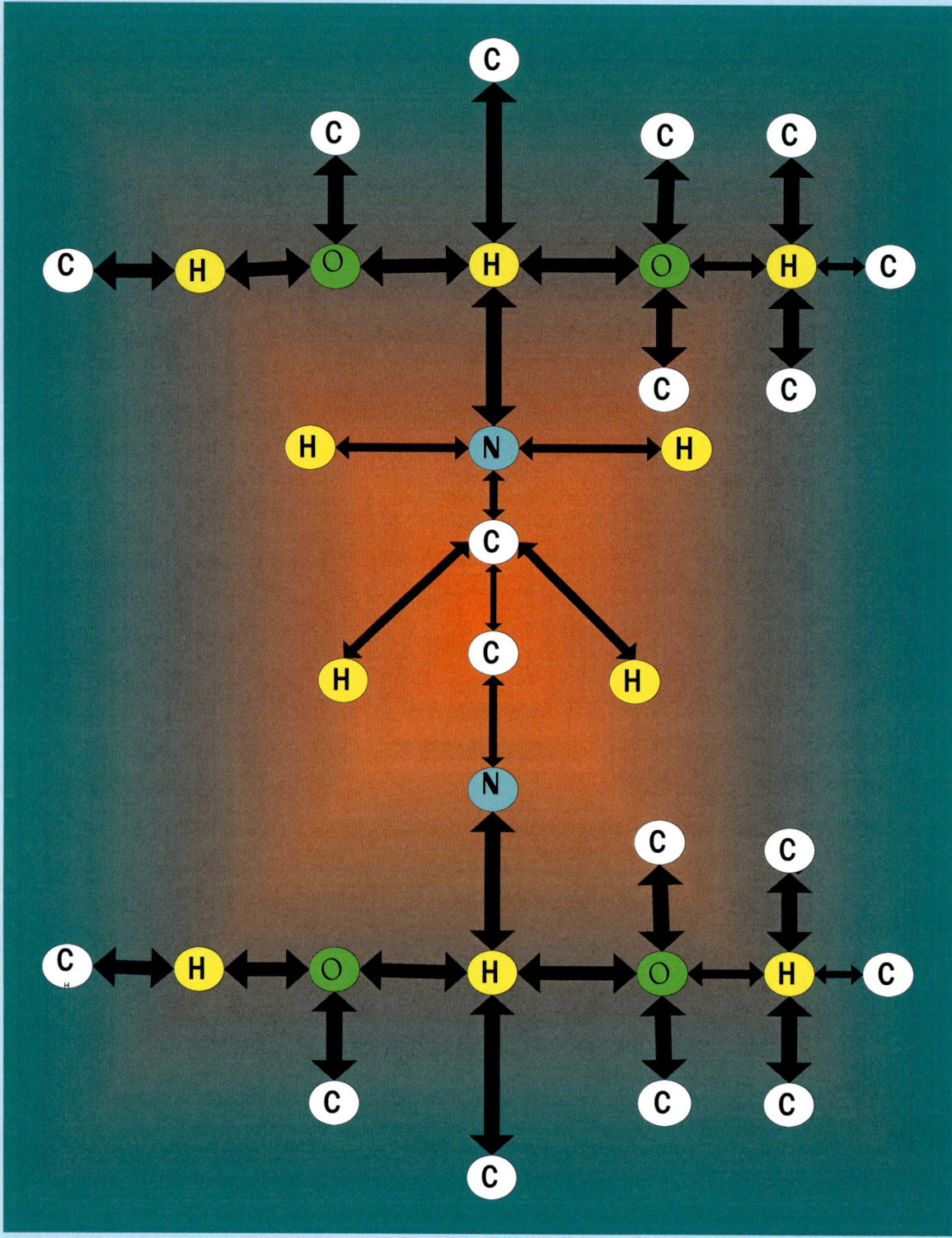

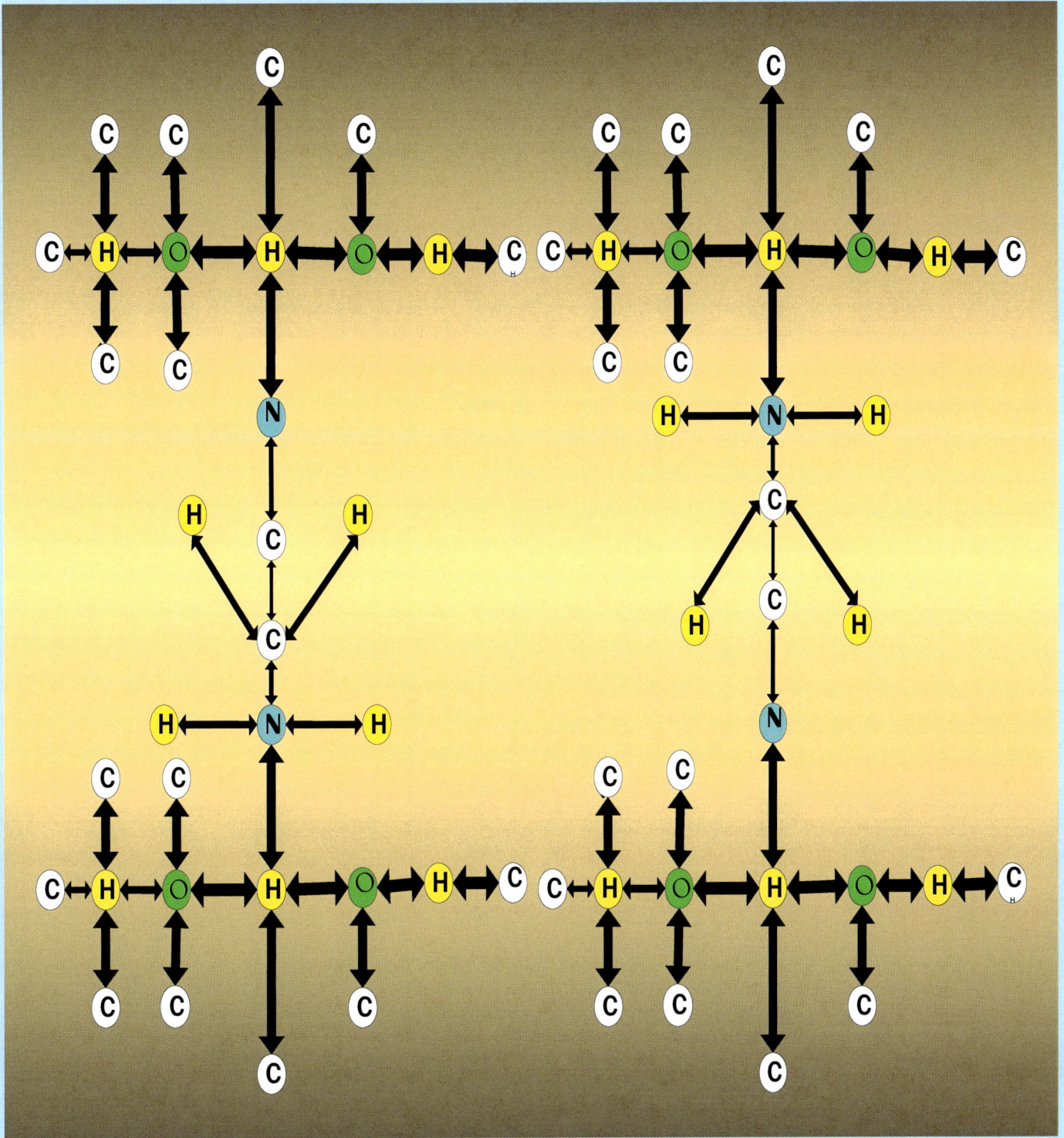

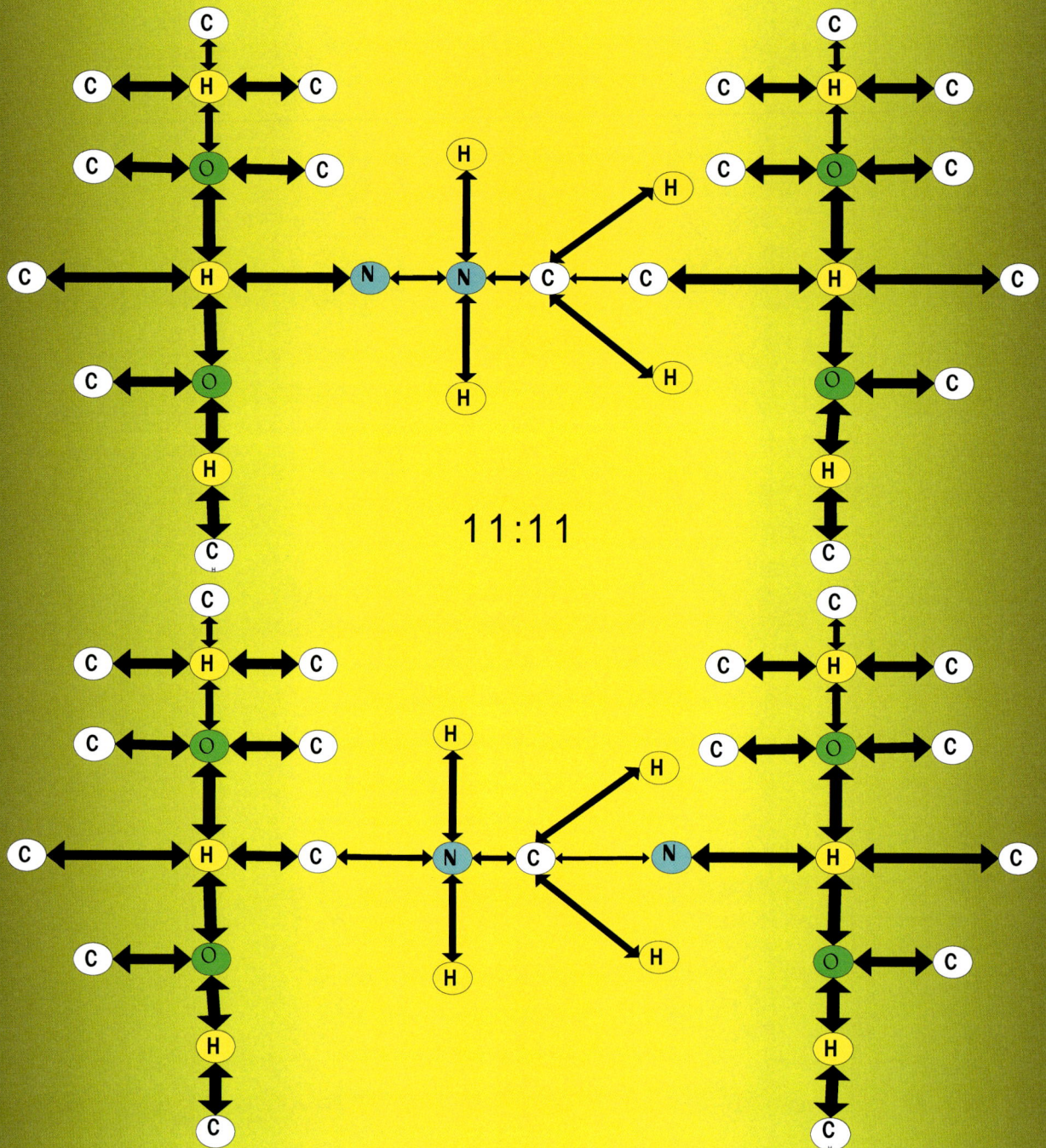

11:11

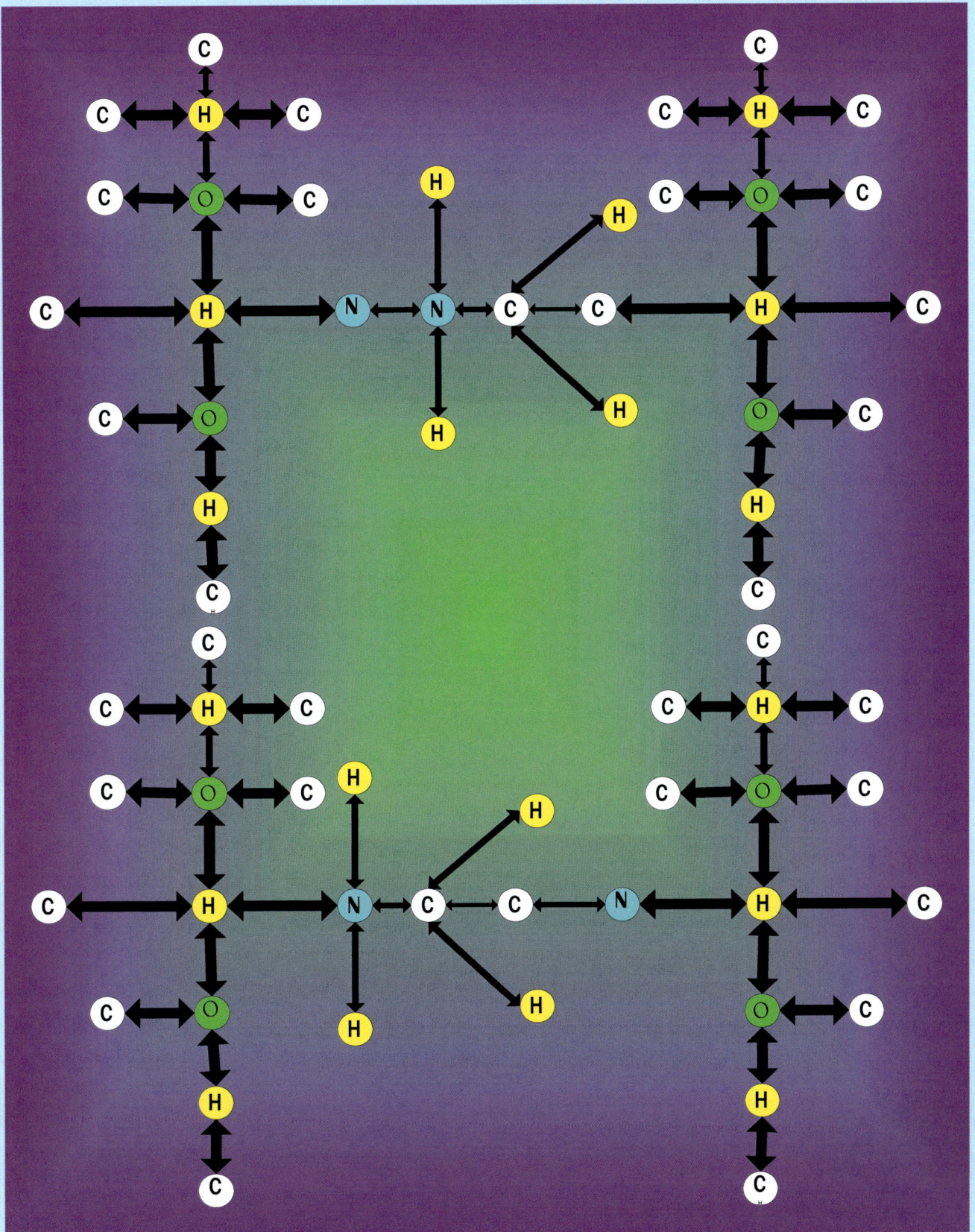

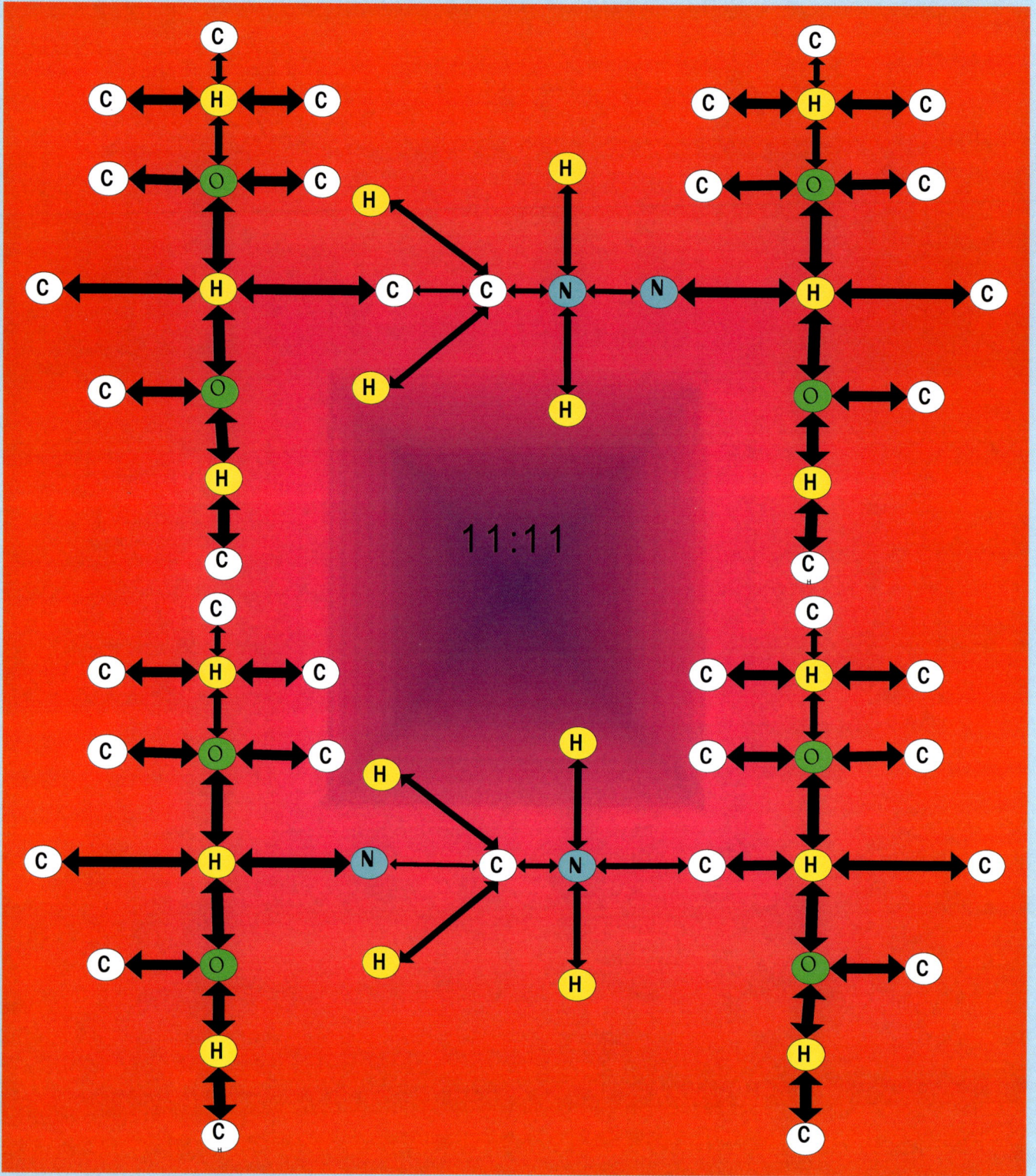

11:11

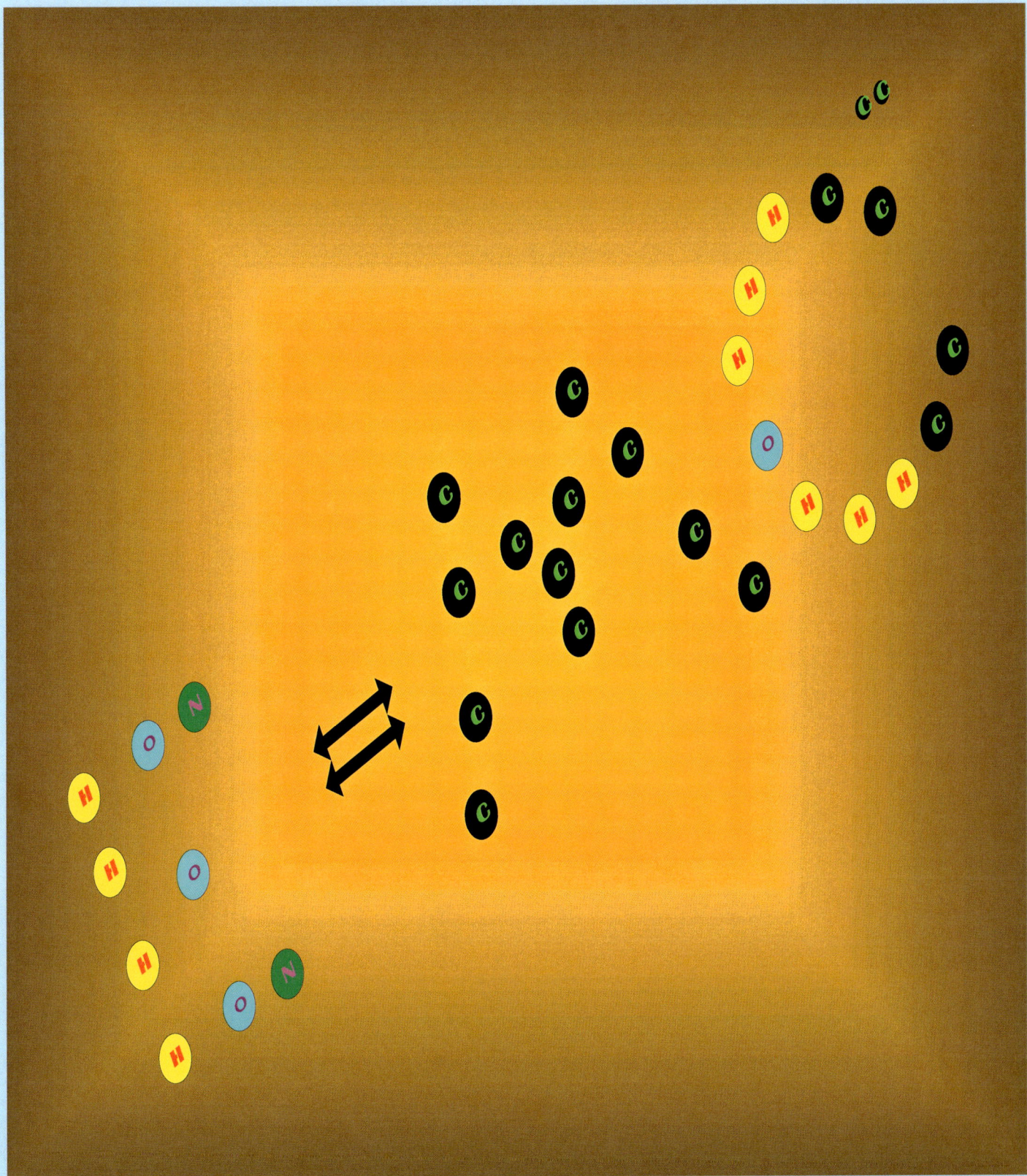

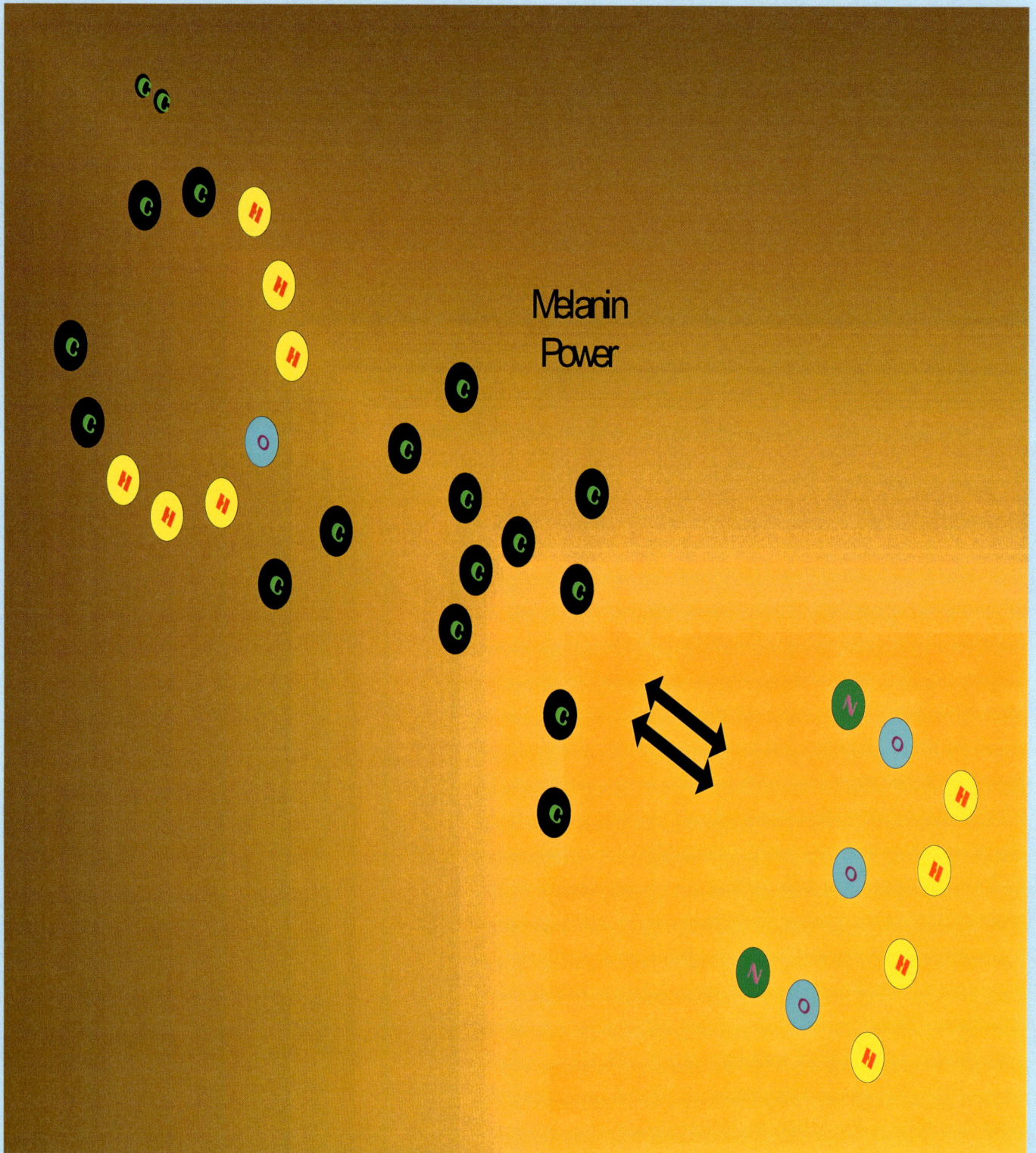

Melanin
Power

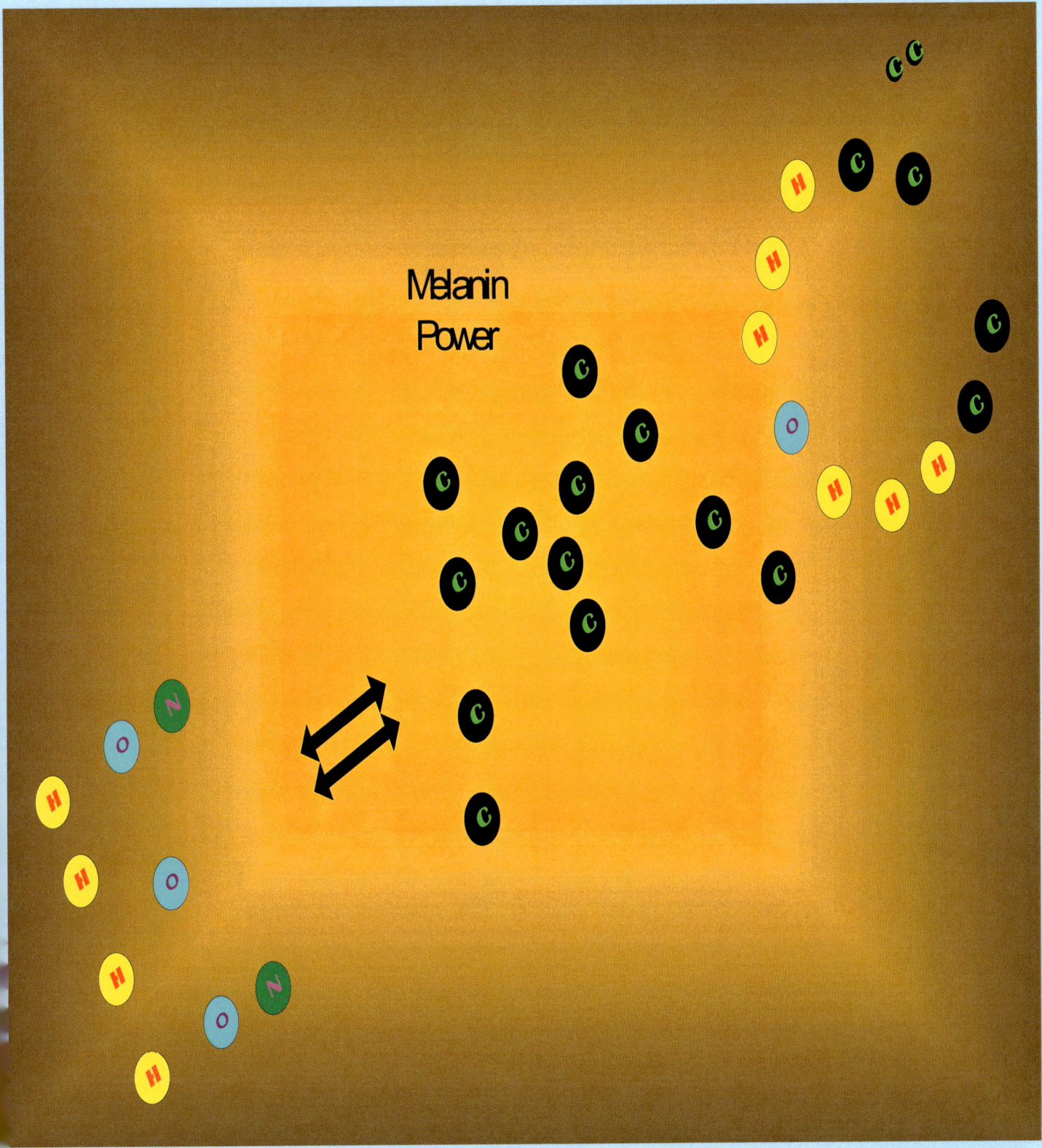

Melanin Power

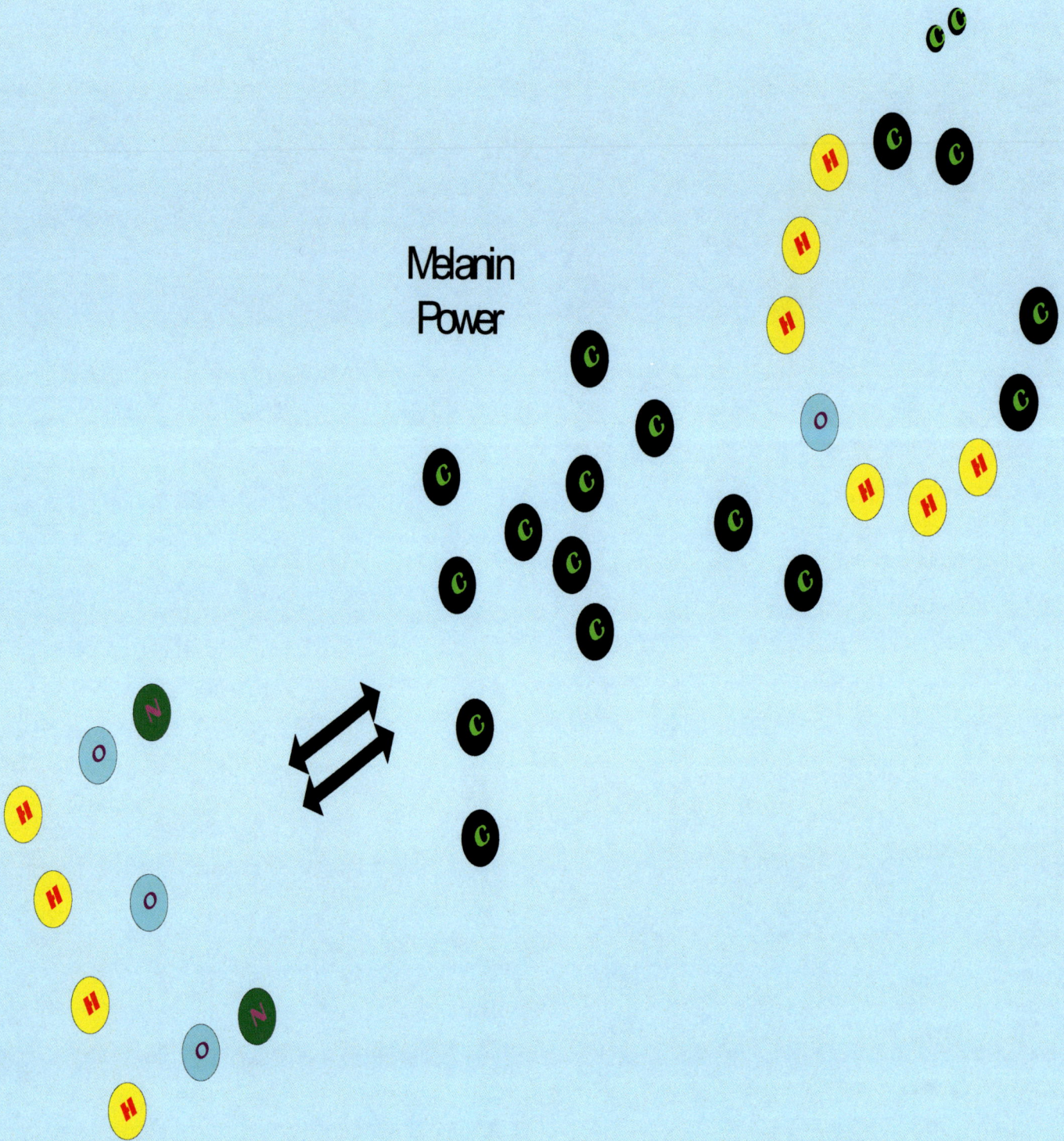

Melanin
Power

42

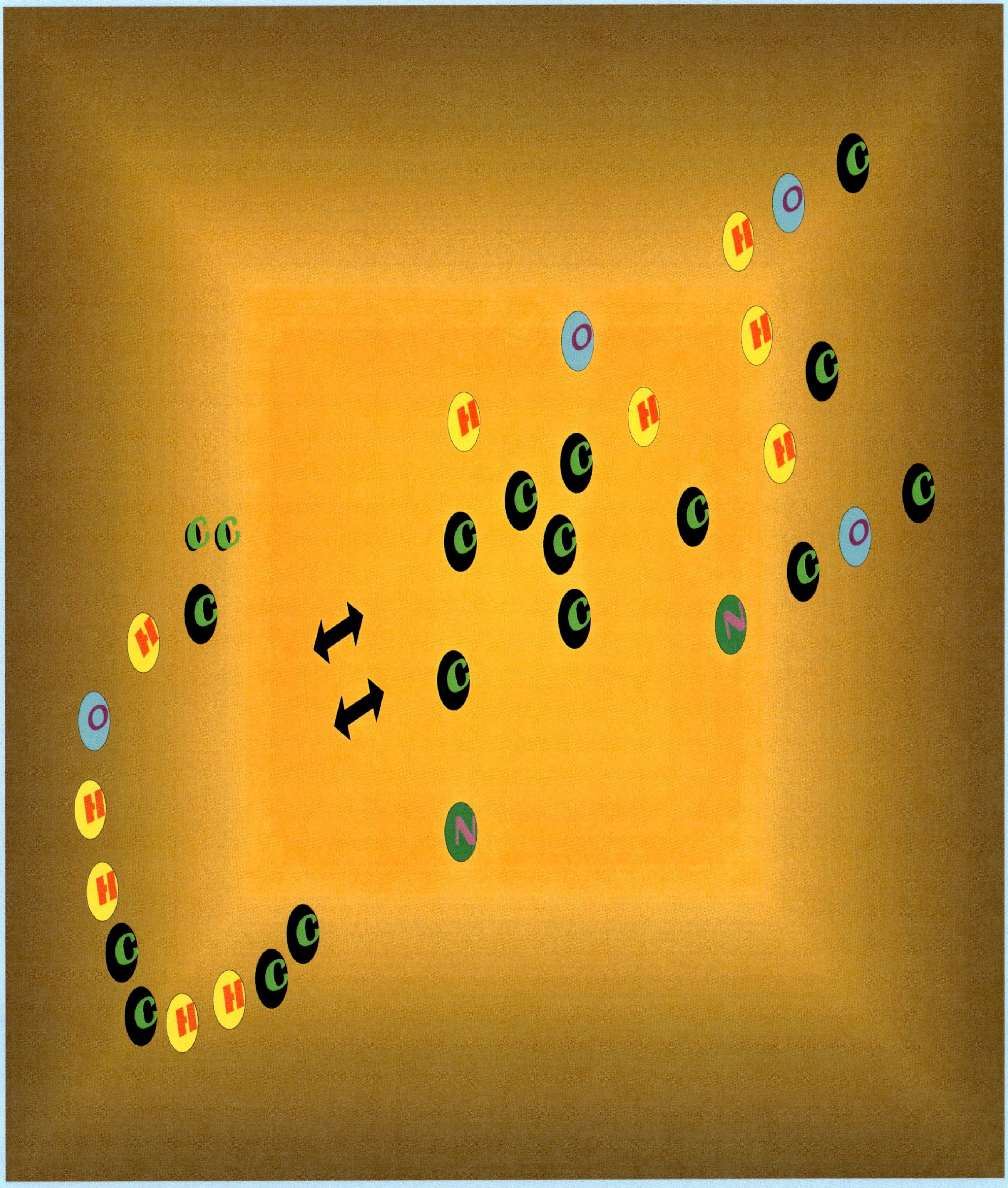

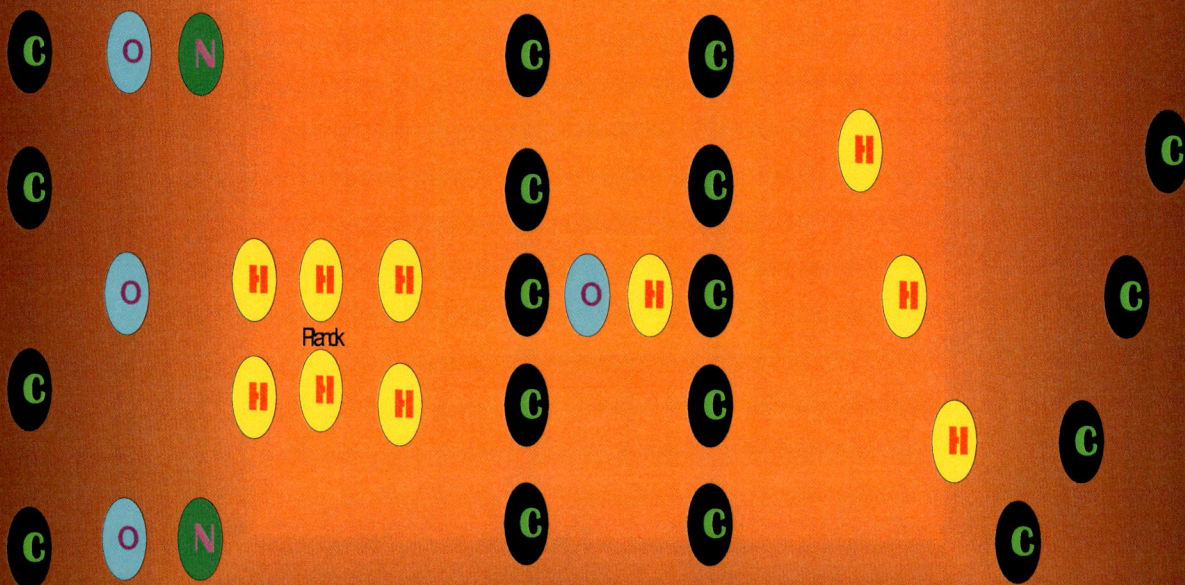

Melanin Power

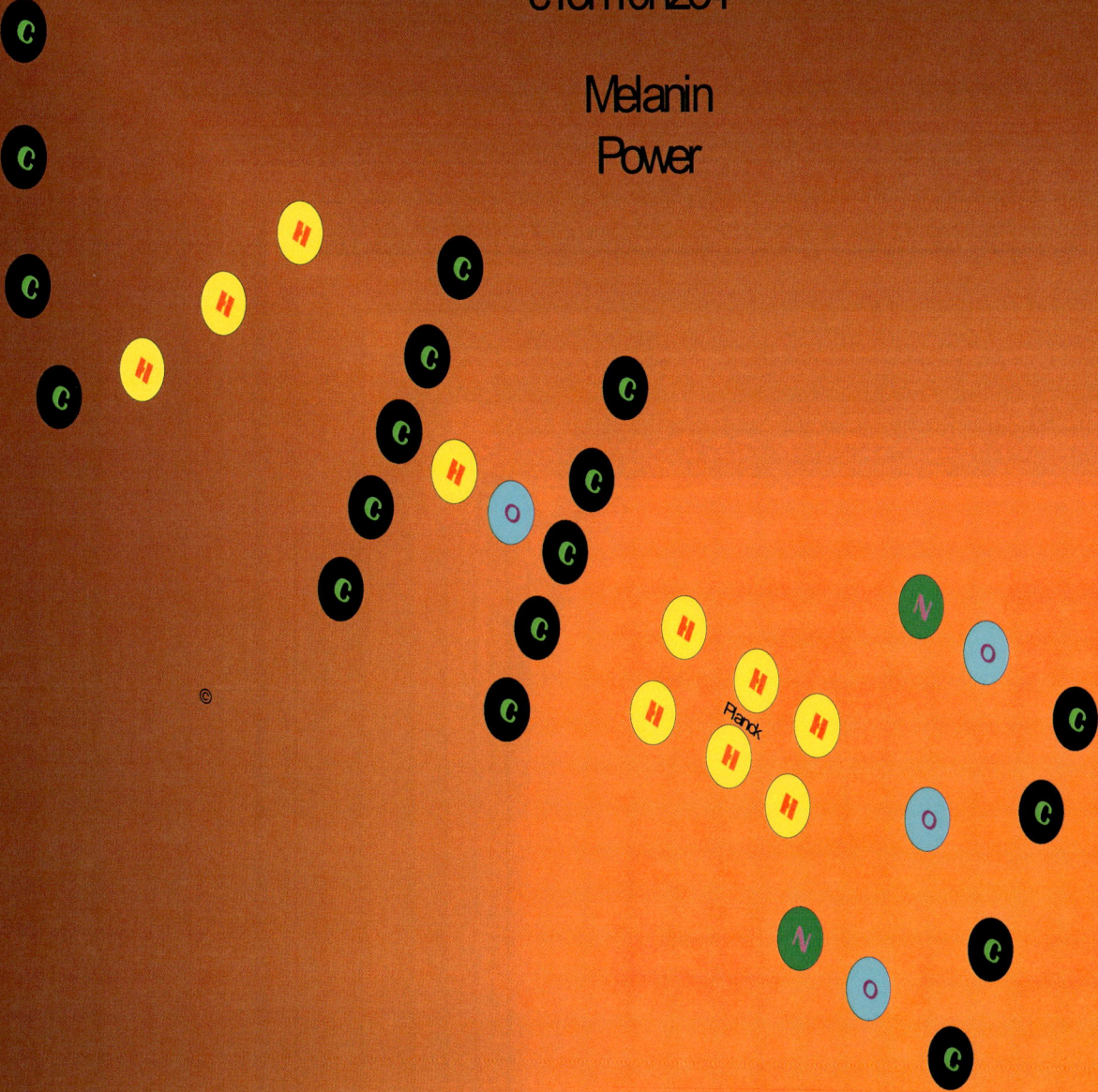

c18h10n2o4

Melanin
Power

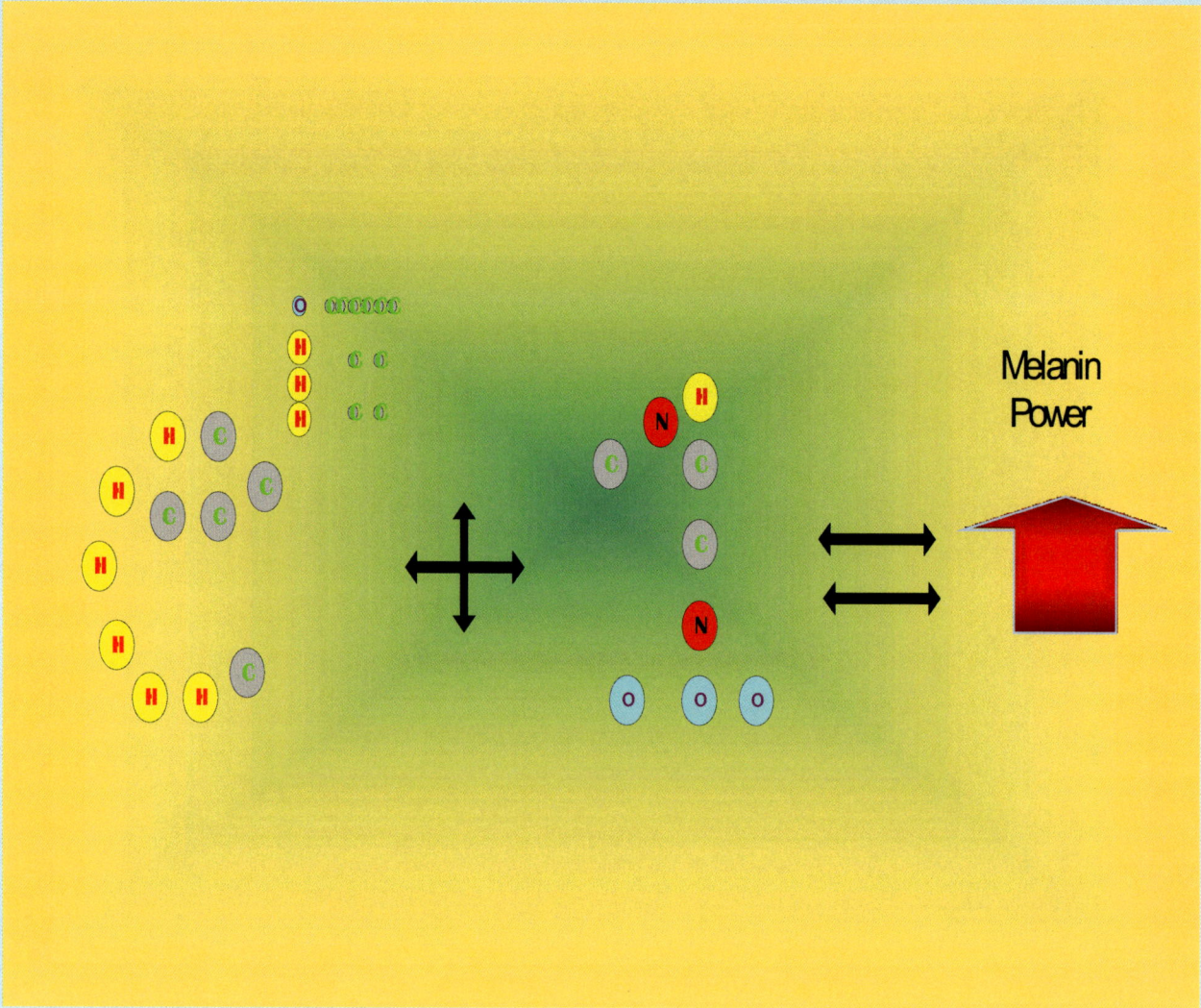

Melanin
Power

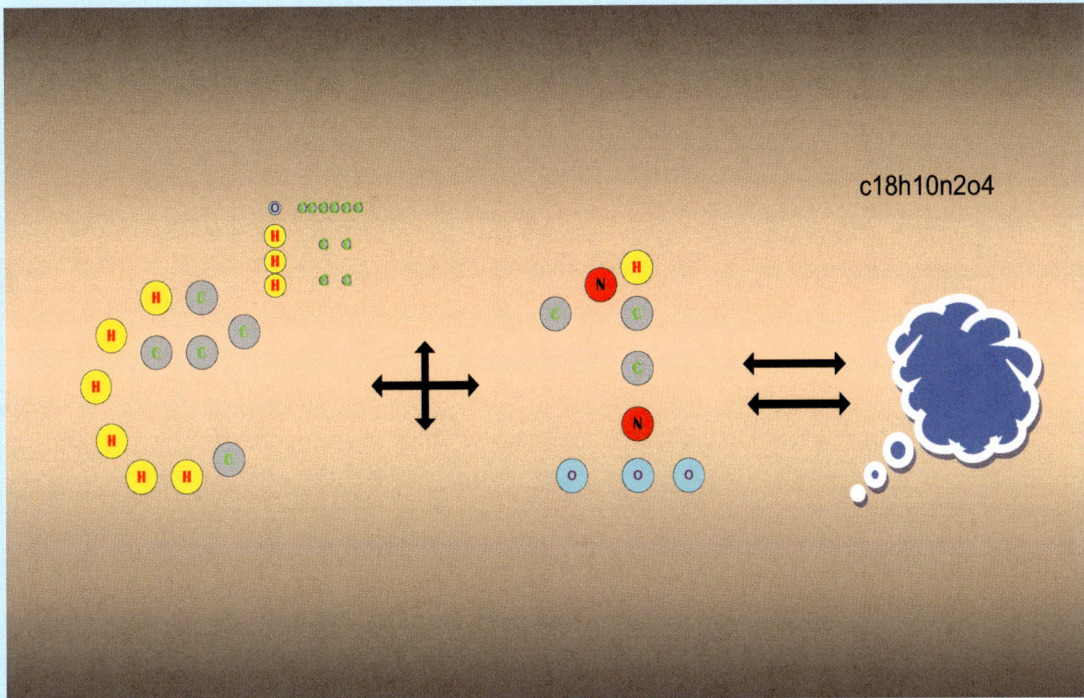

c18h10n2o4

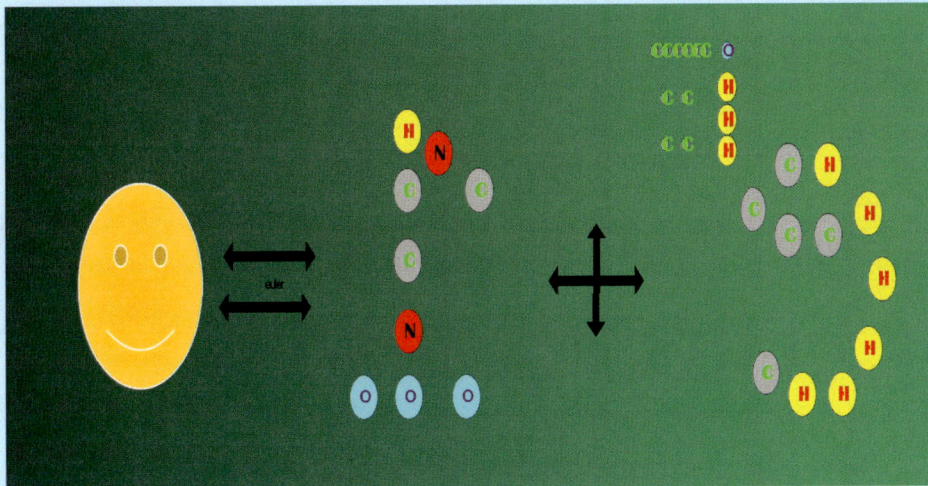

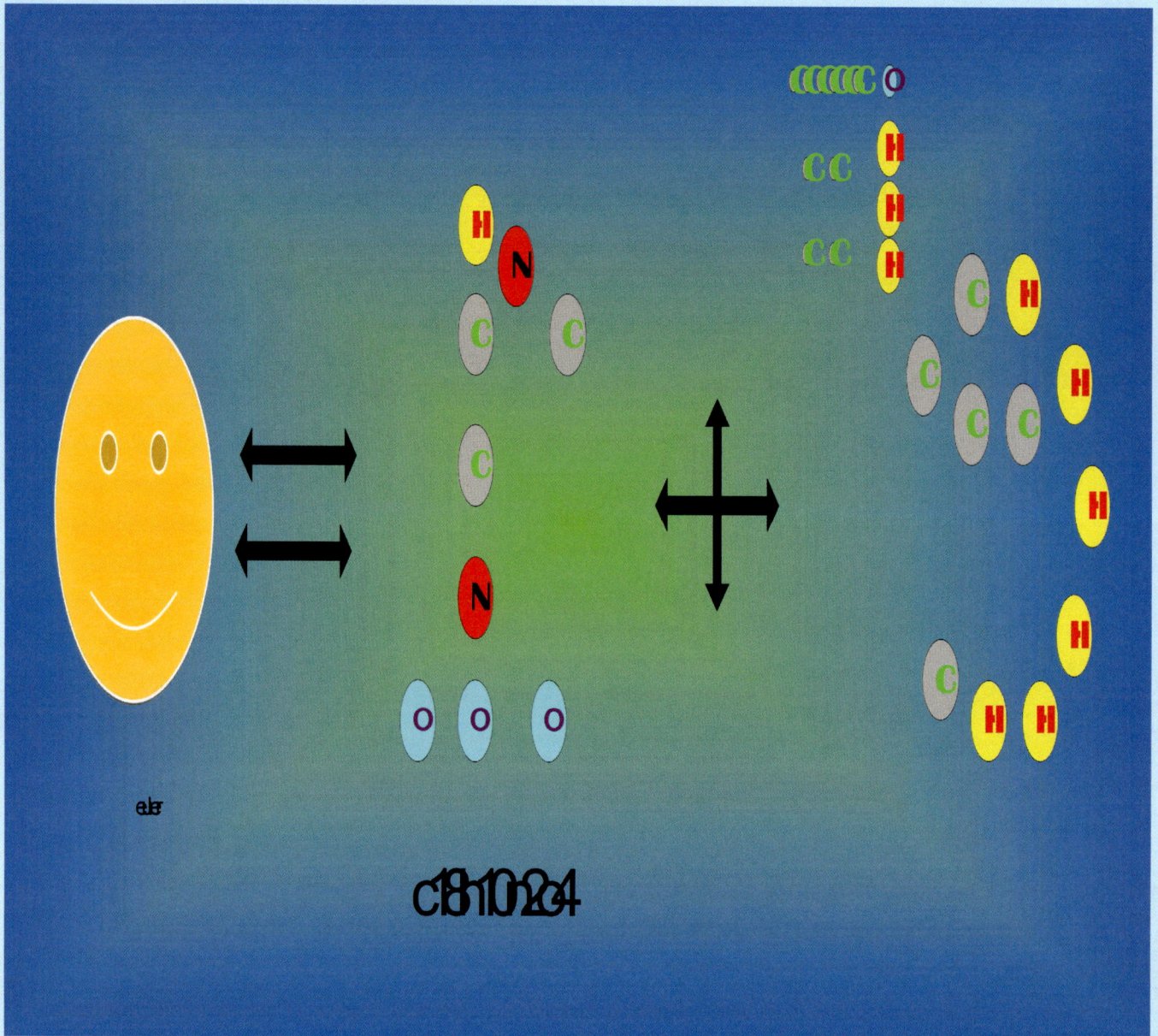

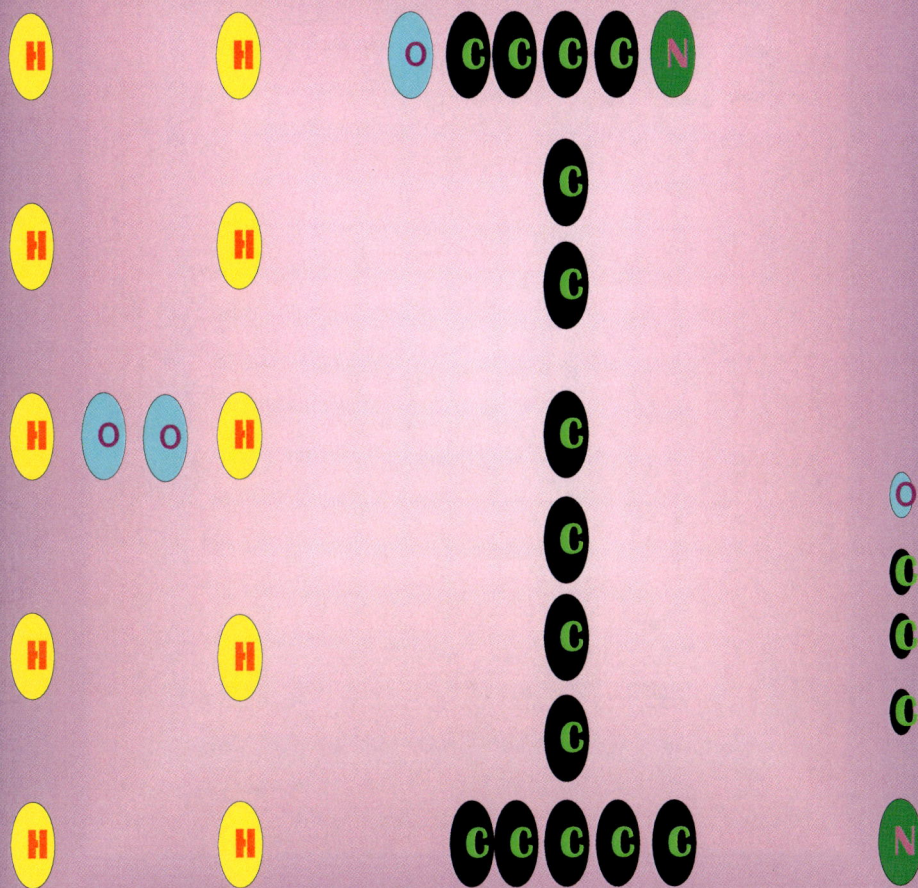

C18H10N2O4

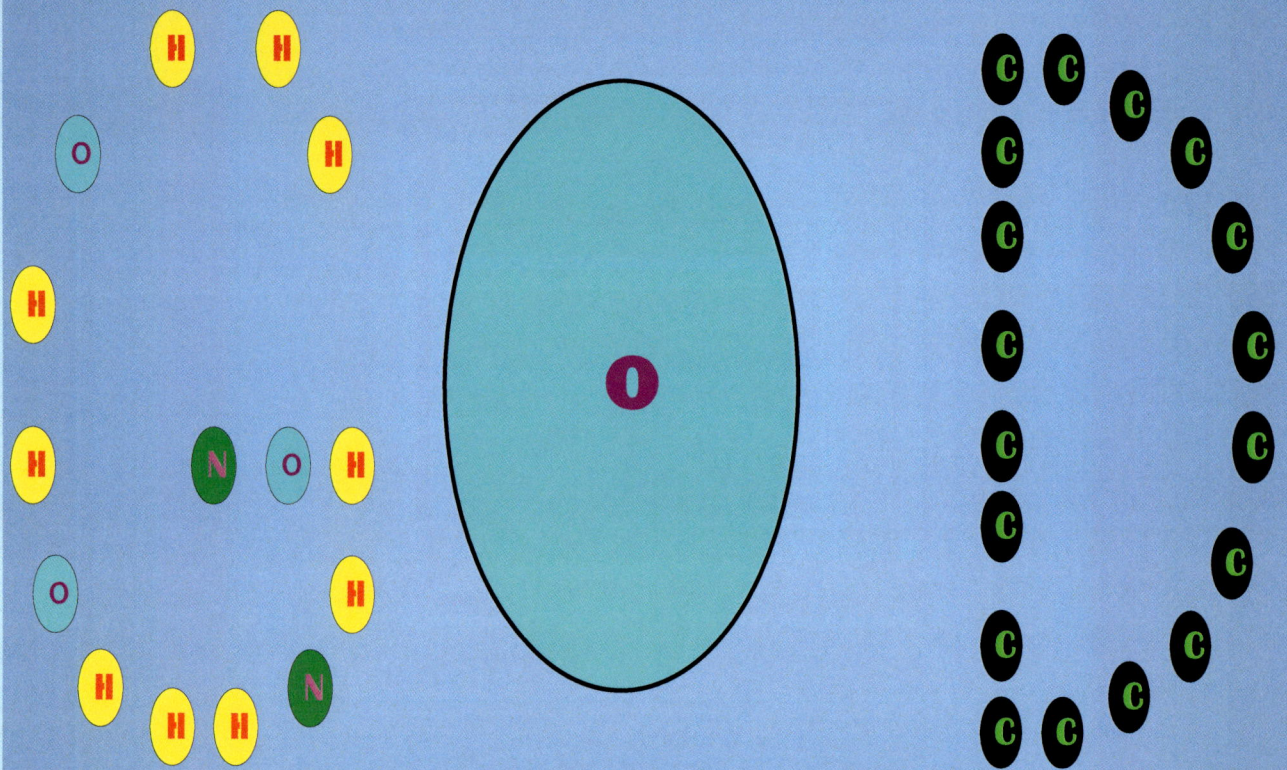

c18h10n2o4

c18h10n2o4

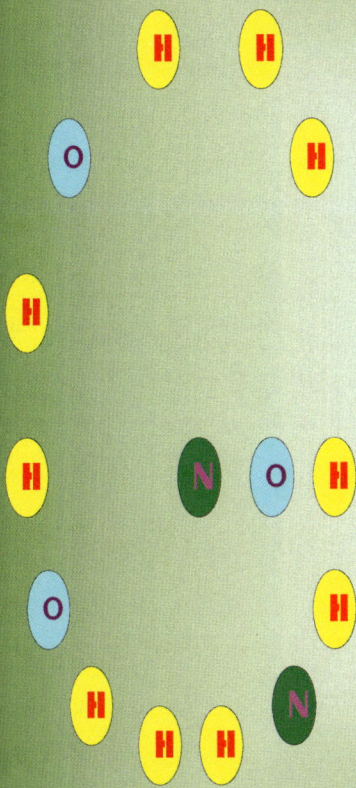
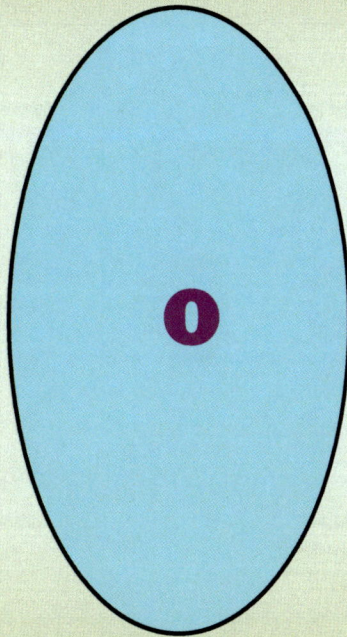

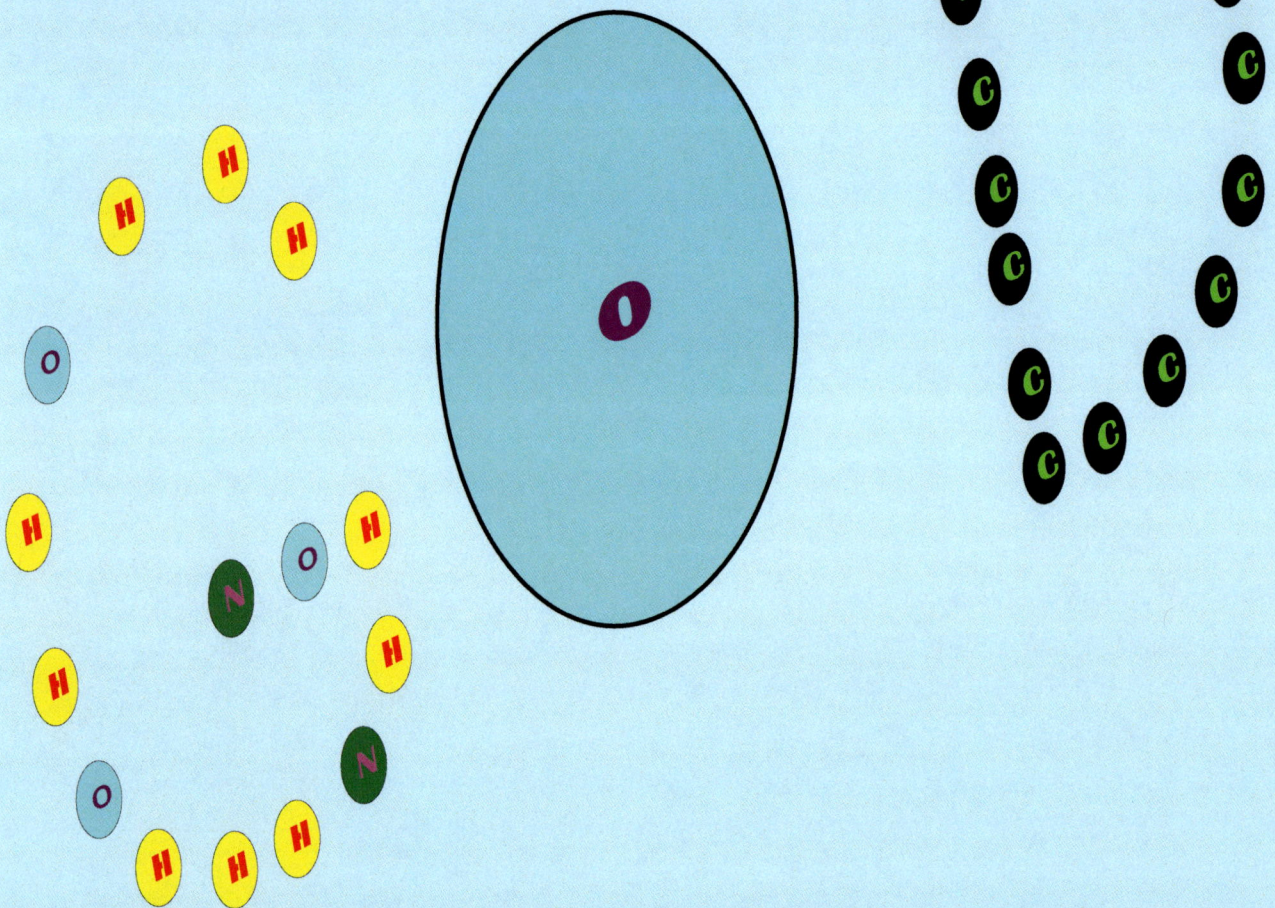

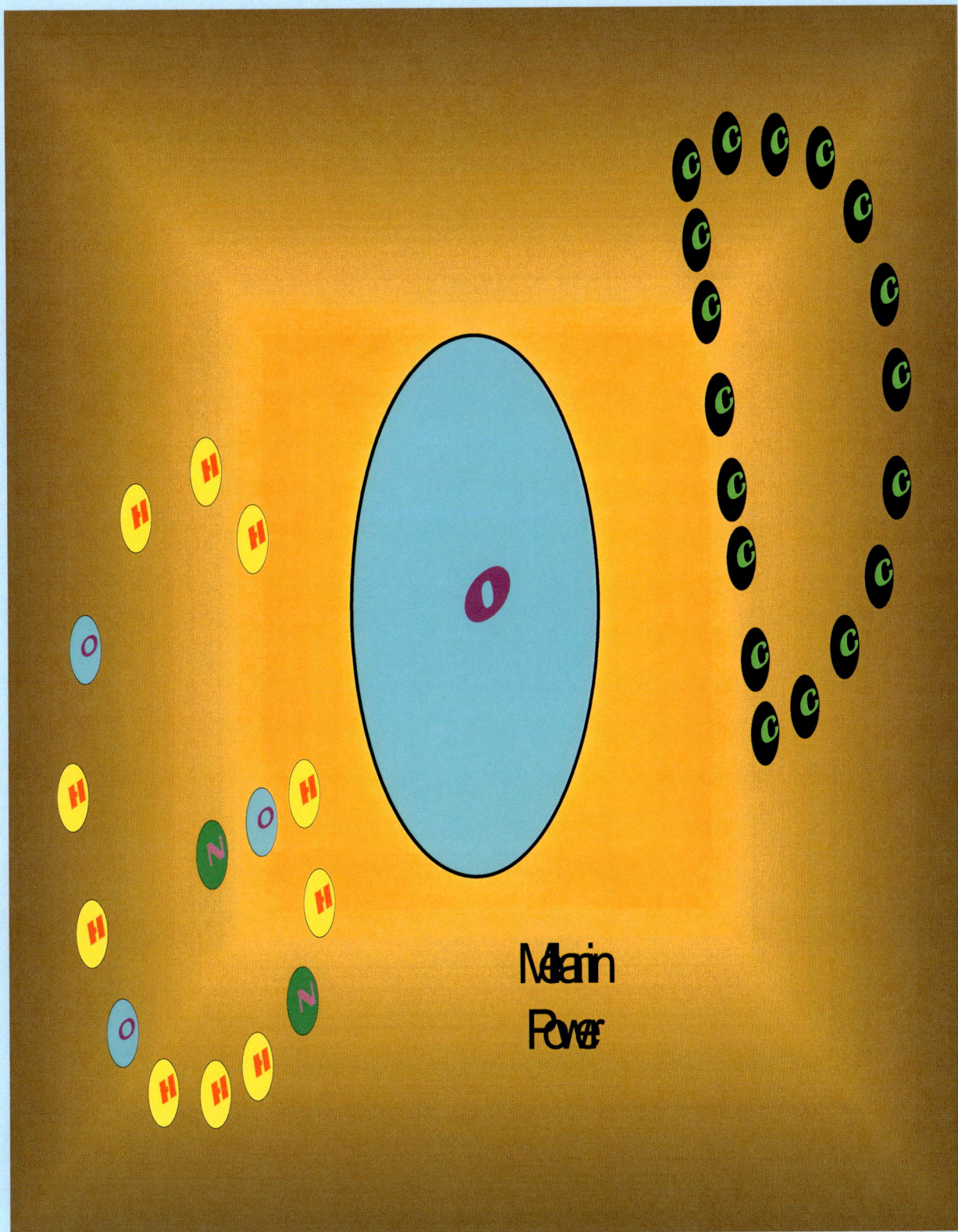

Melanin
Power

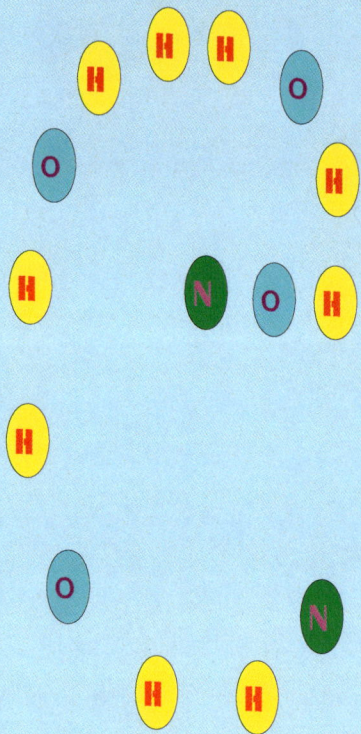

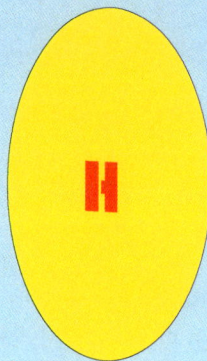

Melanin
Power

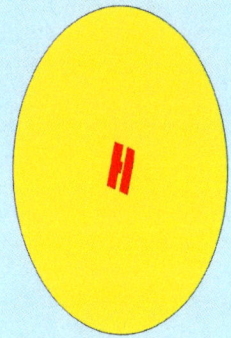

Melanin
Power

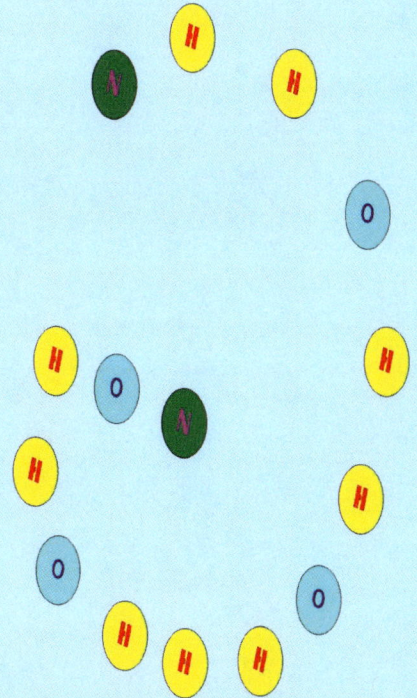

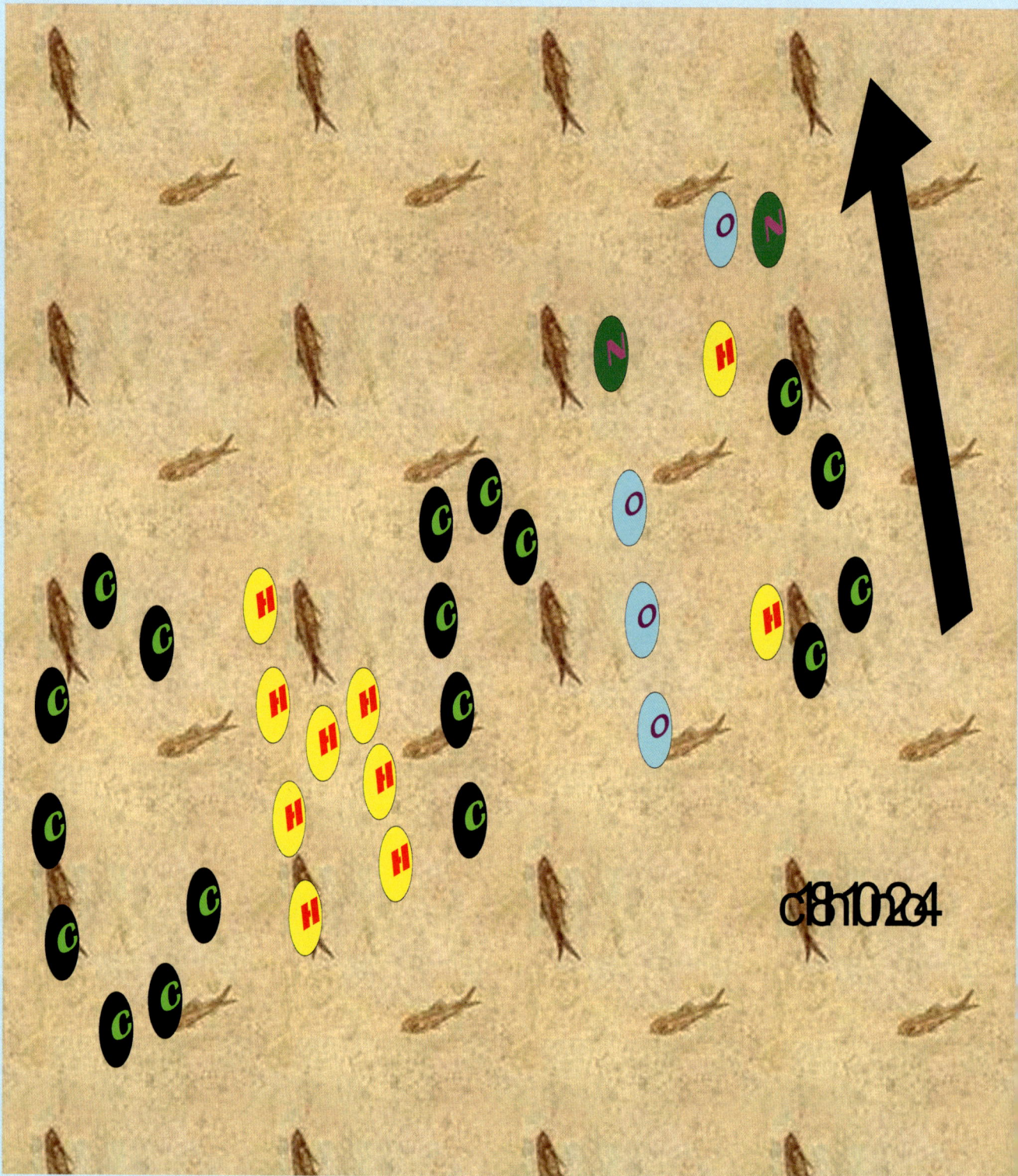

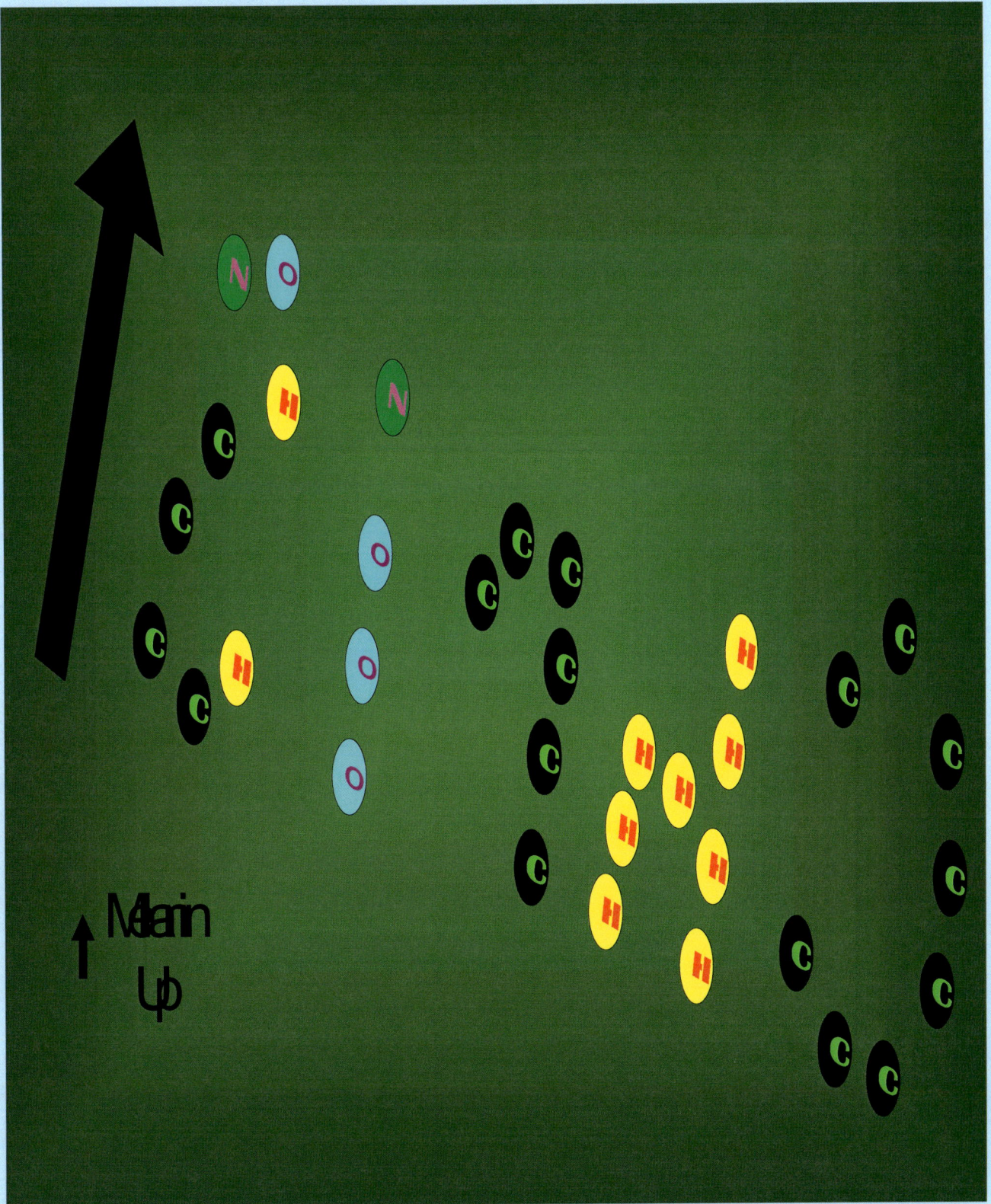

Melanin Up

Melanin
Power.

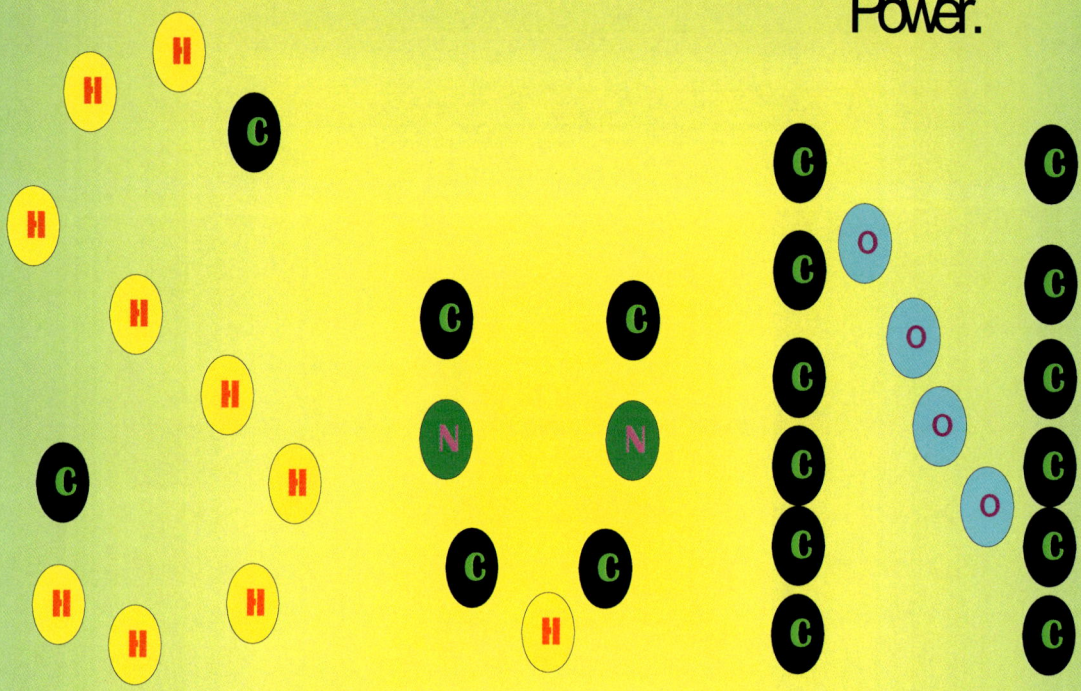

©

58

c18h10n2o4

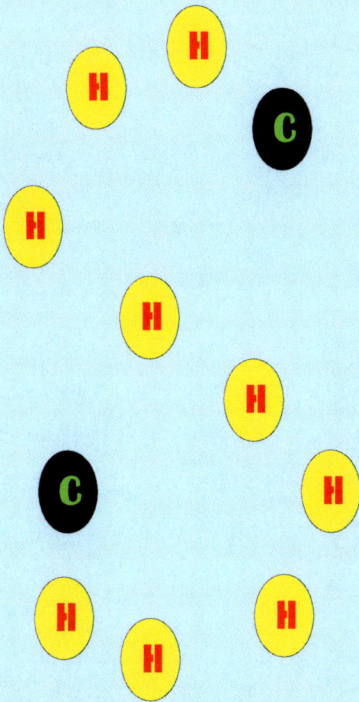 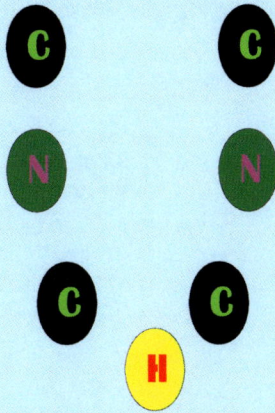 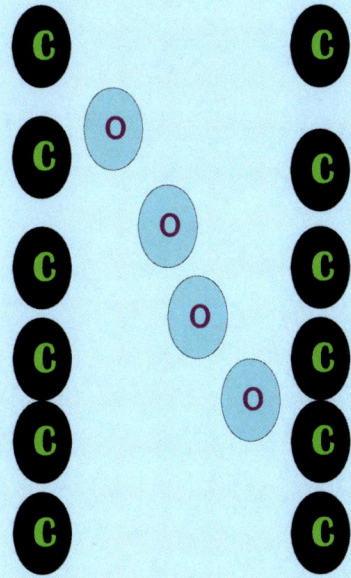

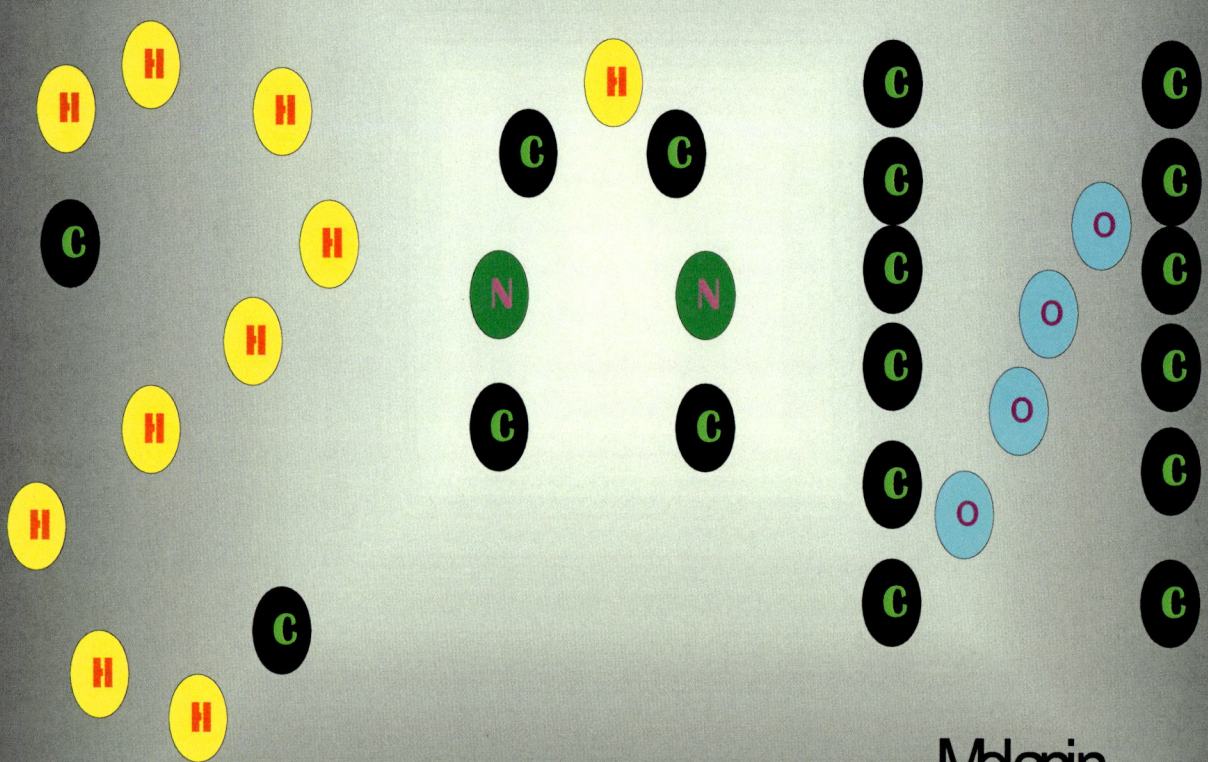

Melanin Power.

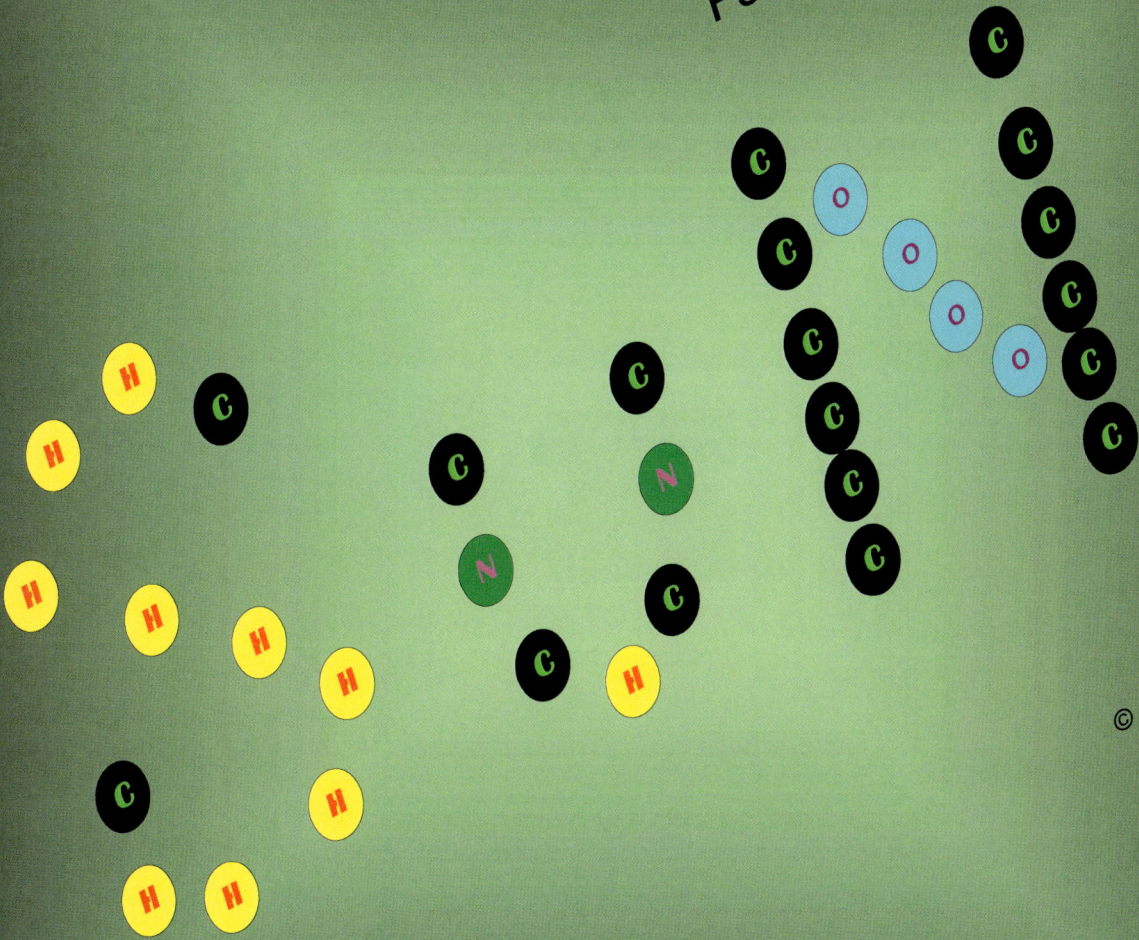

Psalm 84:11

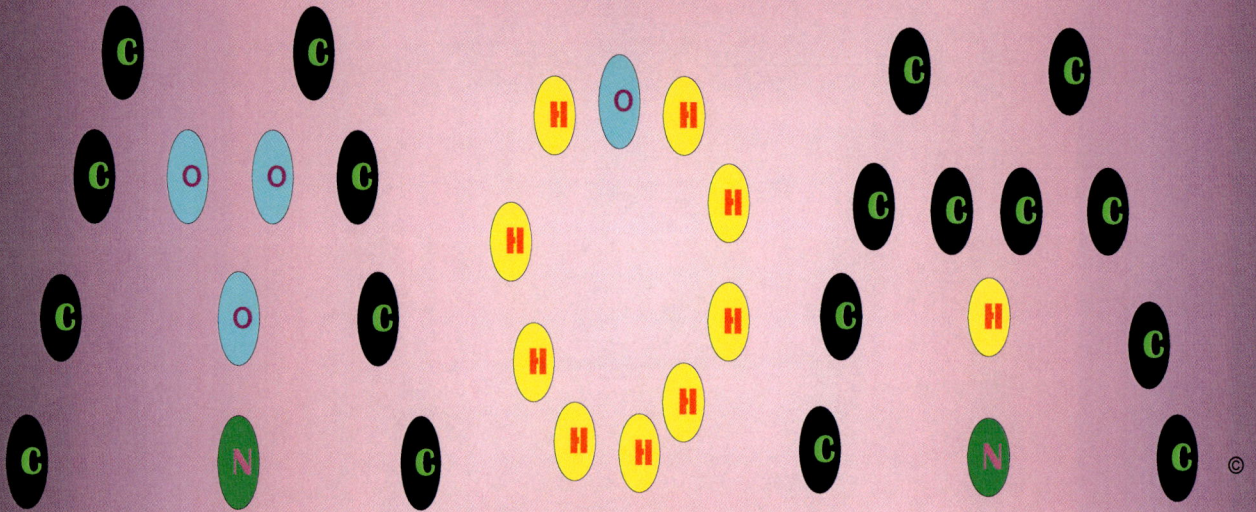

Melanin
Power.

Melanin
Power.

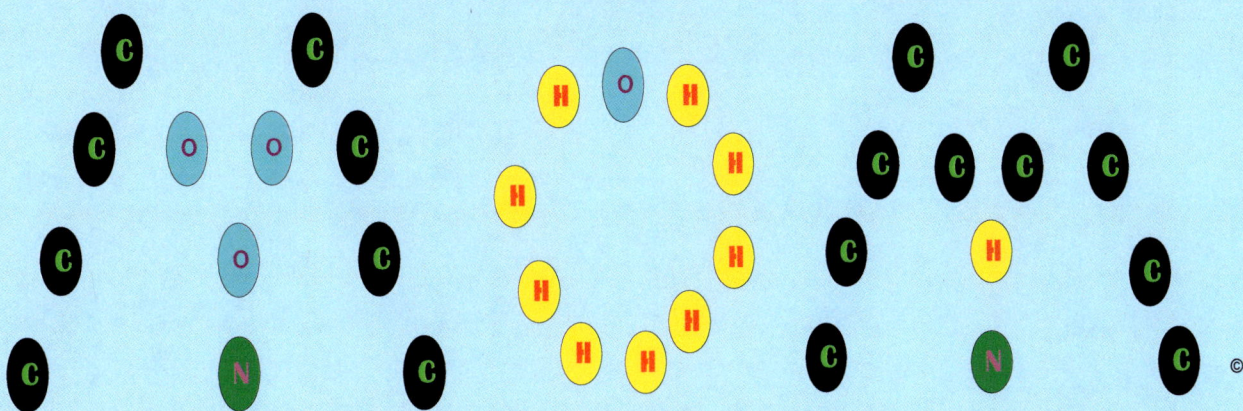

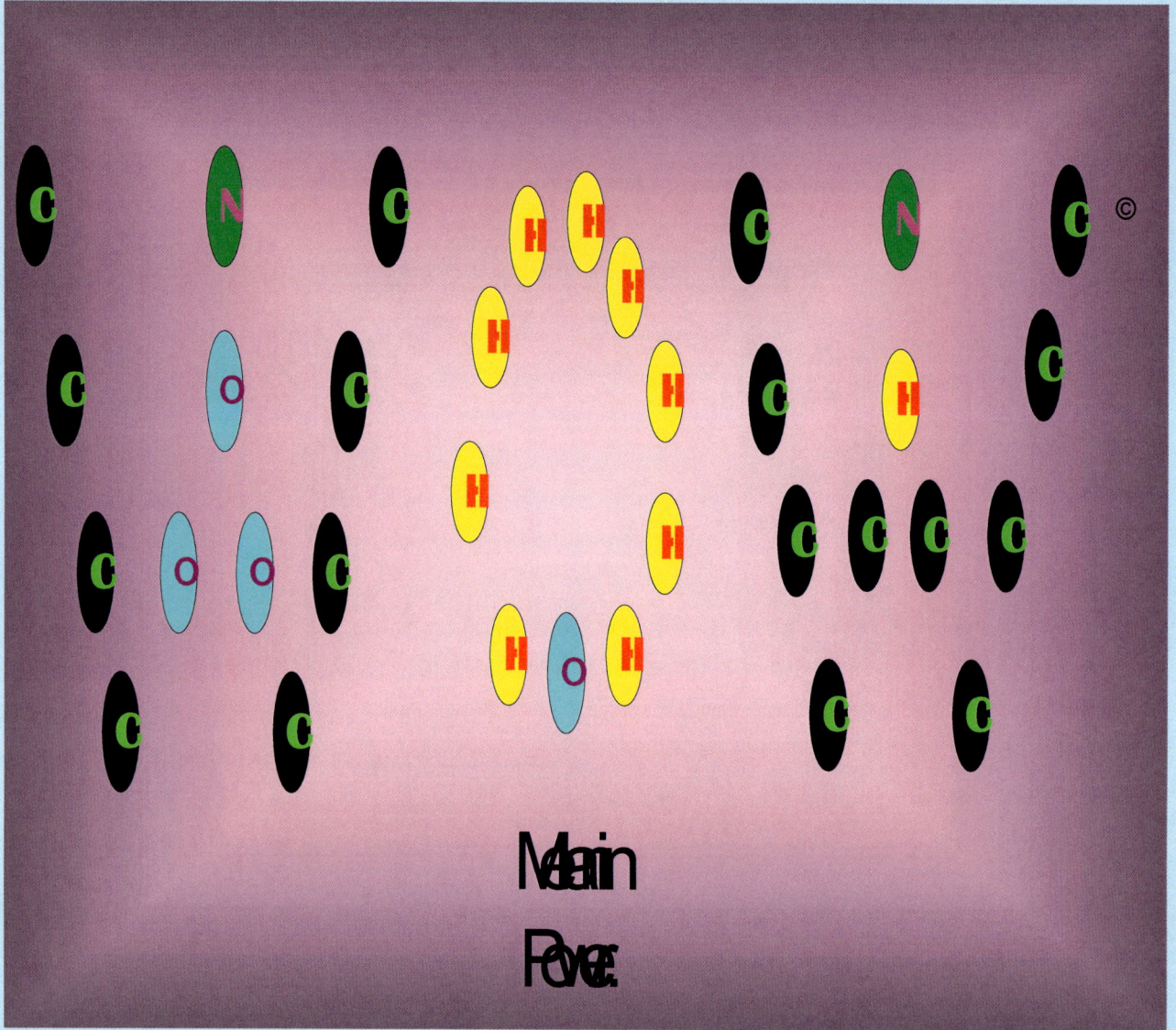

Melatonin

Power

Melanin
Power.

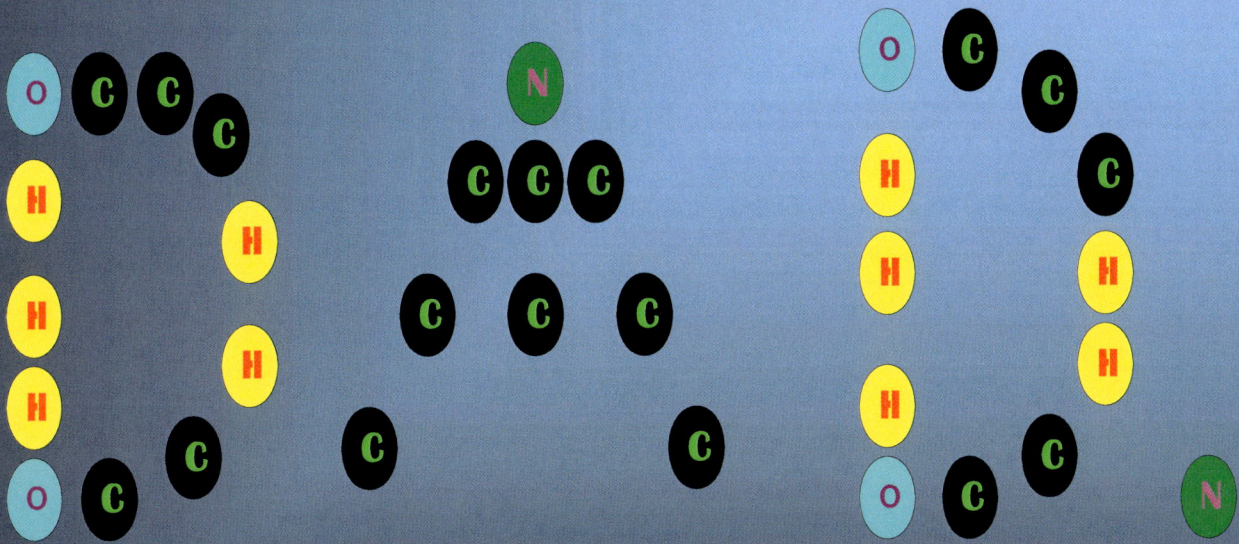

65

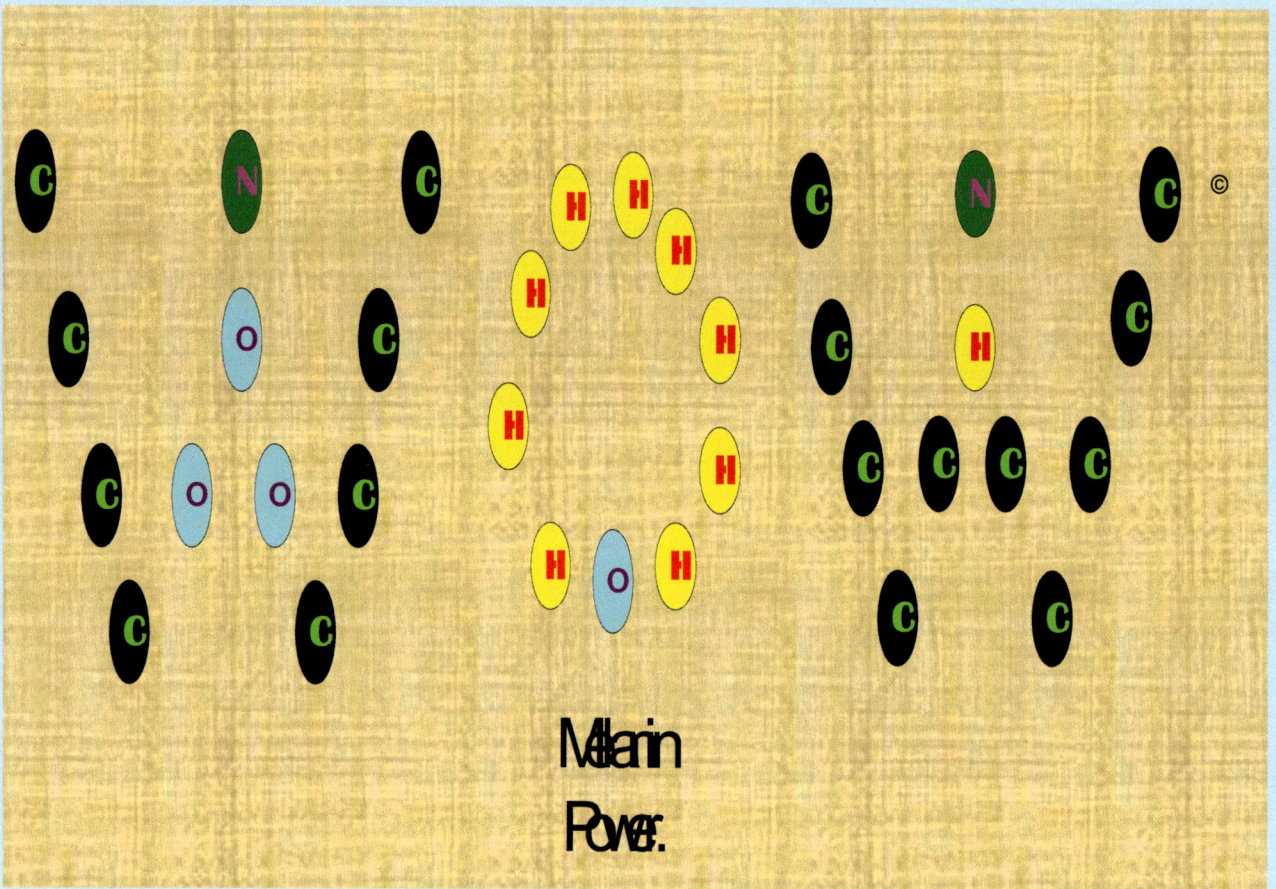

Melanin
Power.

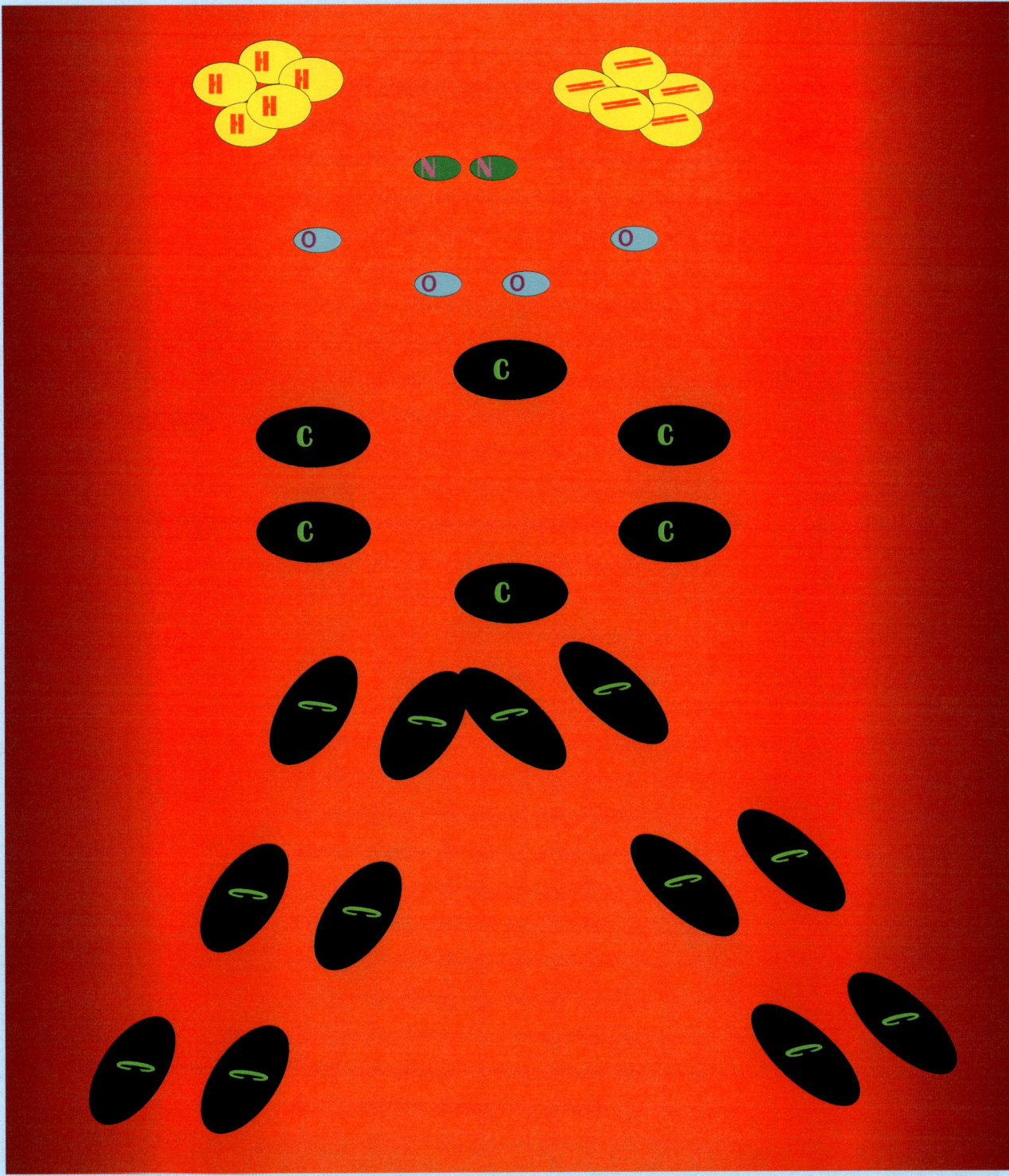

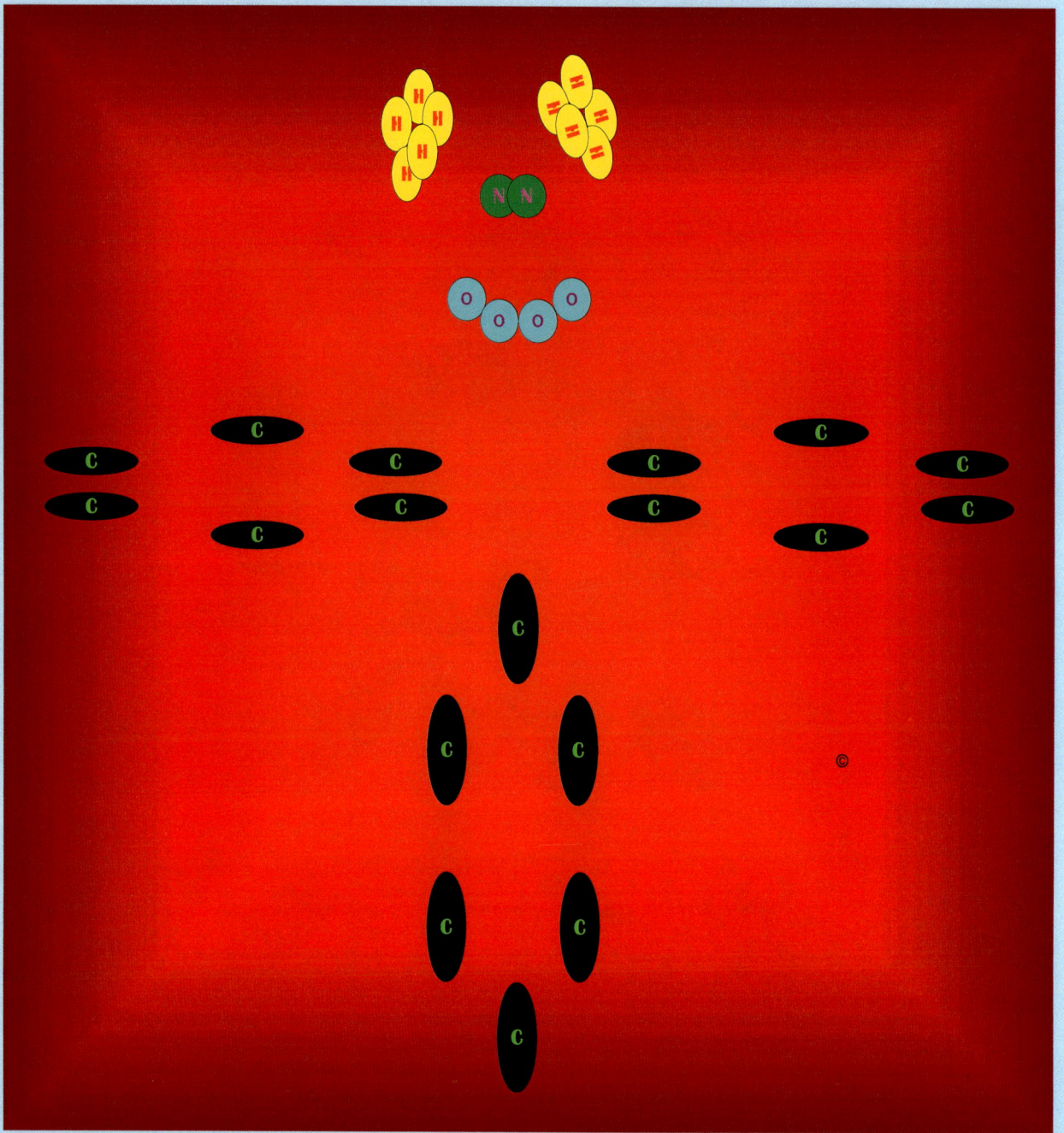

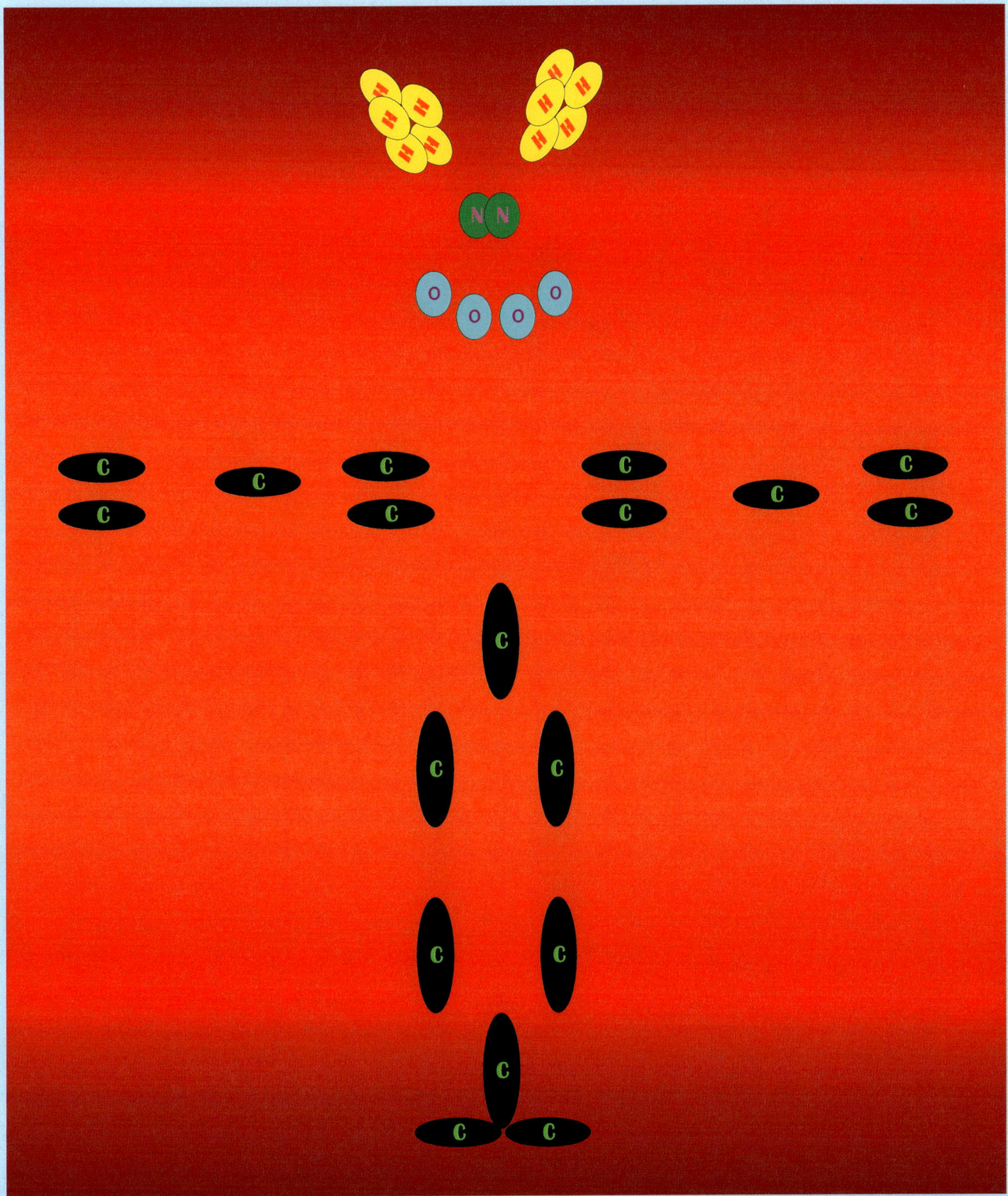

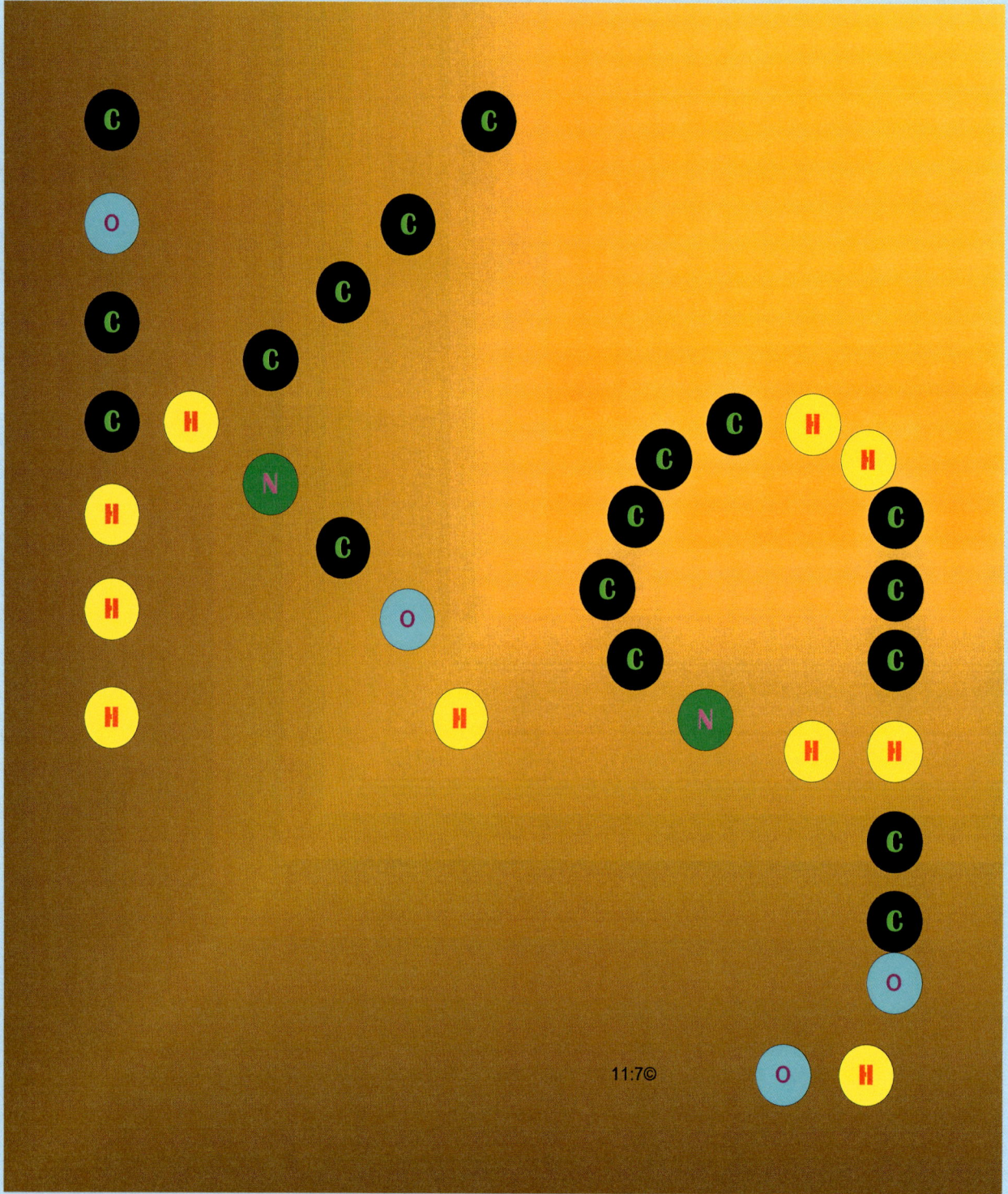

11:7©

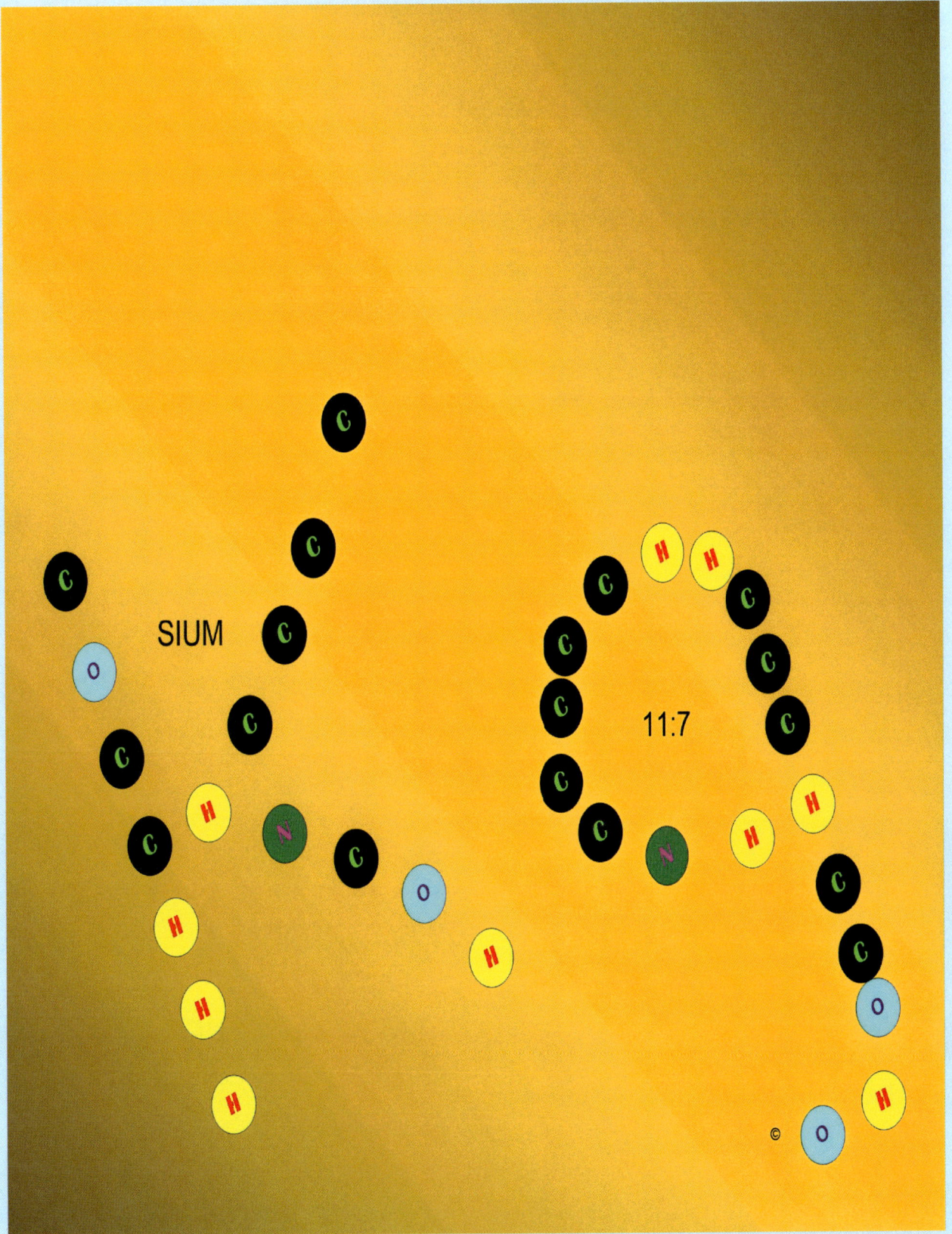

SIUM

11:7

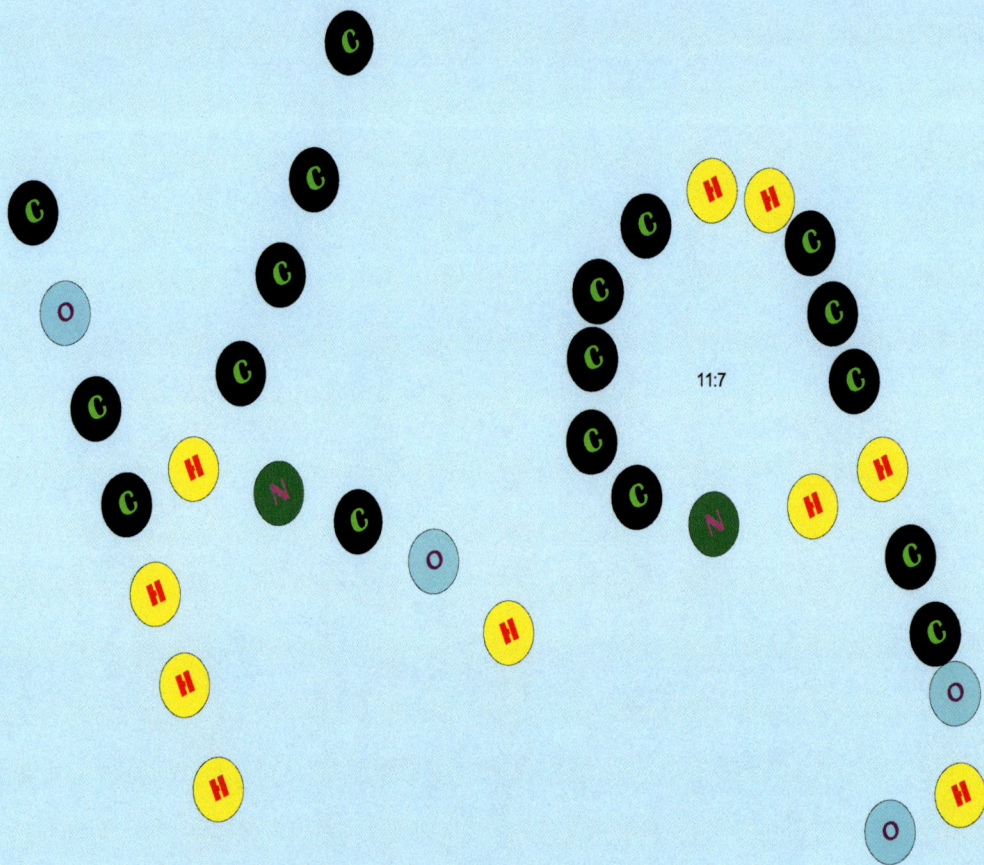

11:7

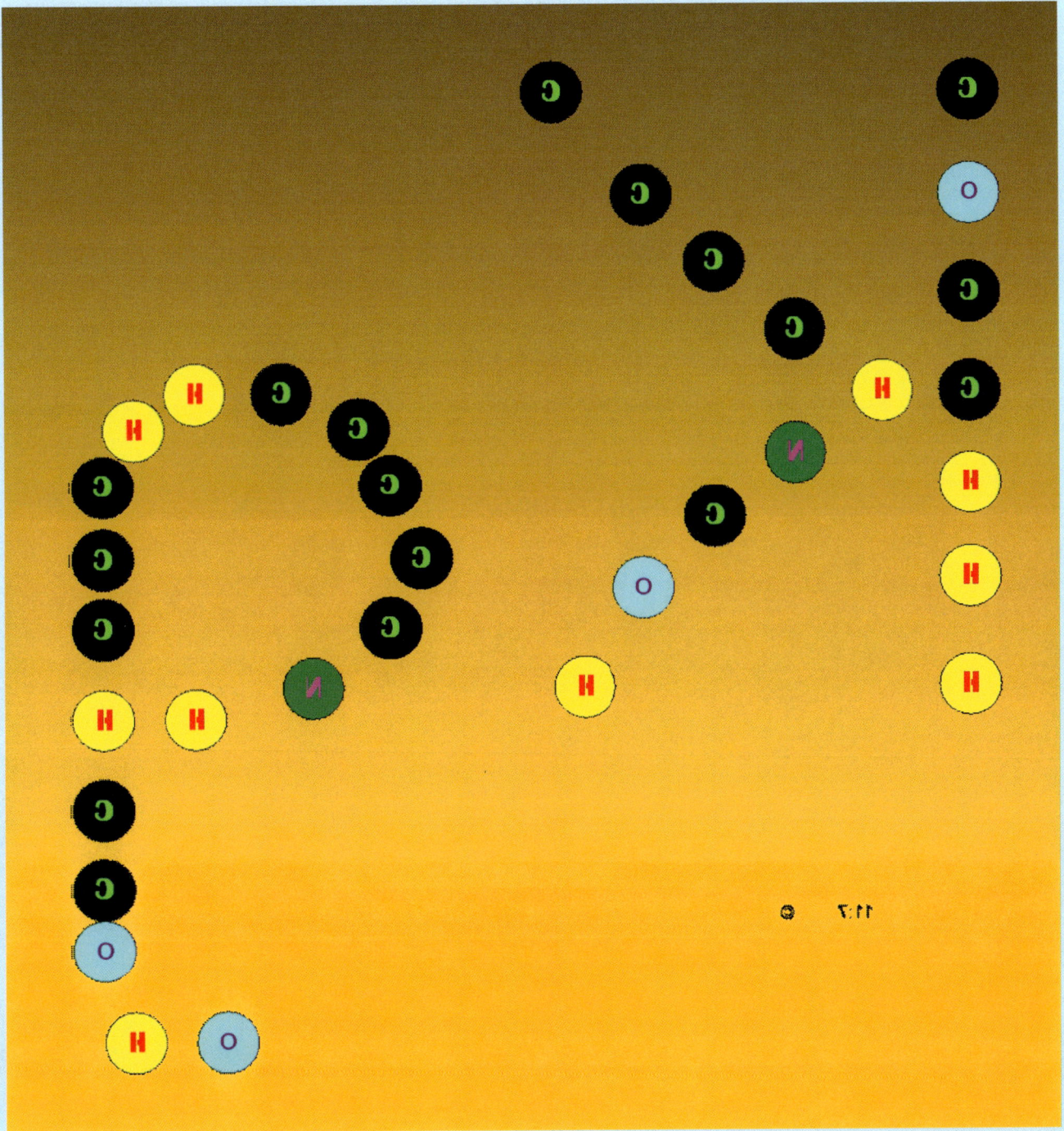

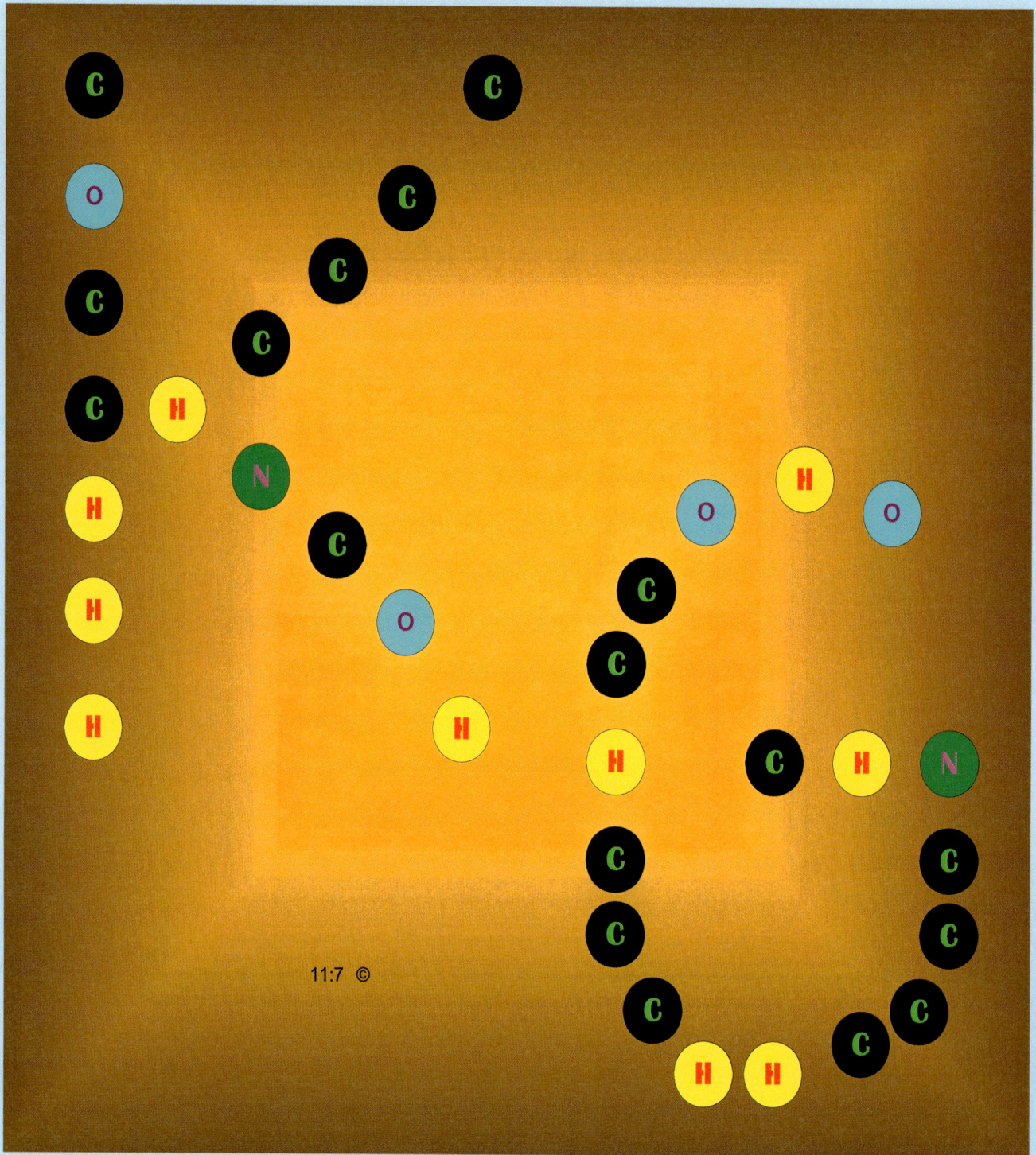

11:7 ©

74

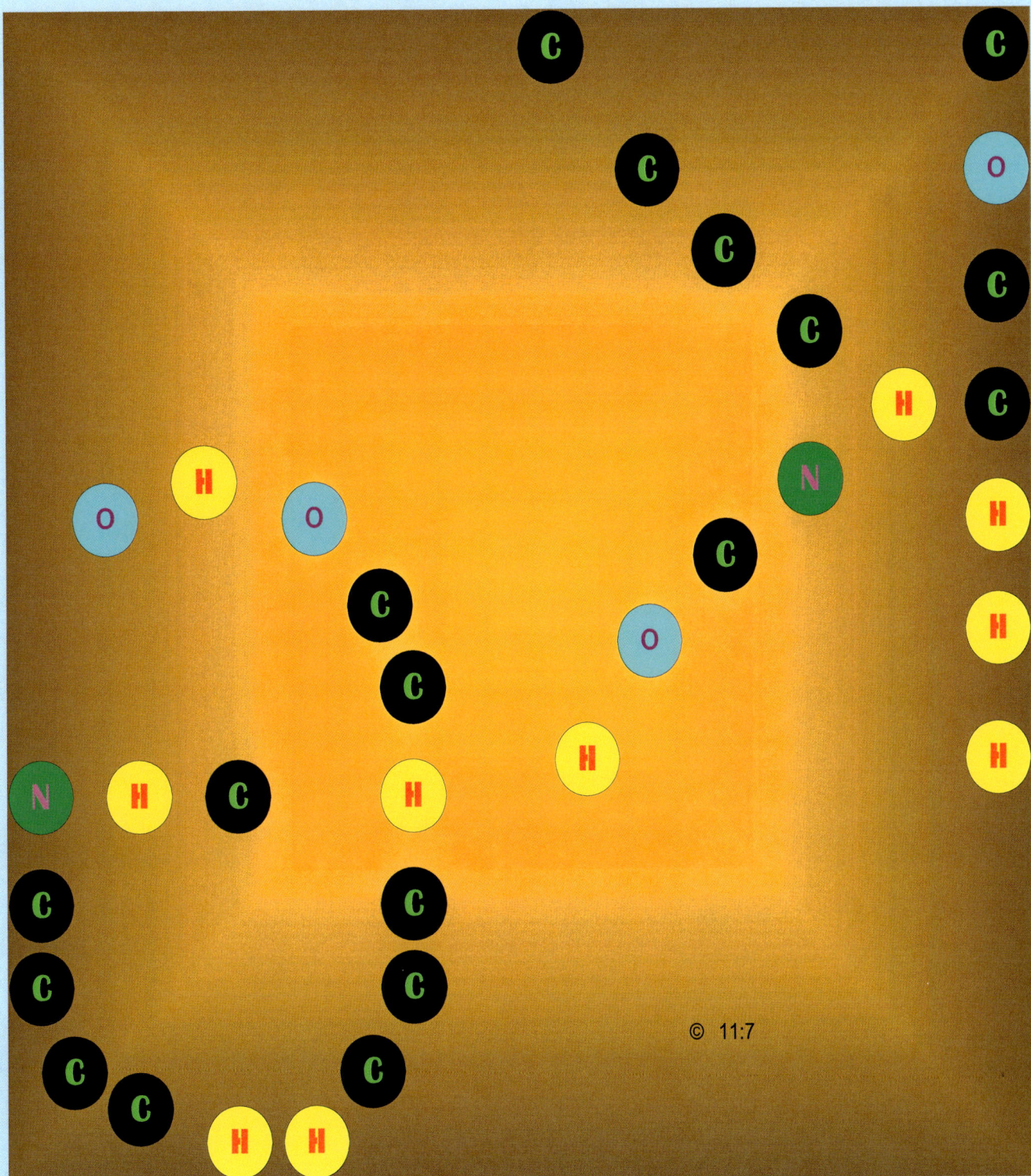

© 11:7

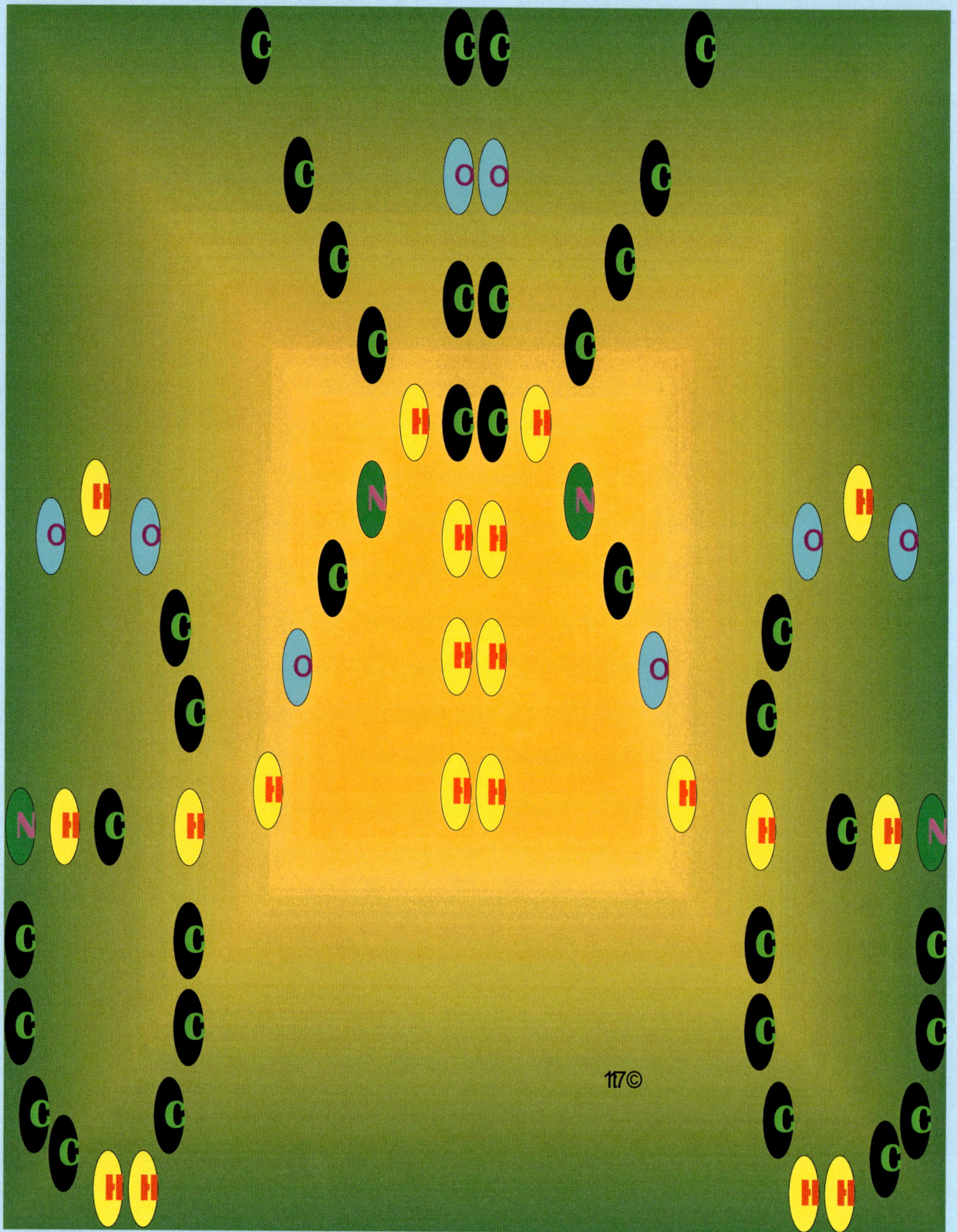

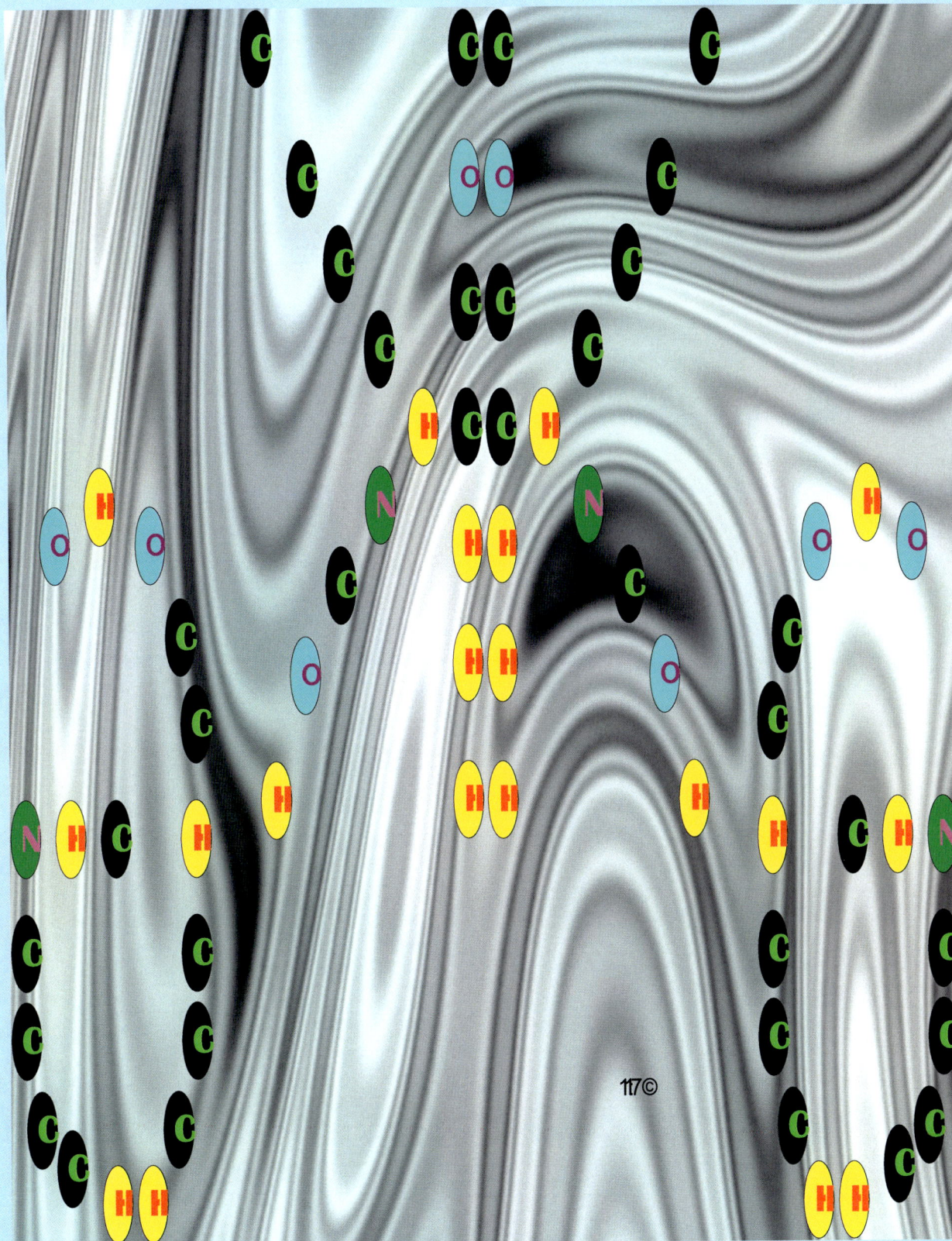

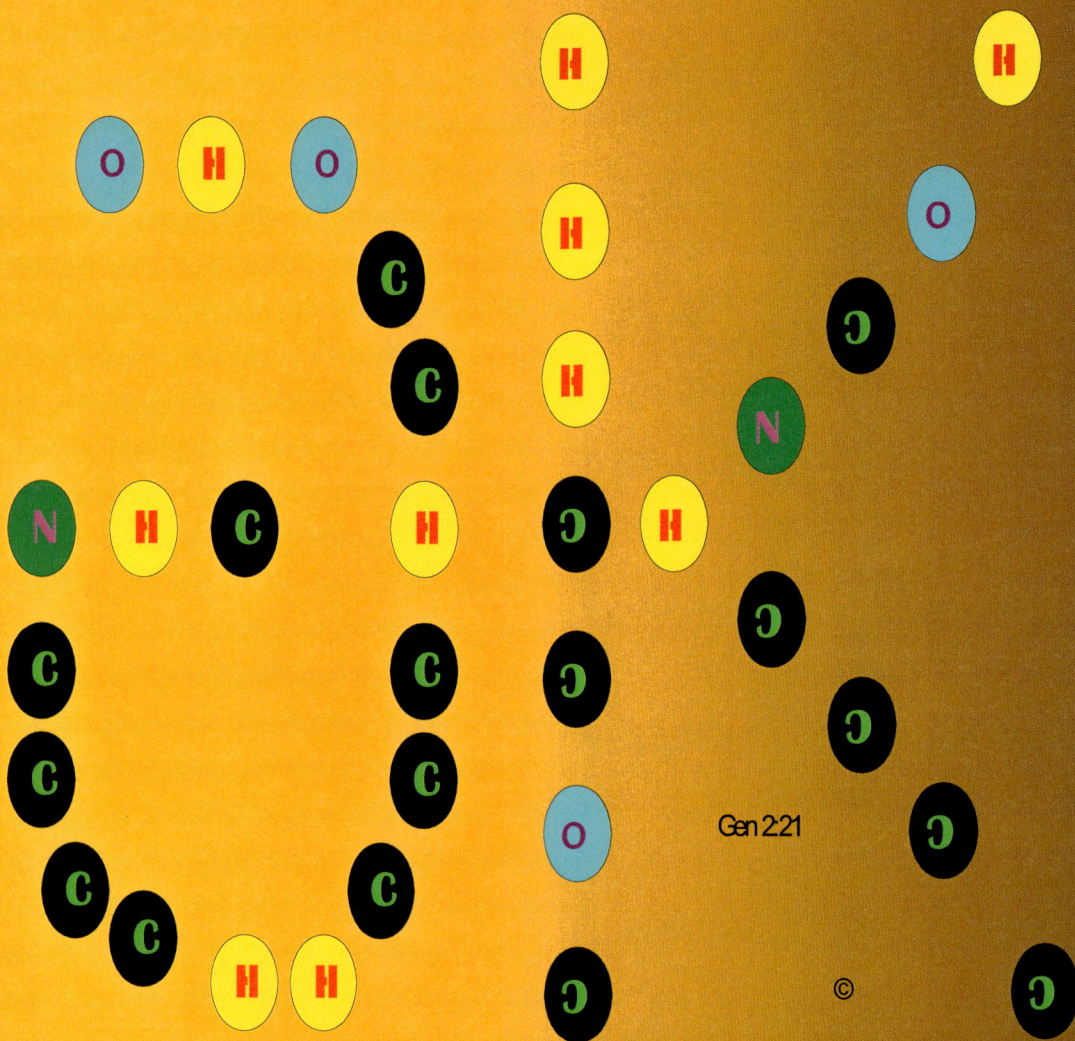

Gen 2:21

©

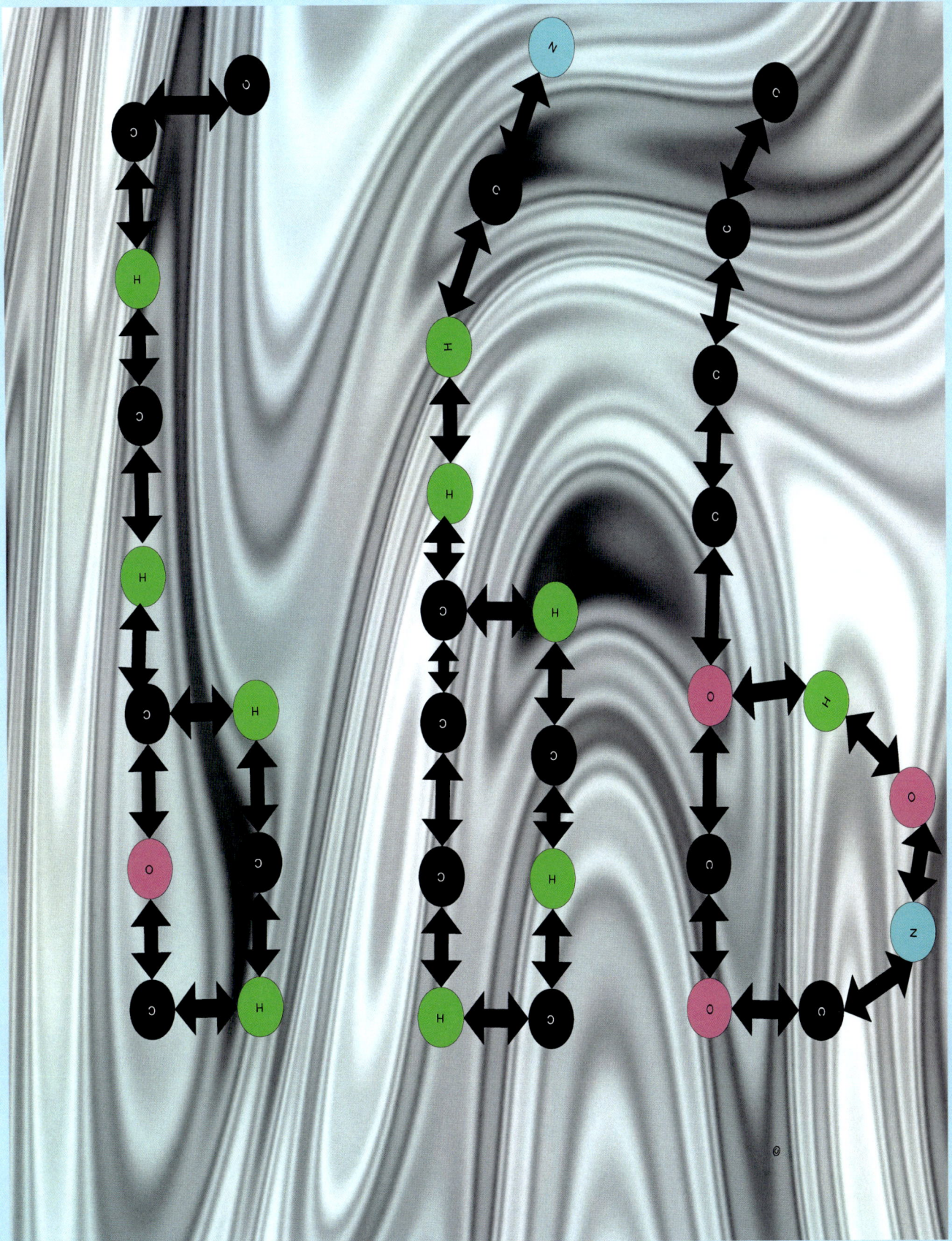

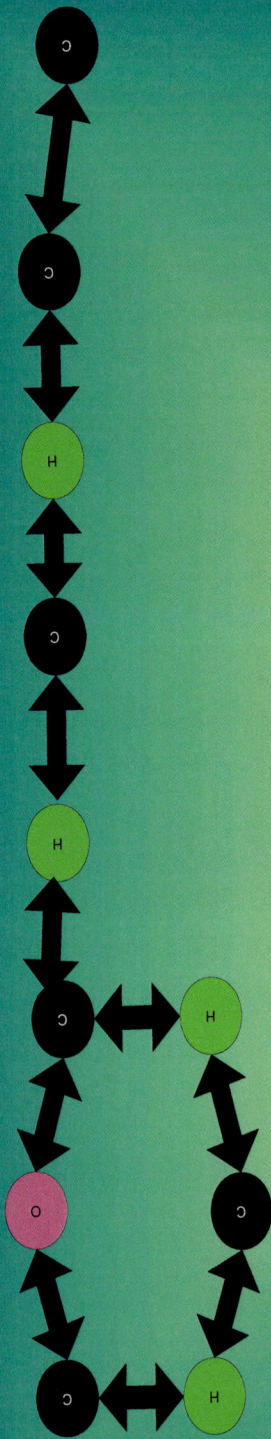

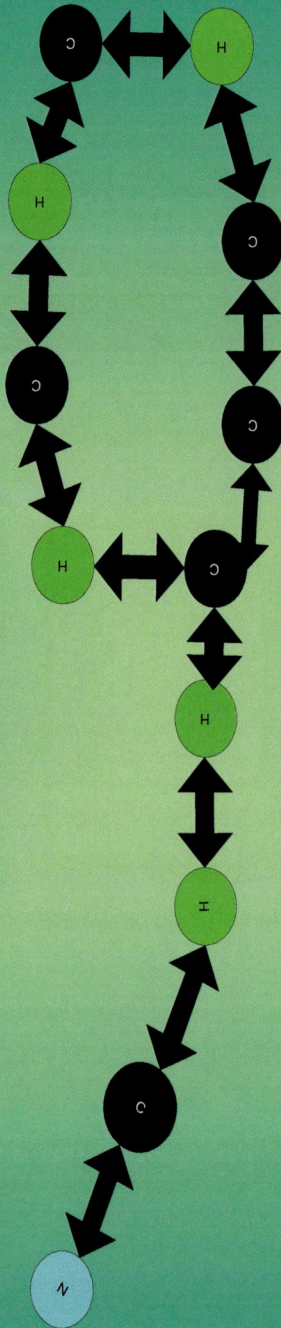

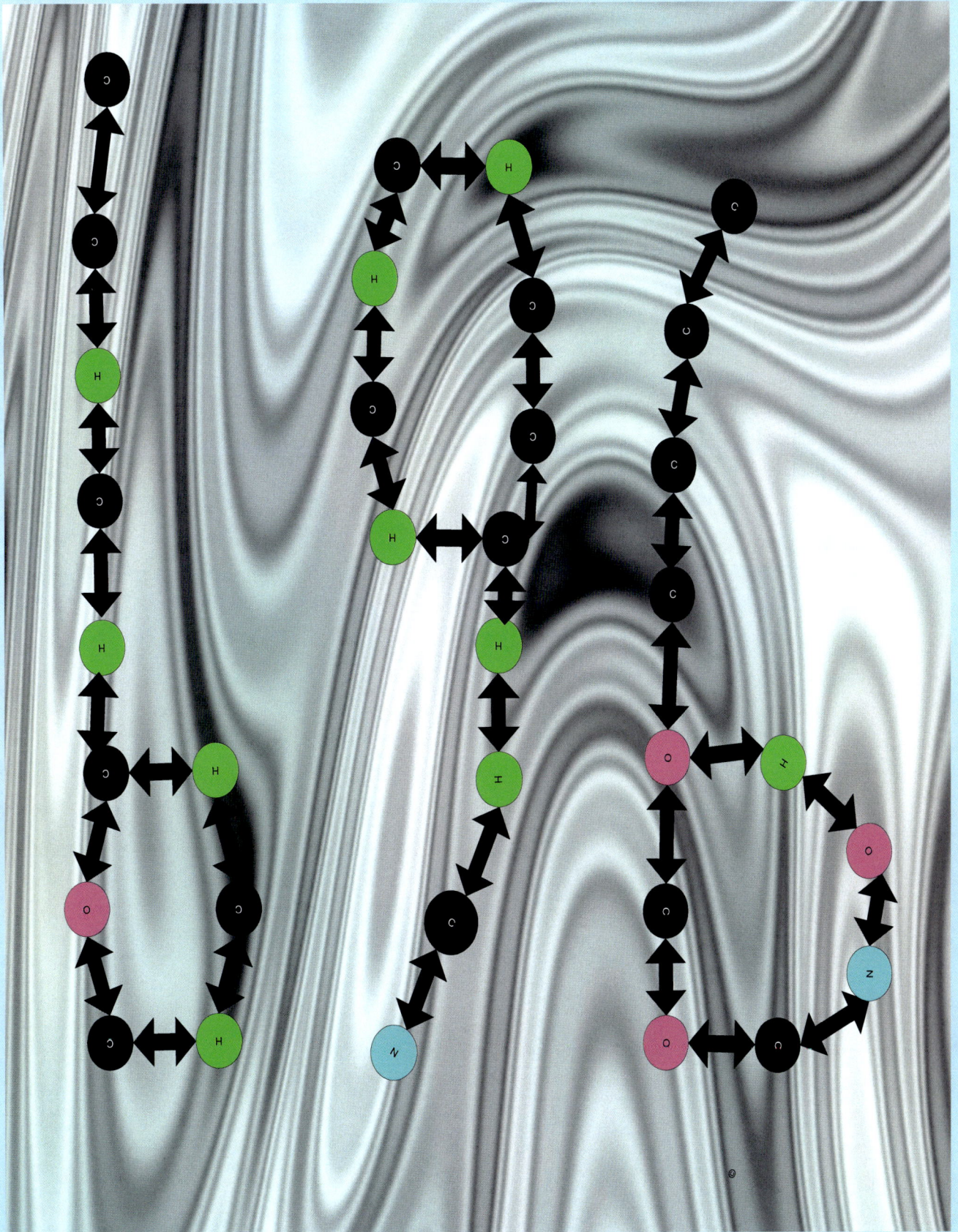

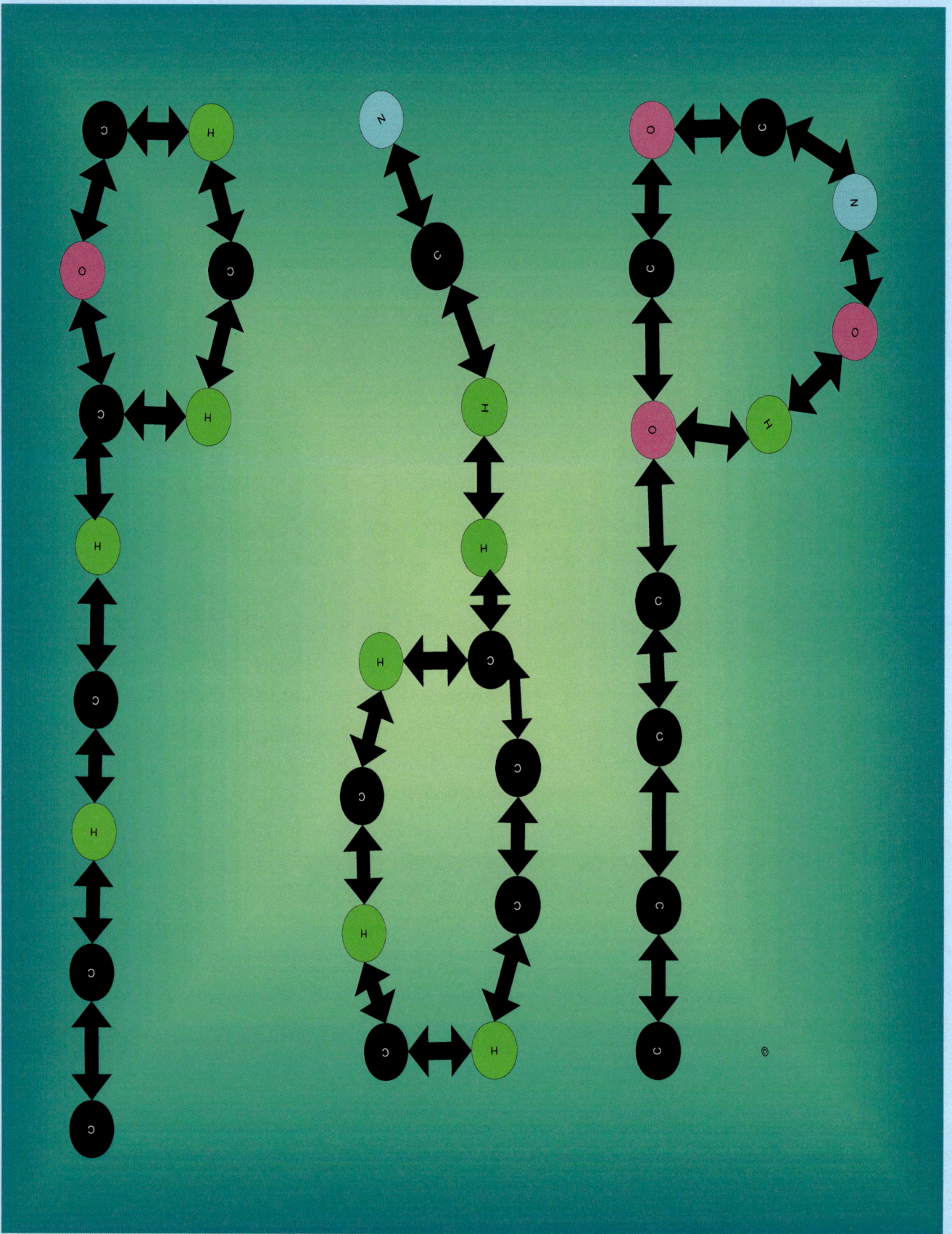

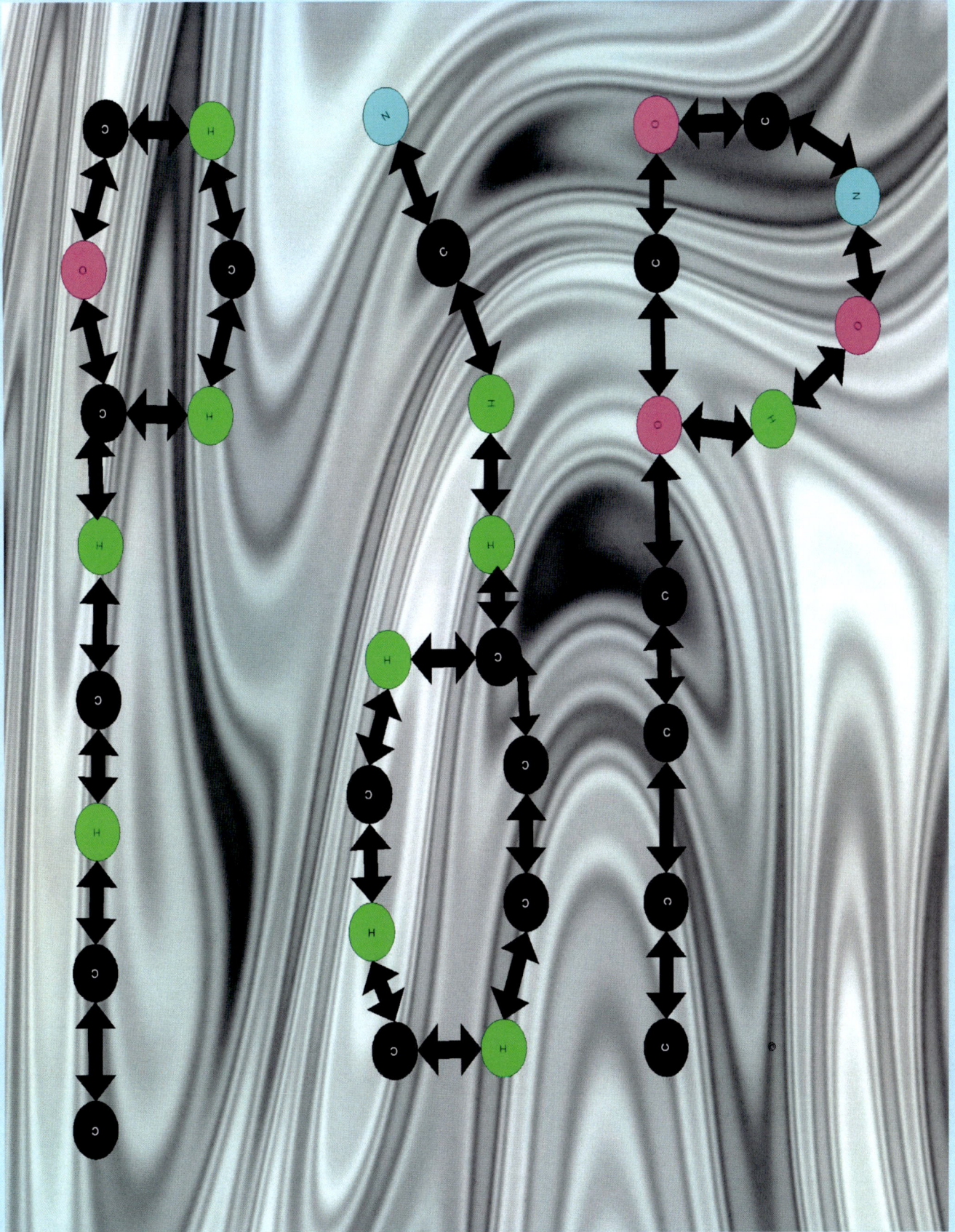

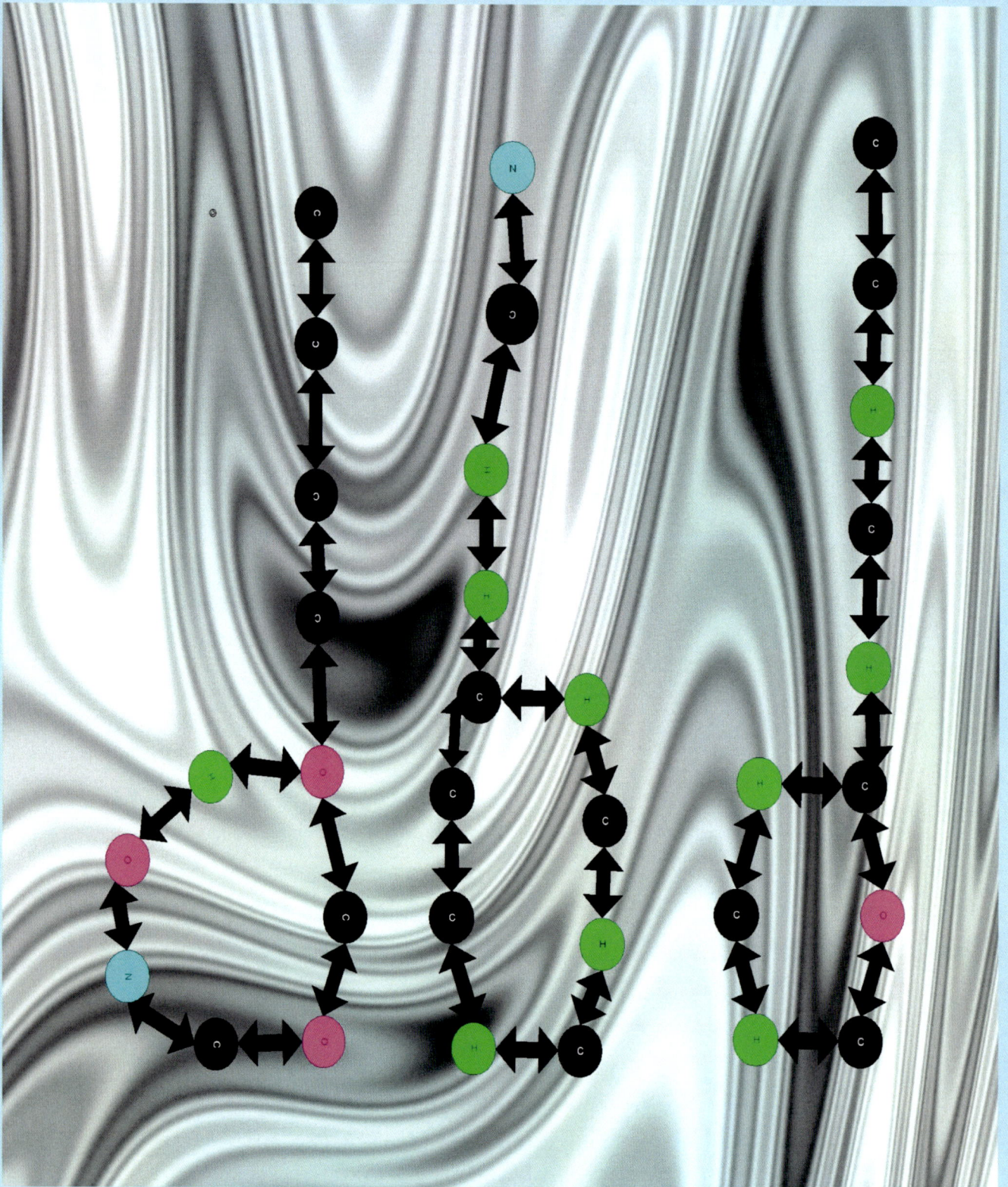

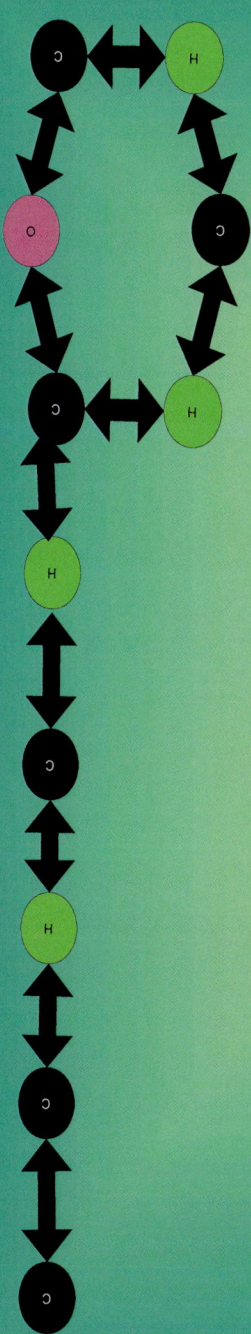
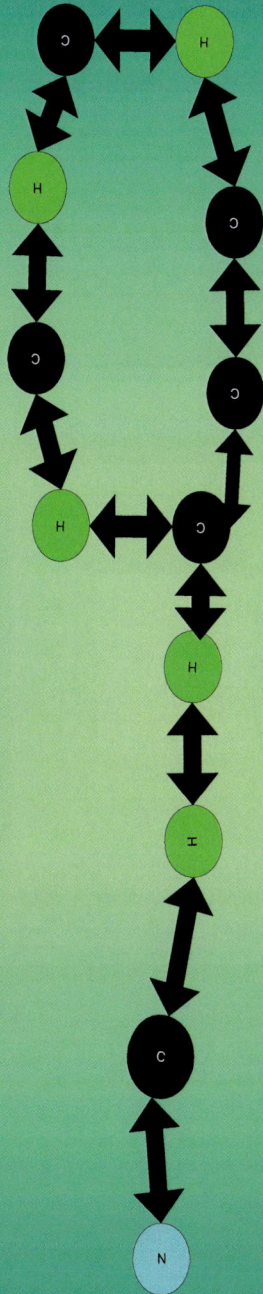
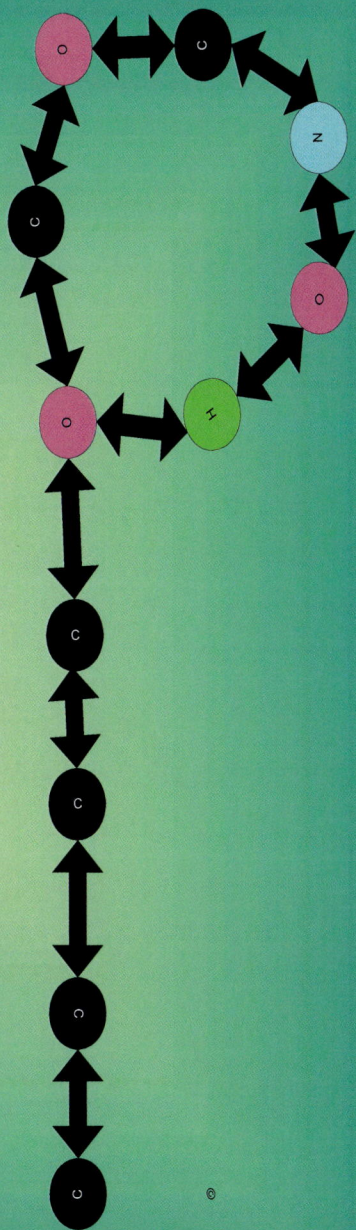

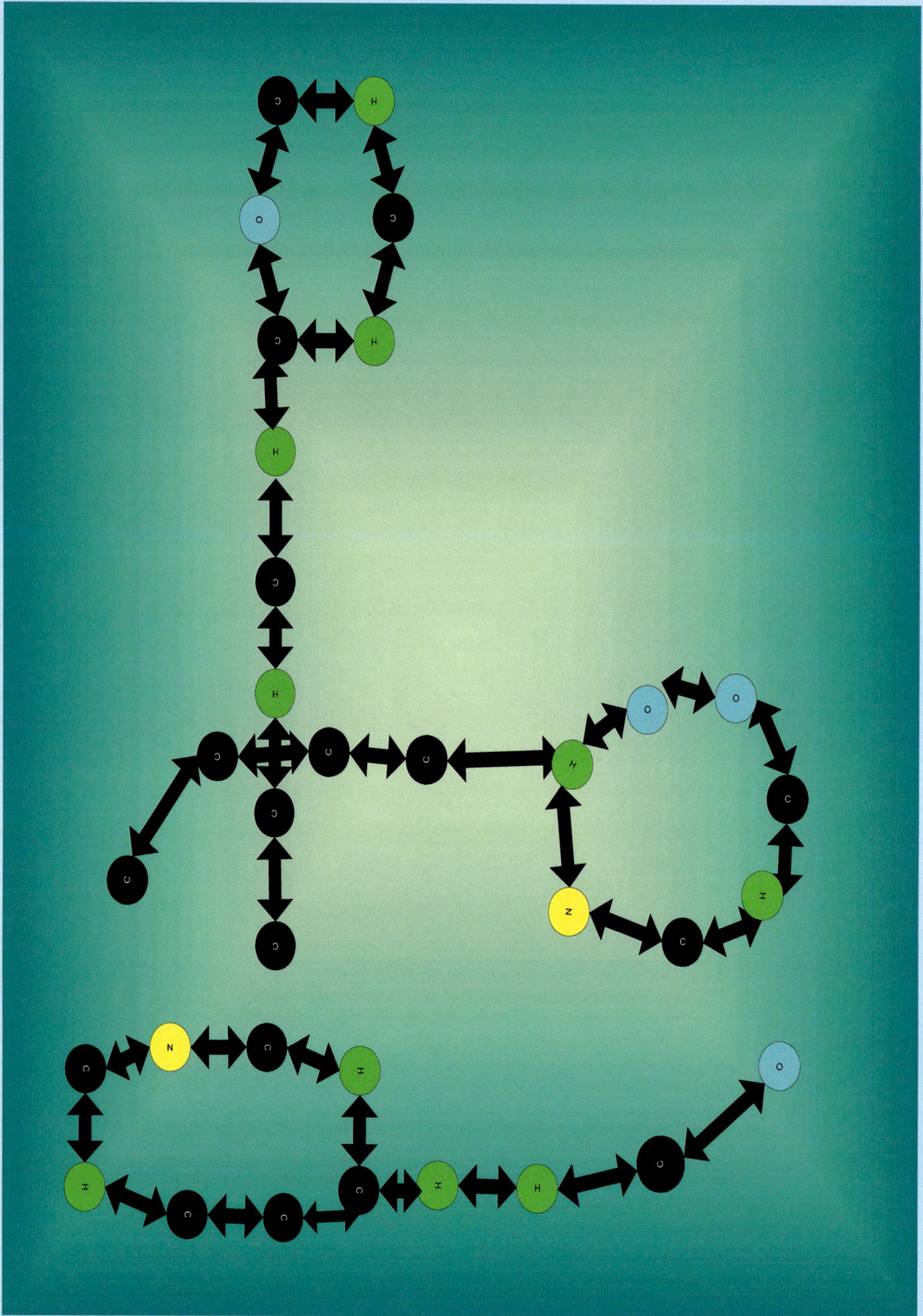

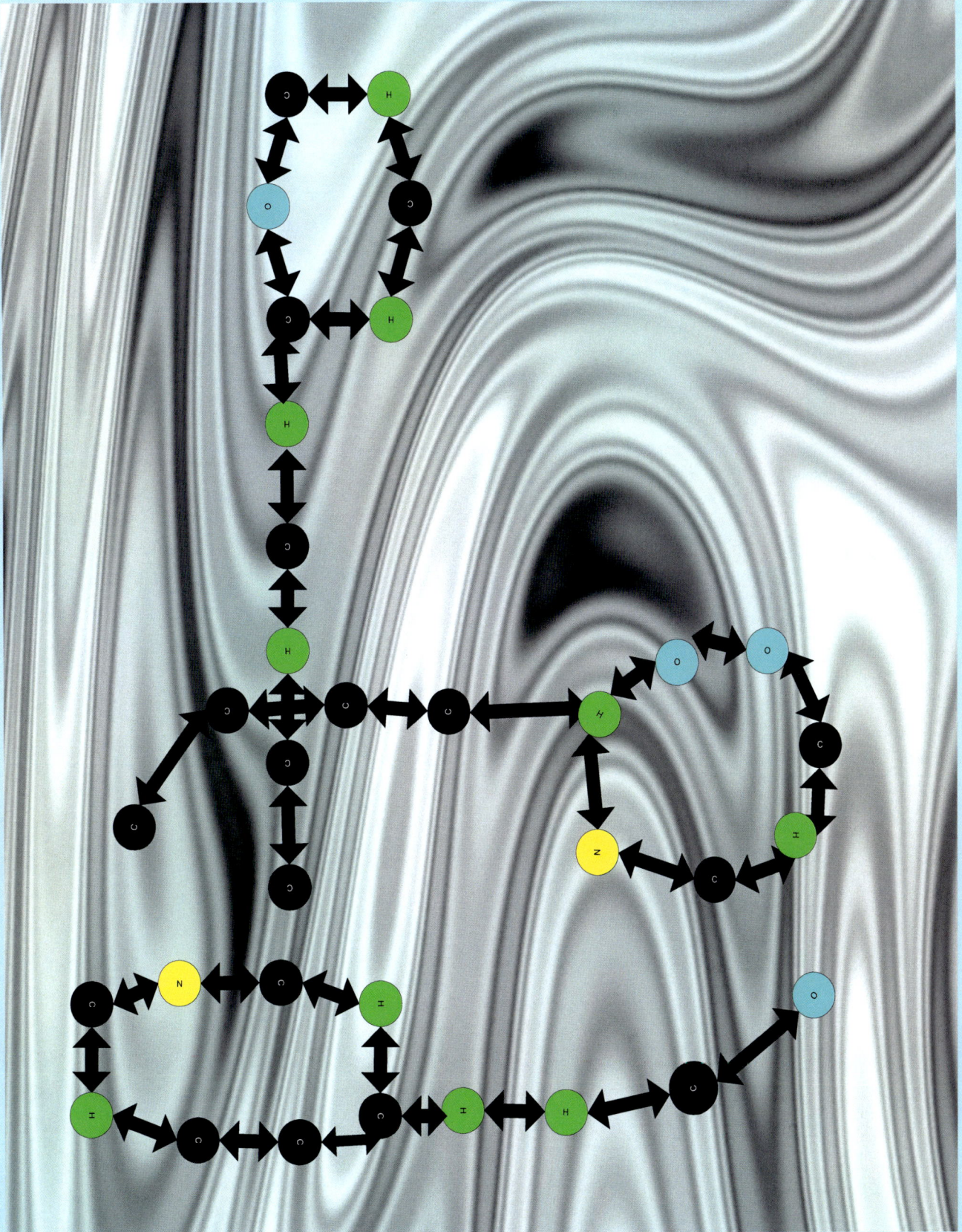

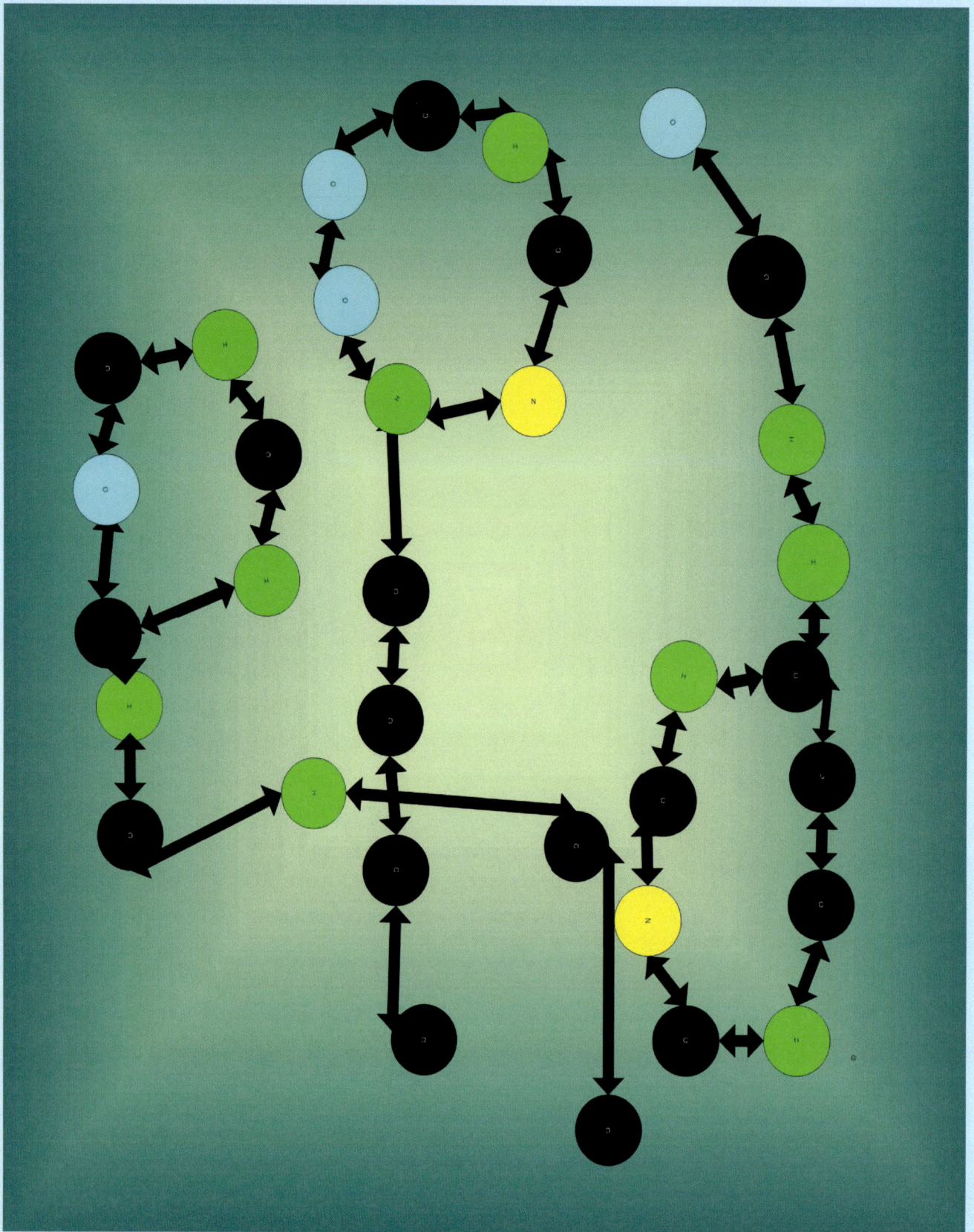

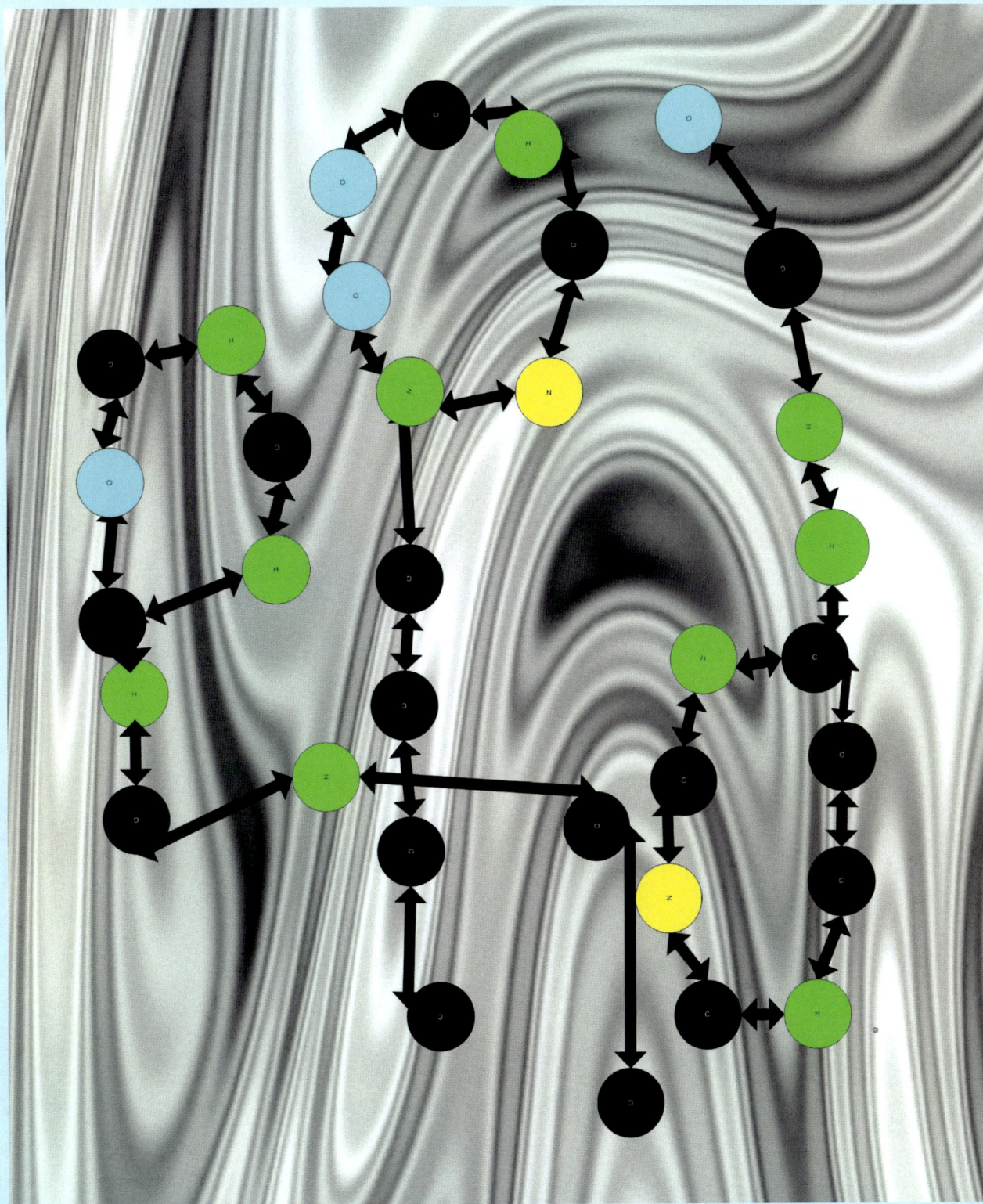

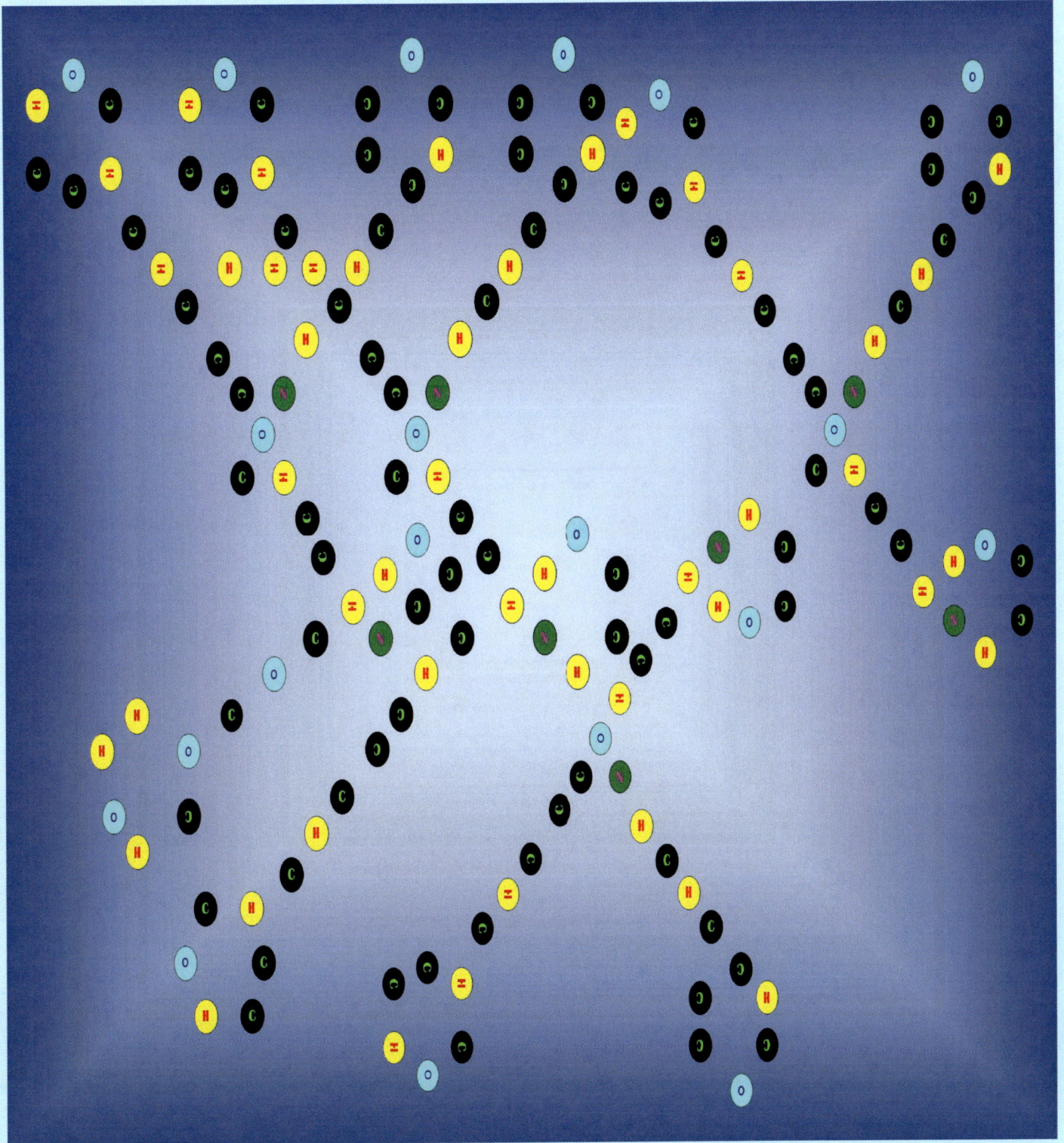

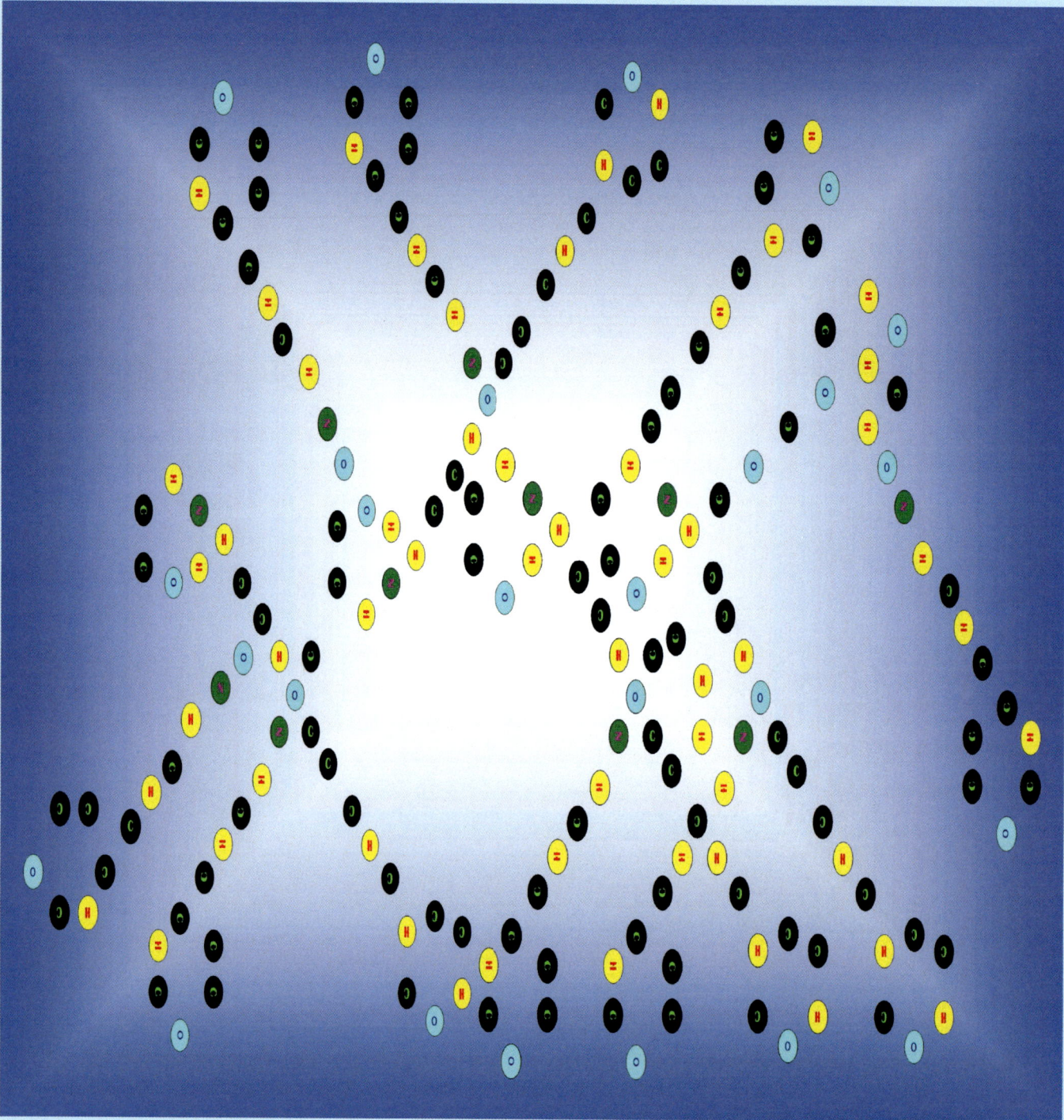

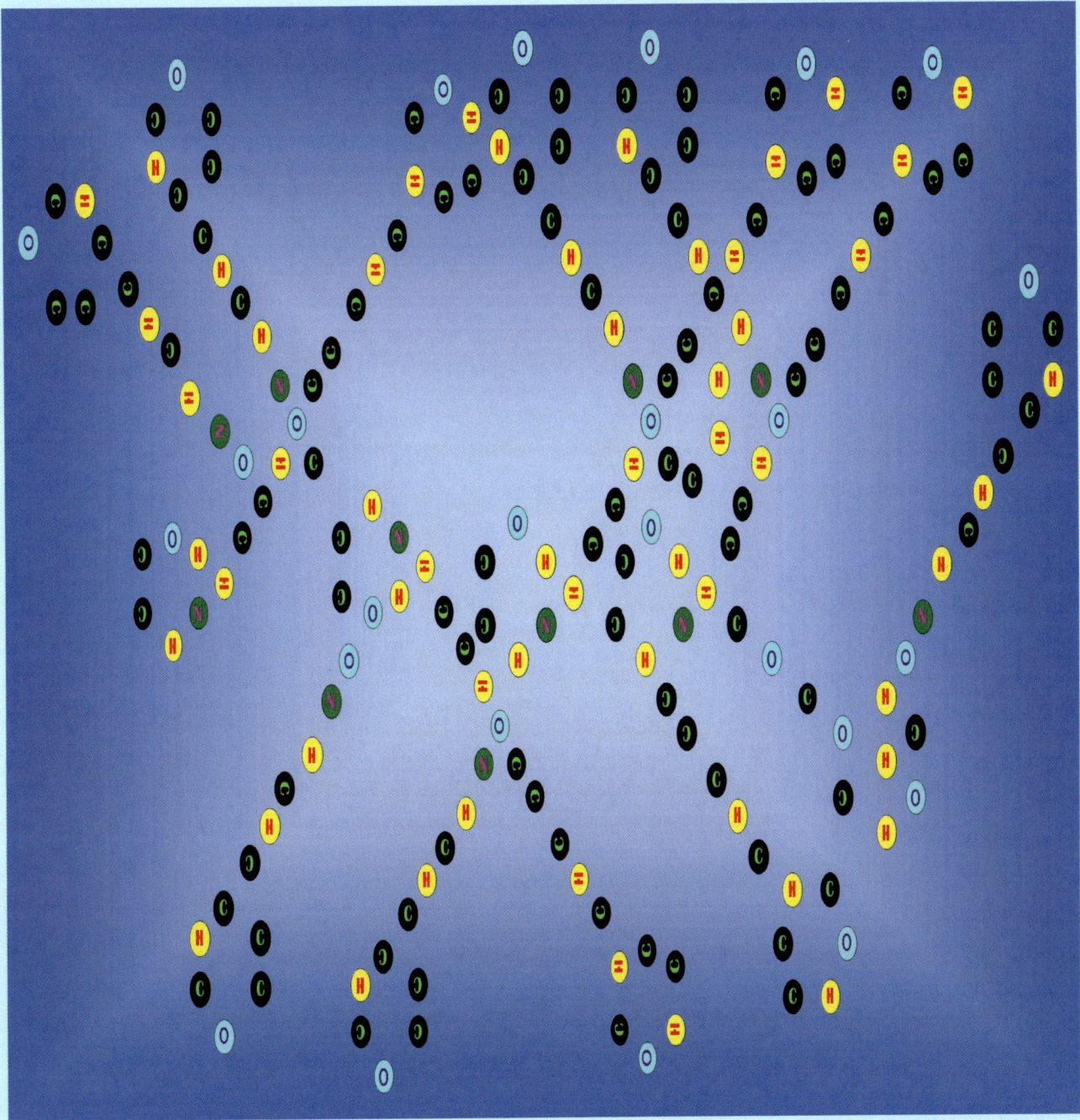

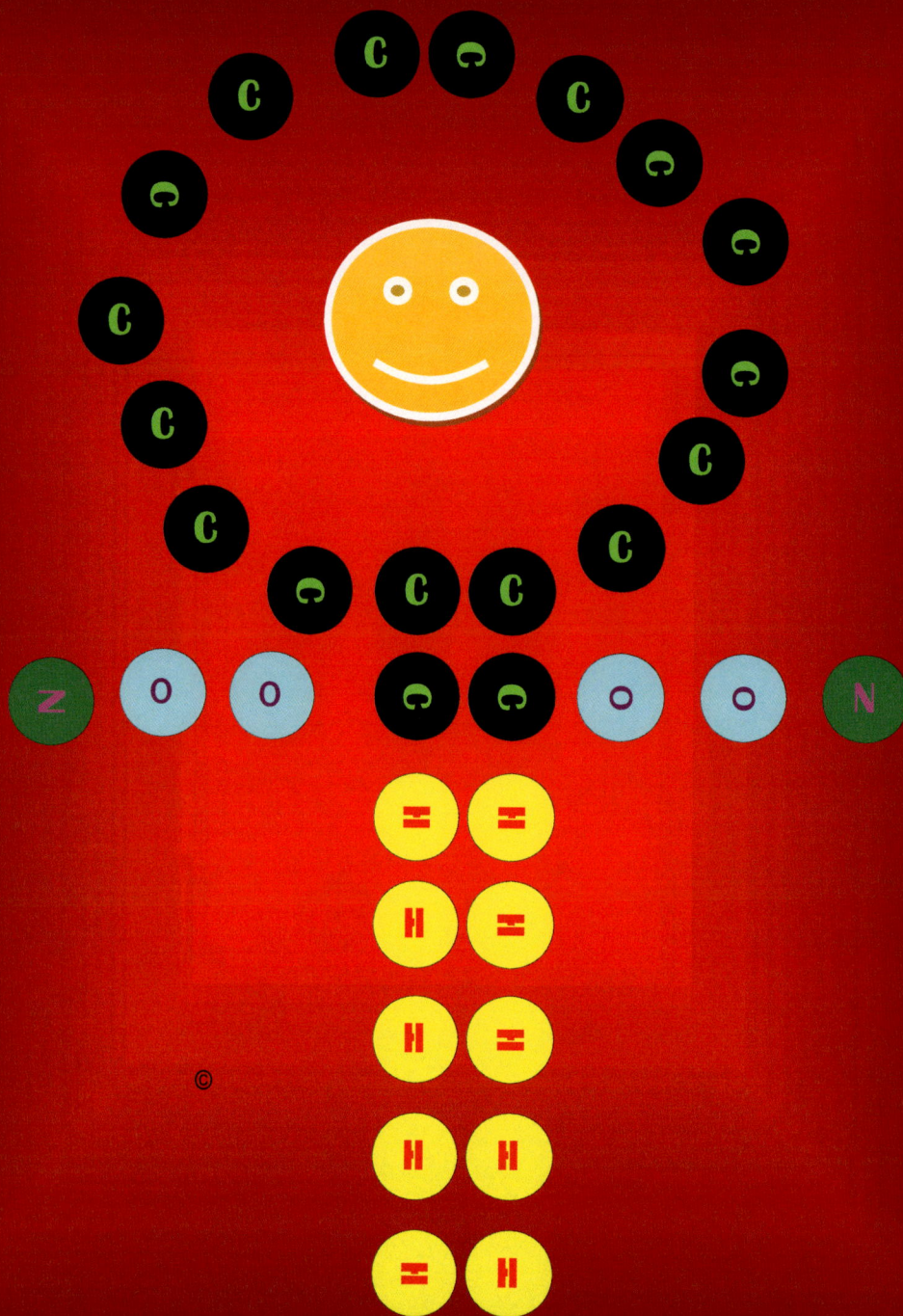

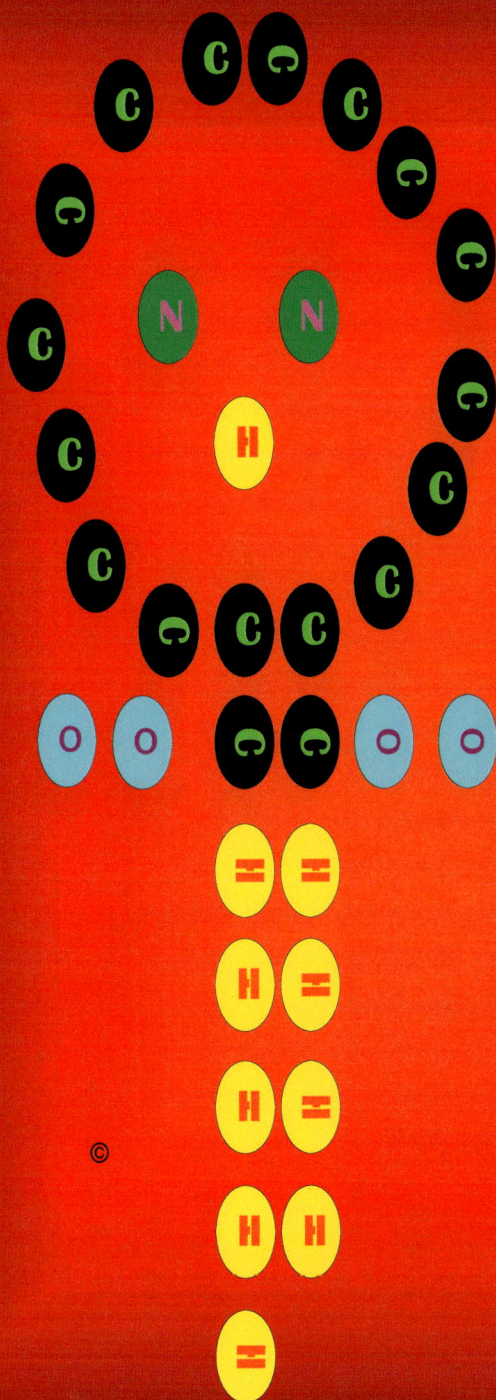

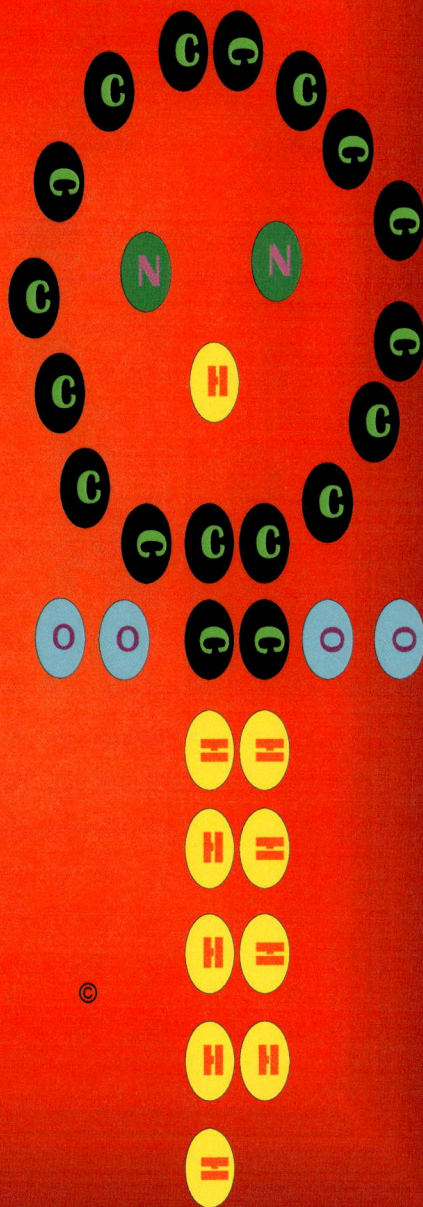

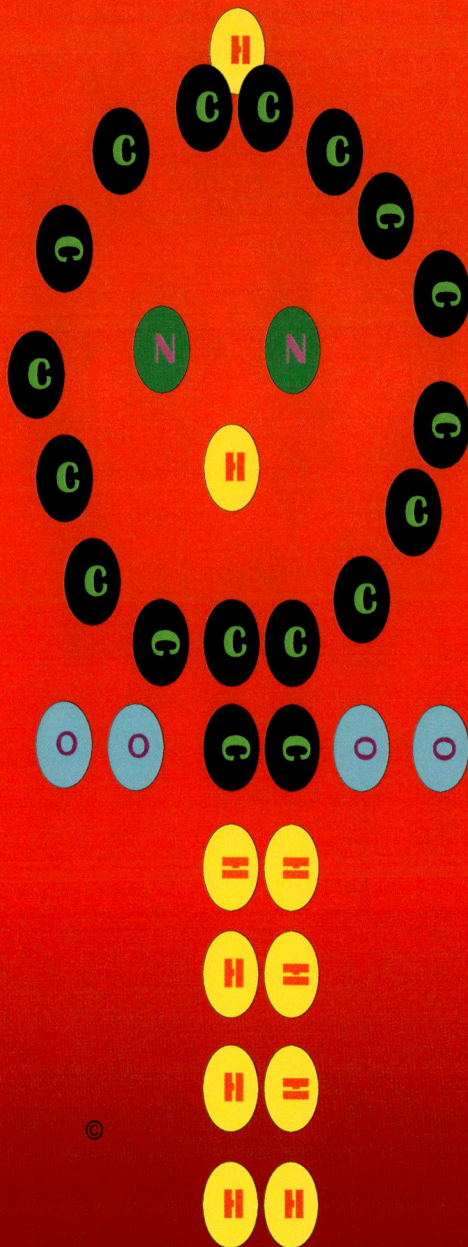
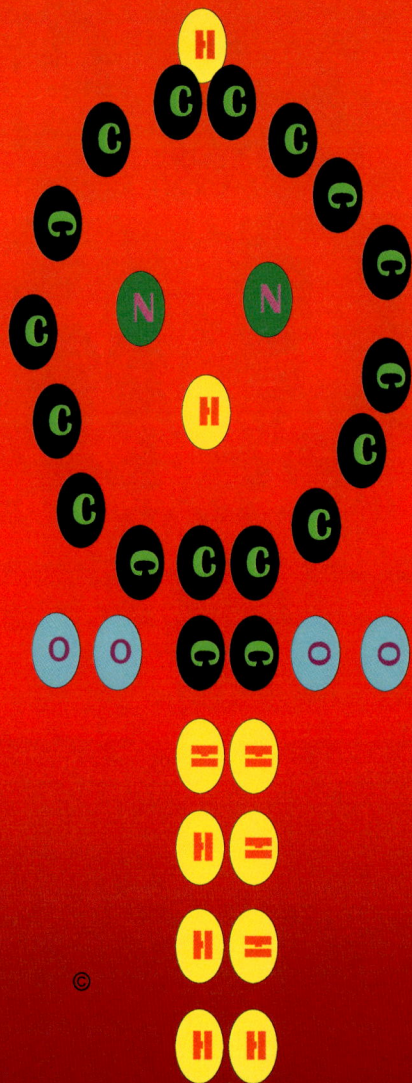

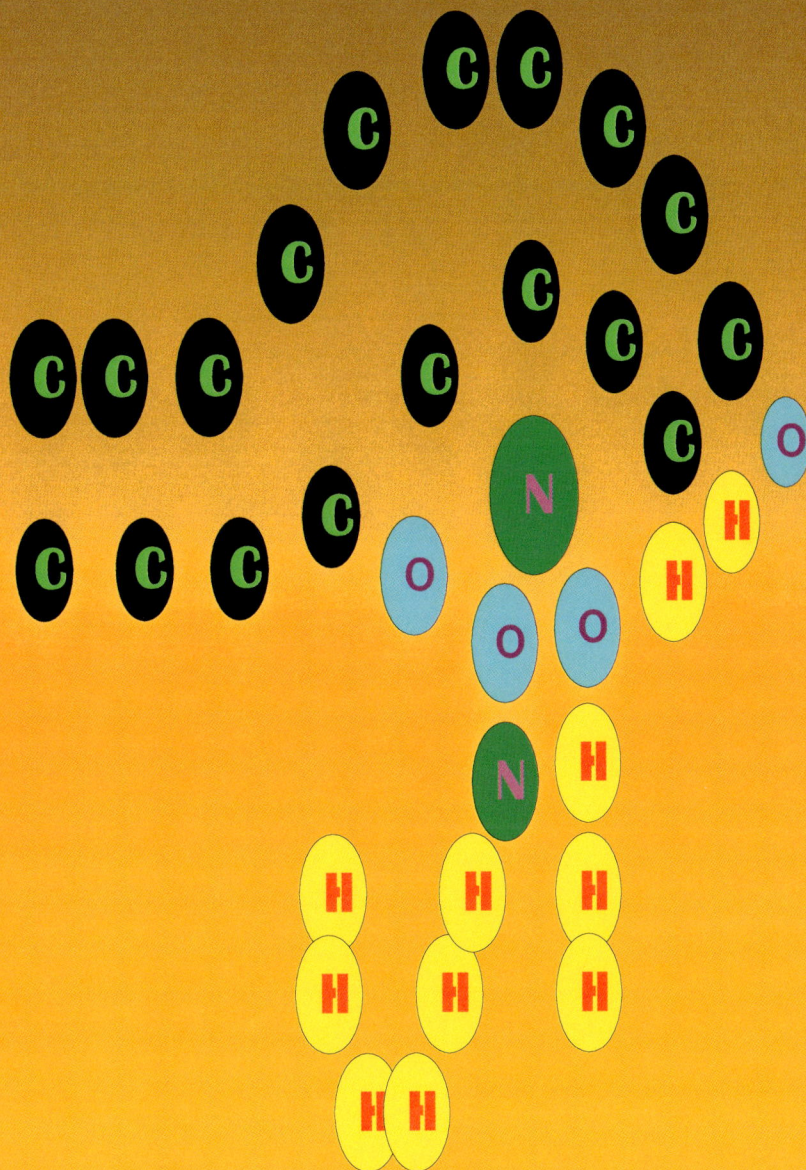

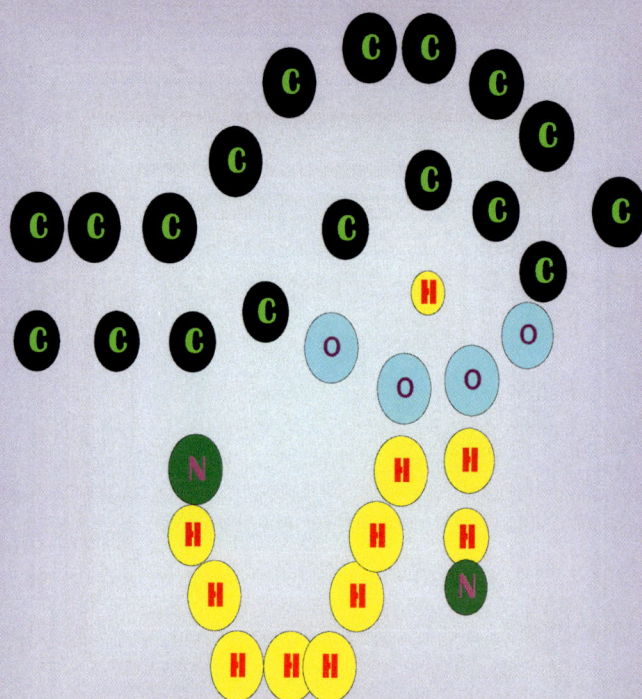

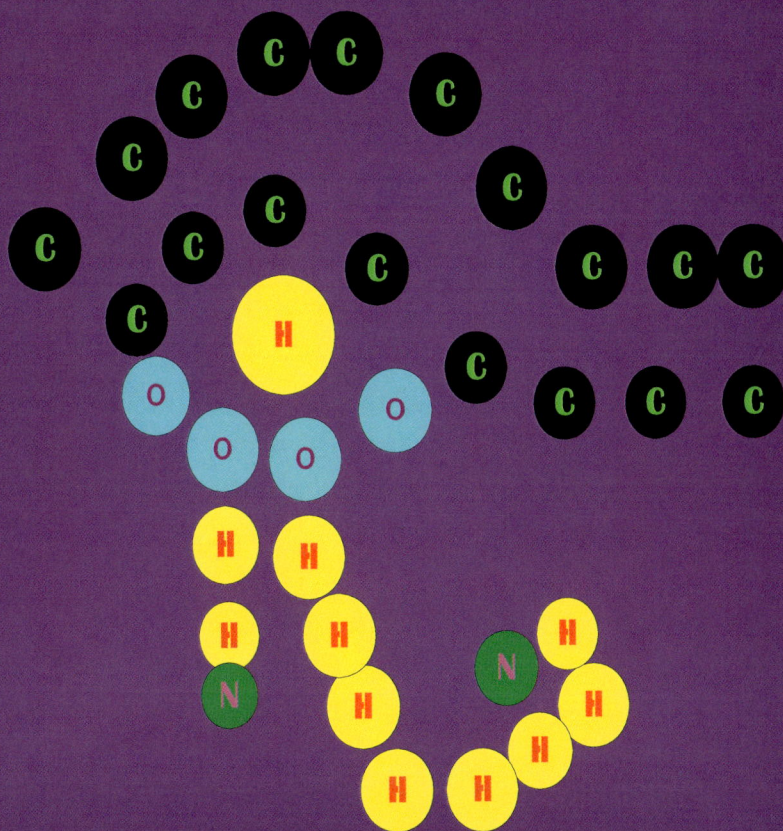

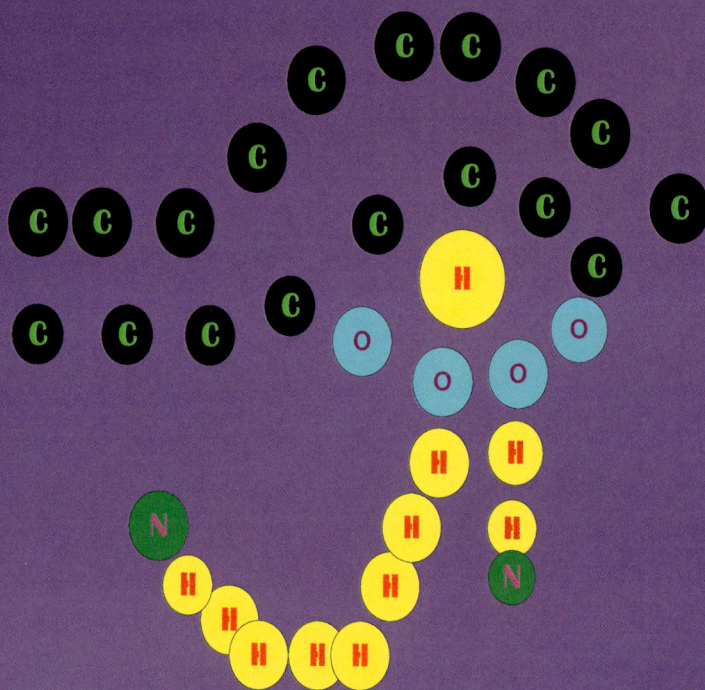

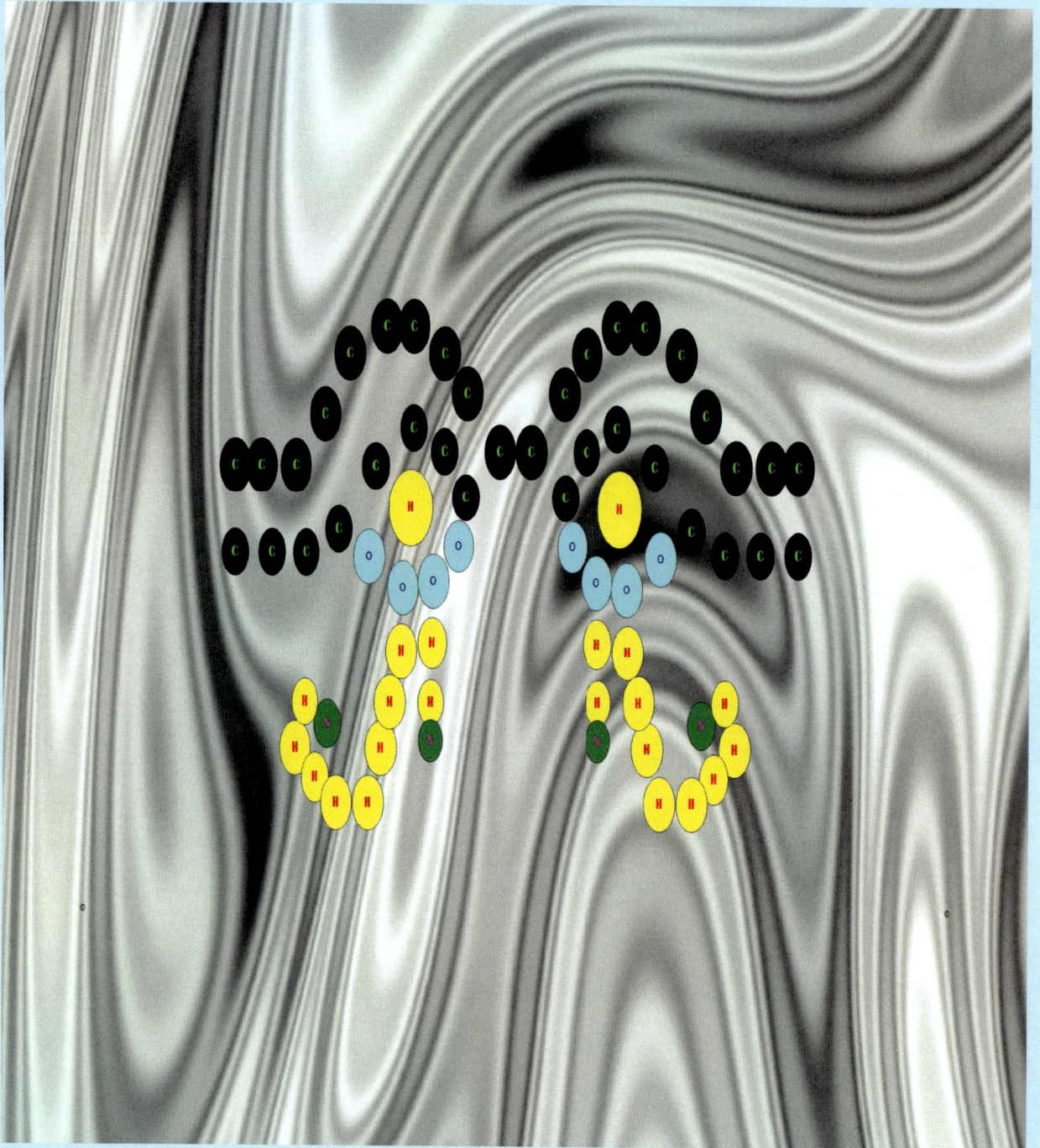

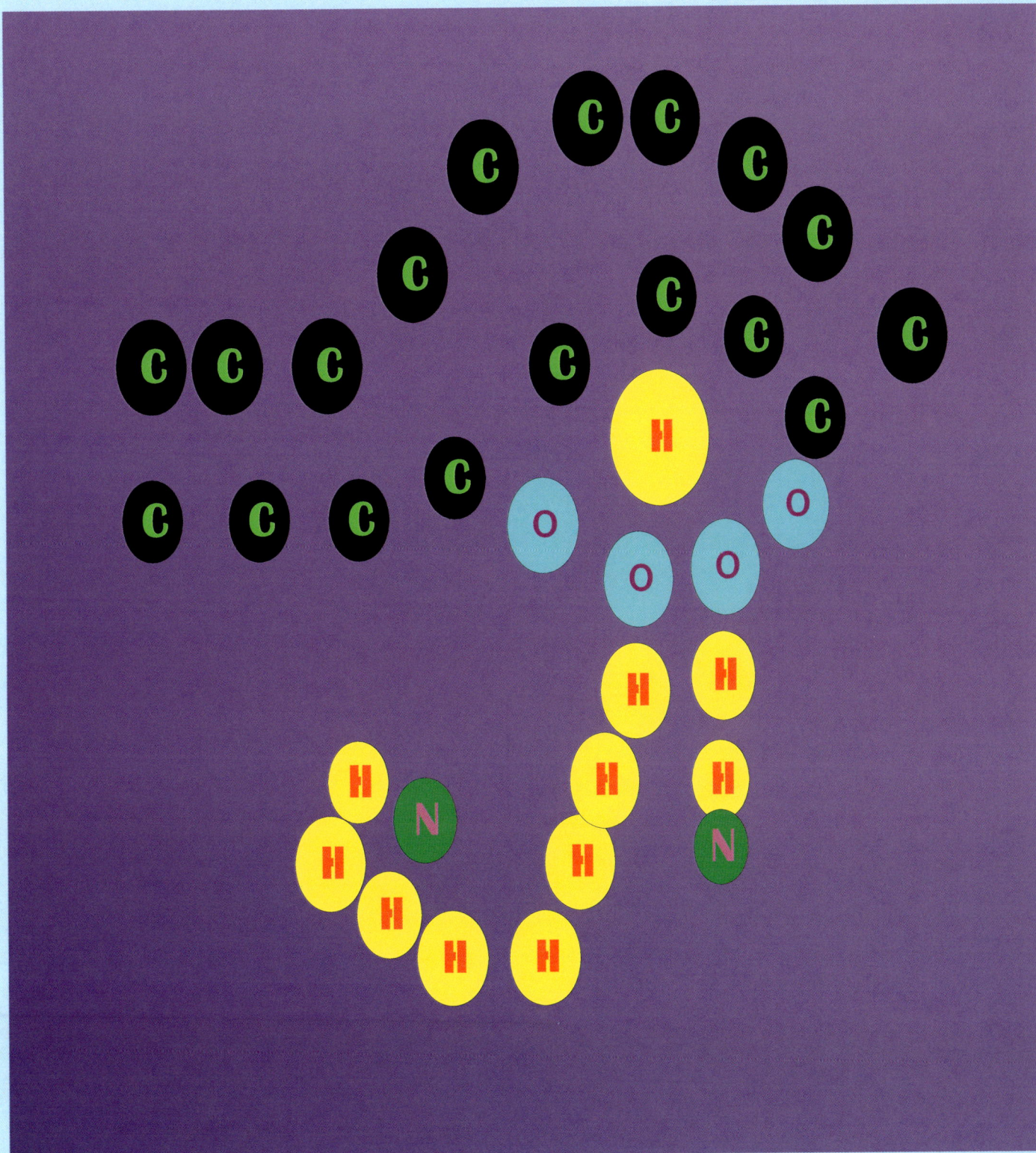

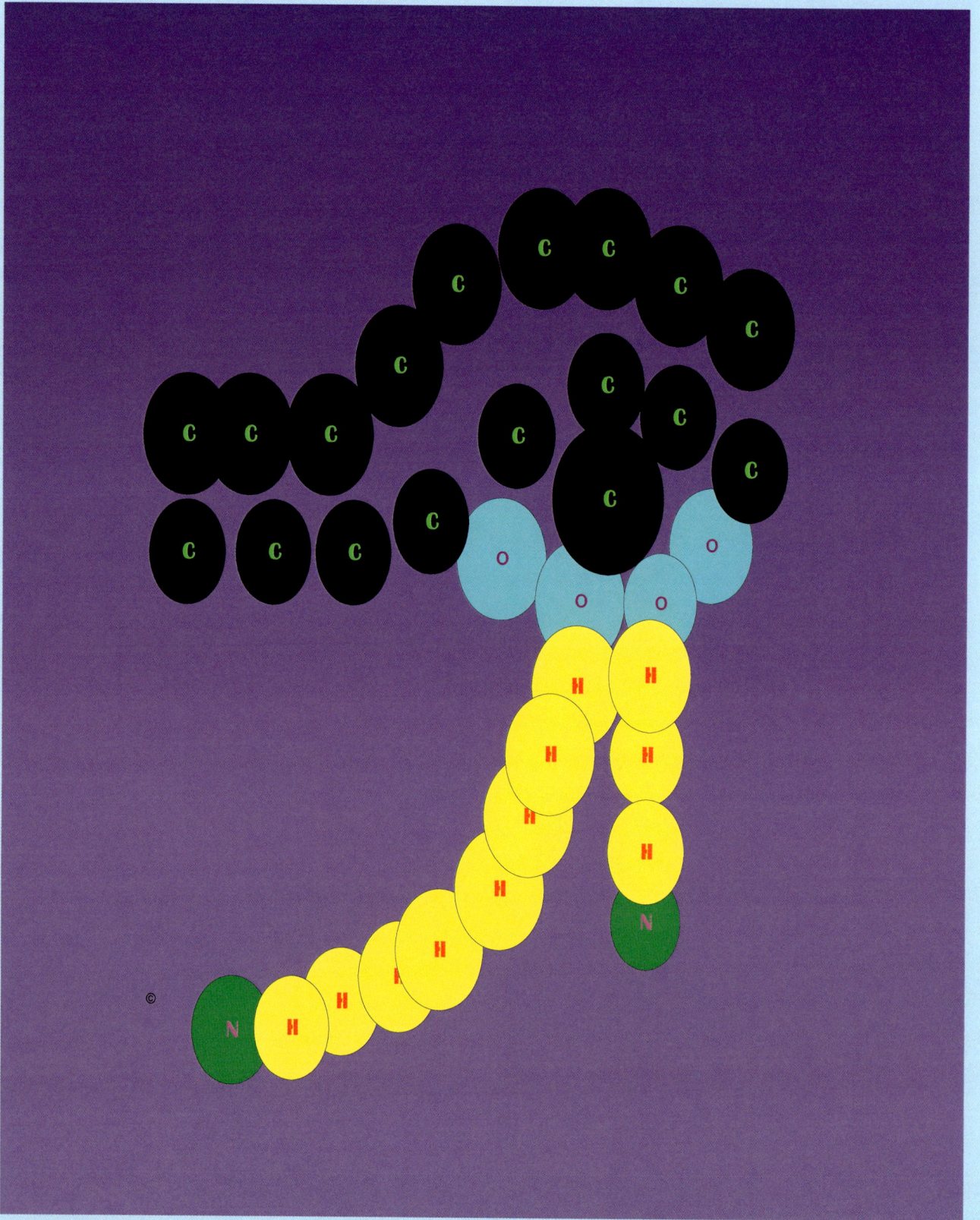

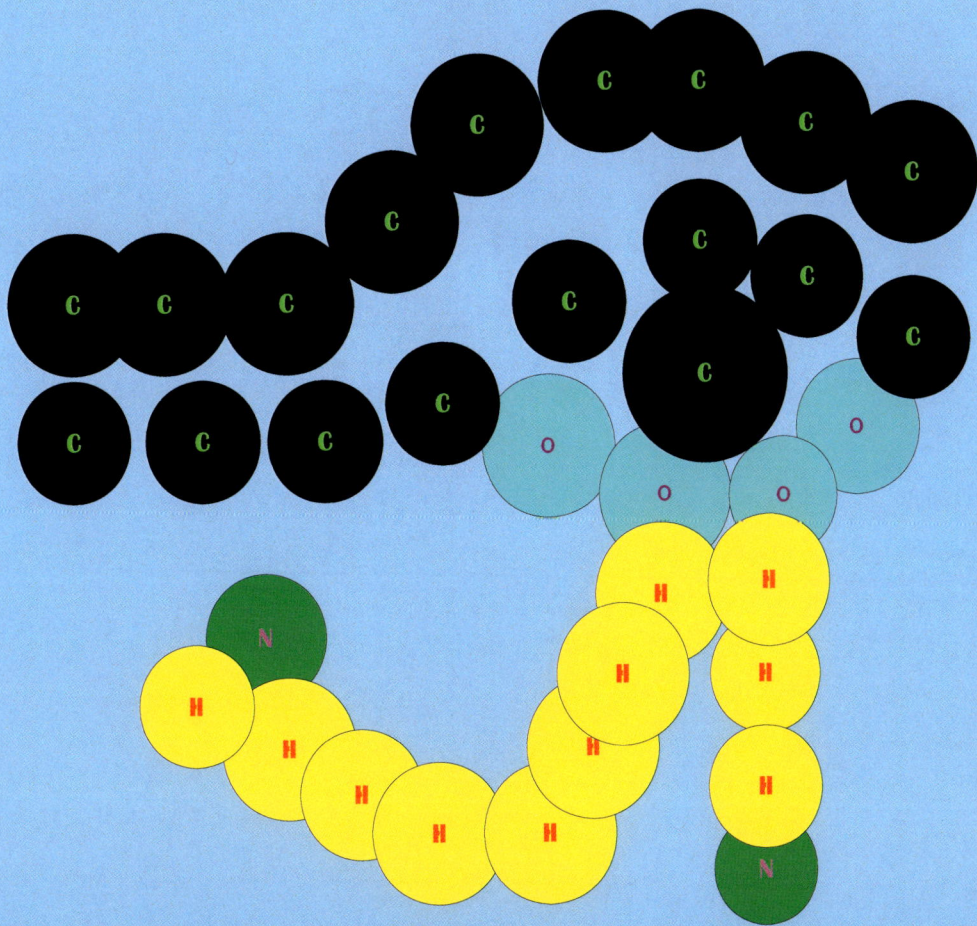

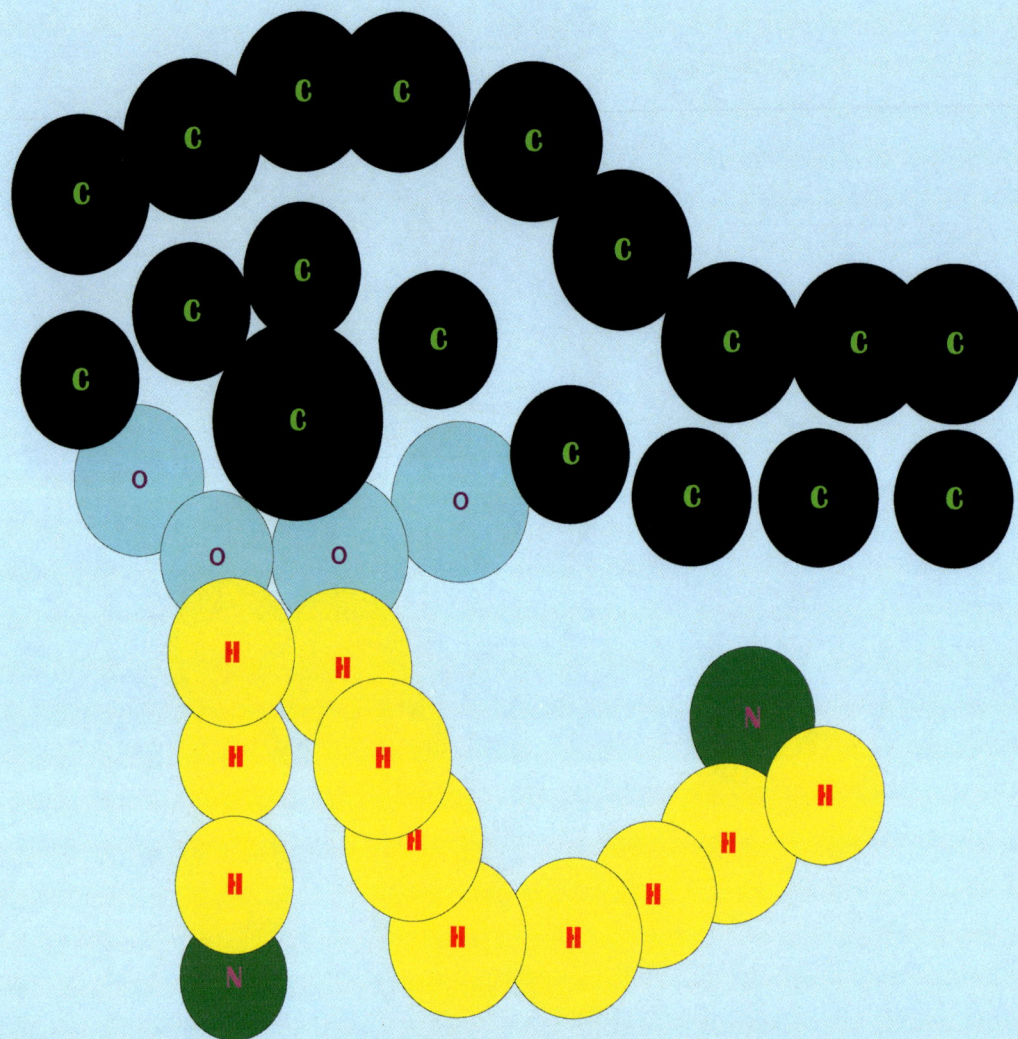

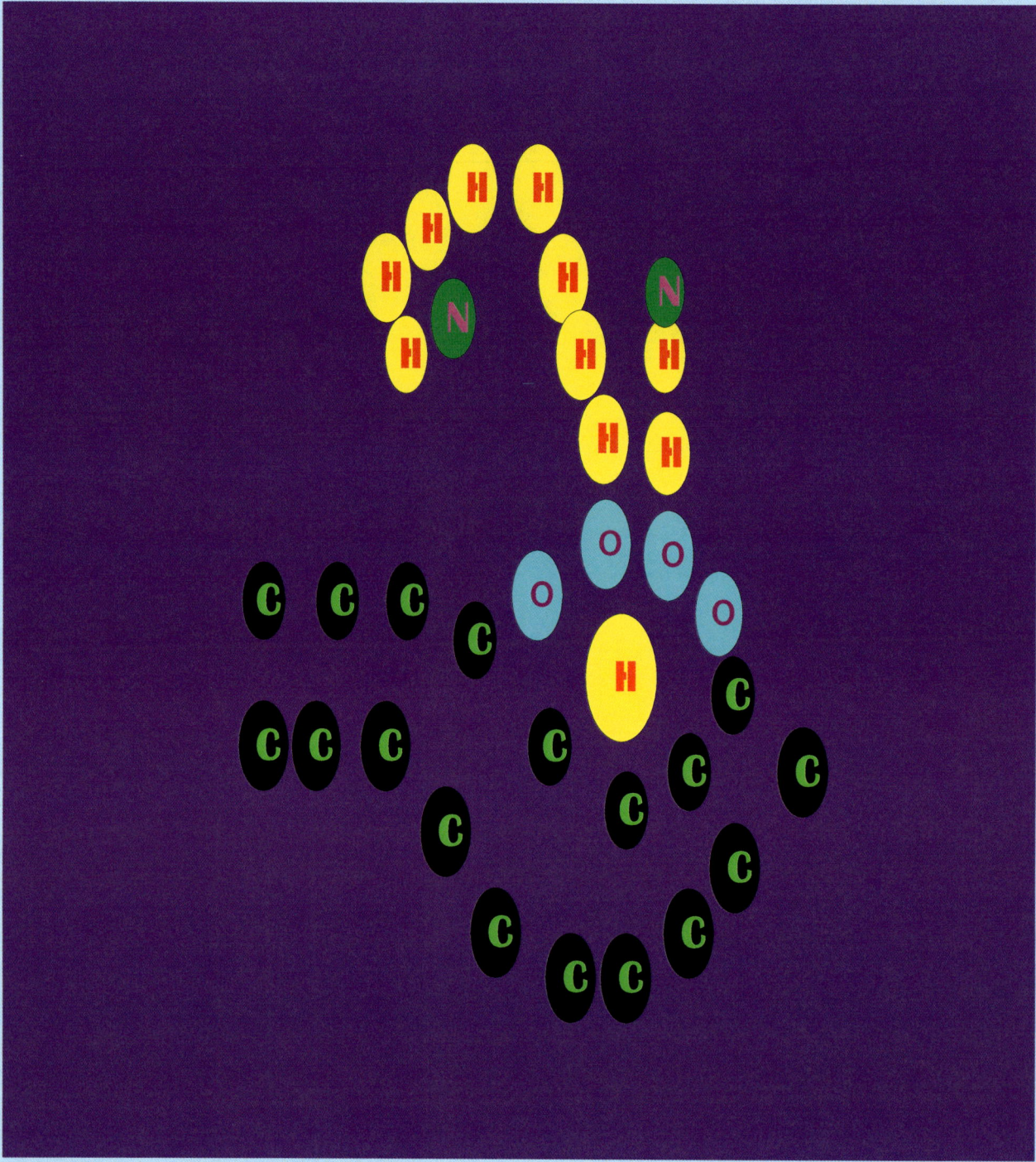

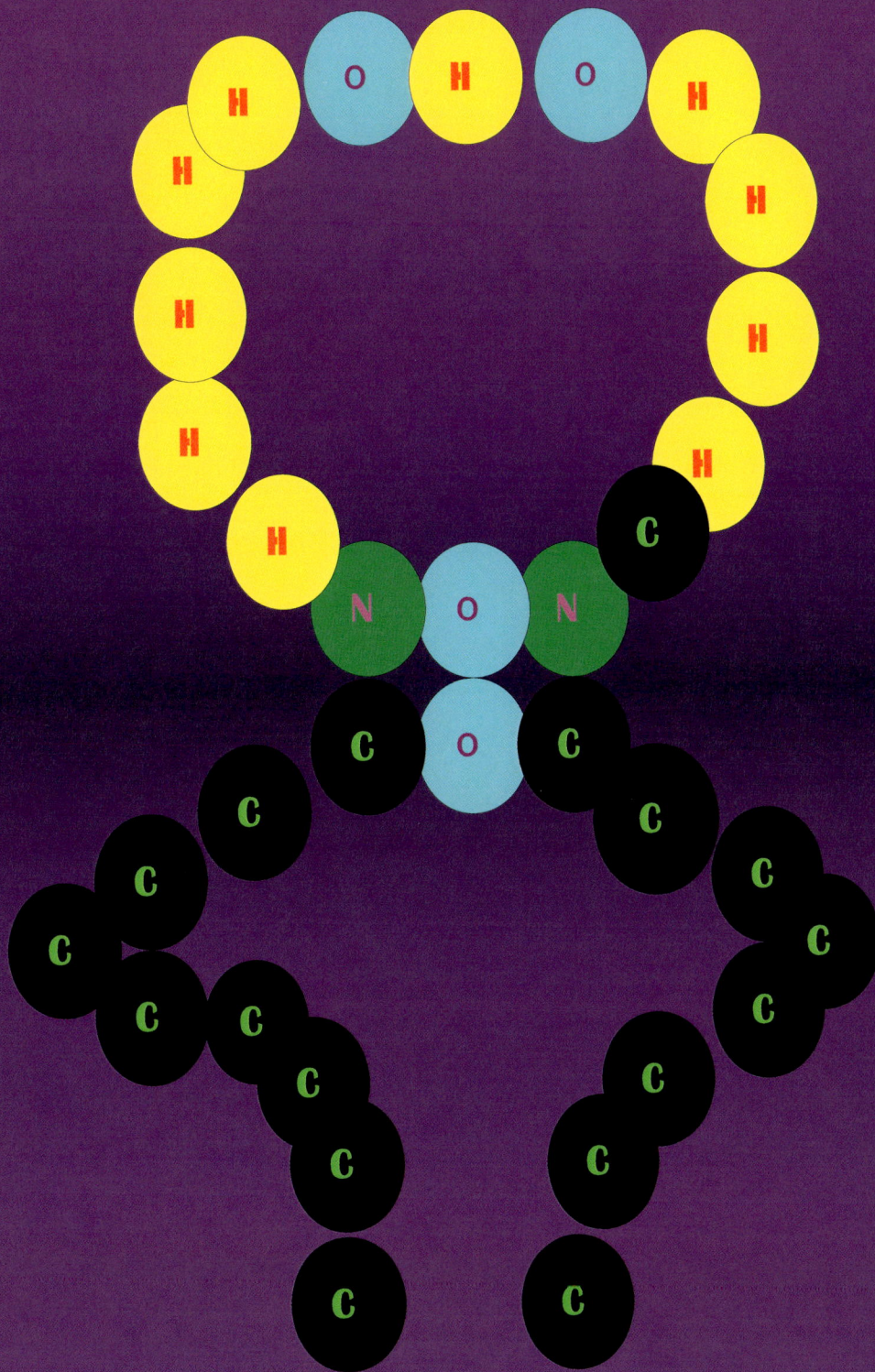

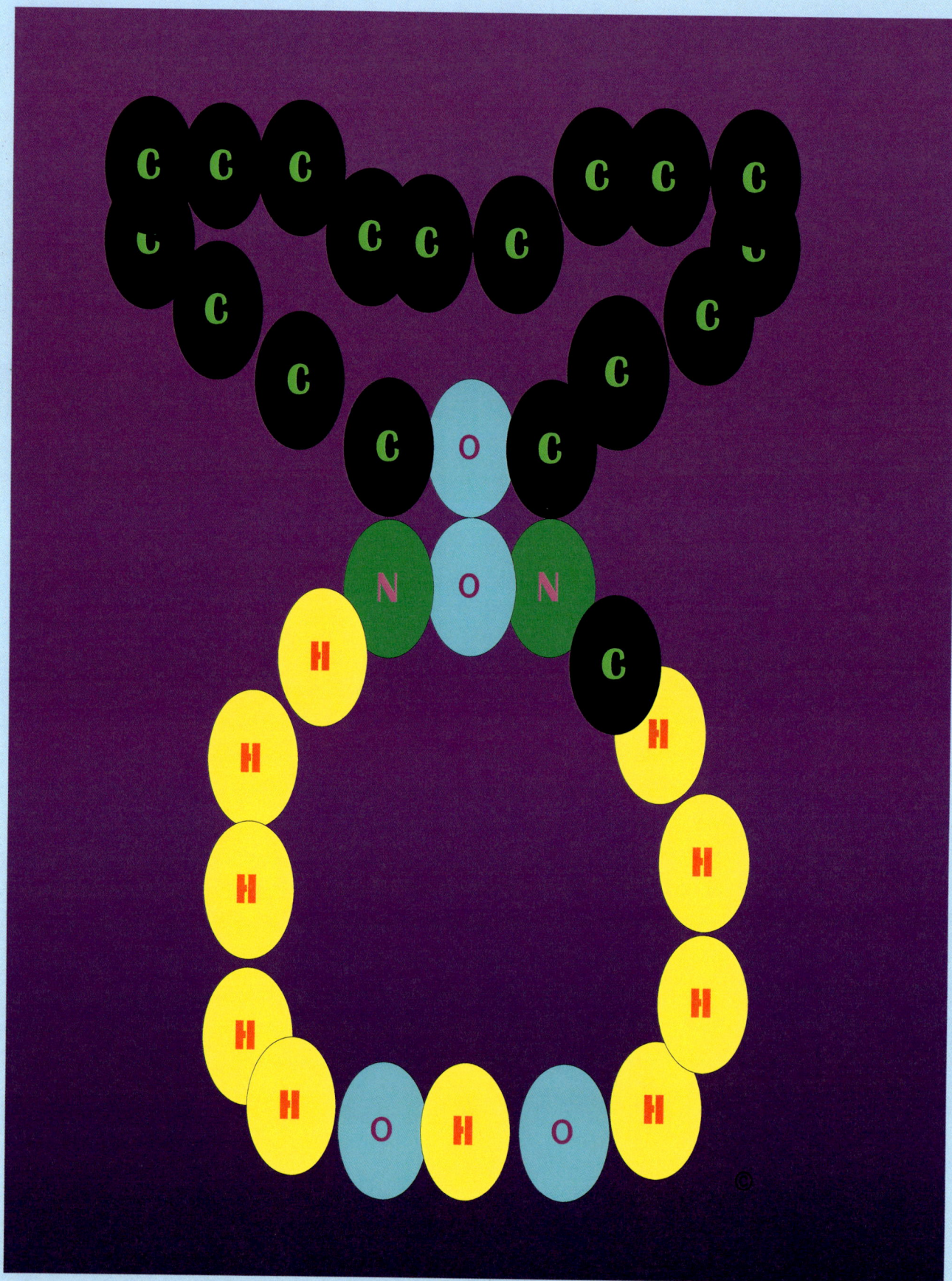

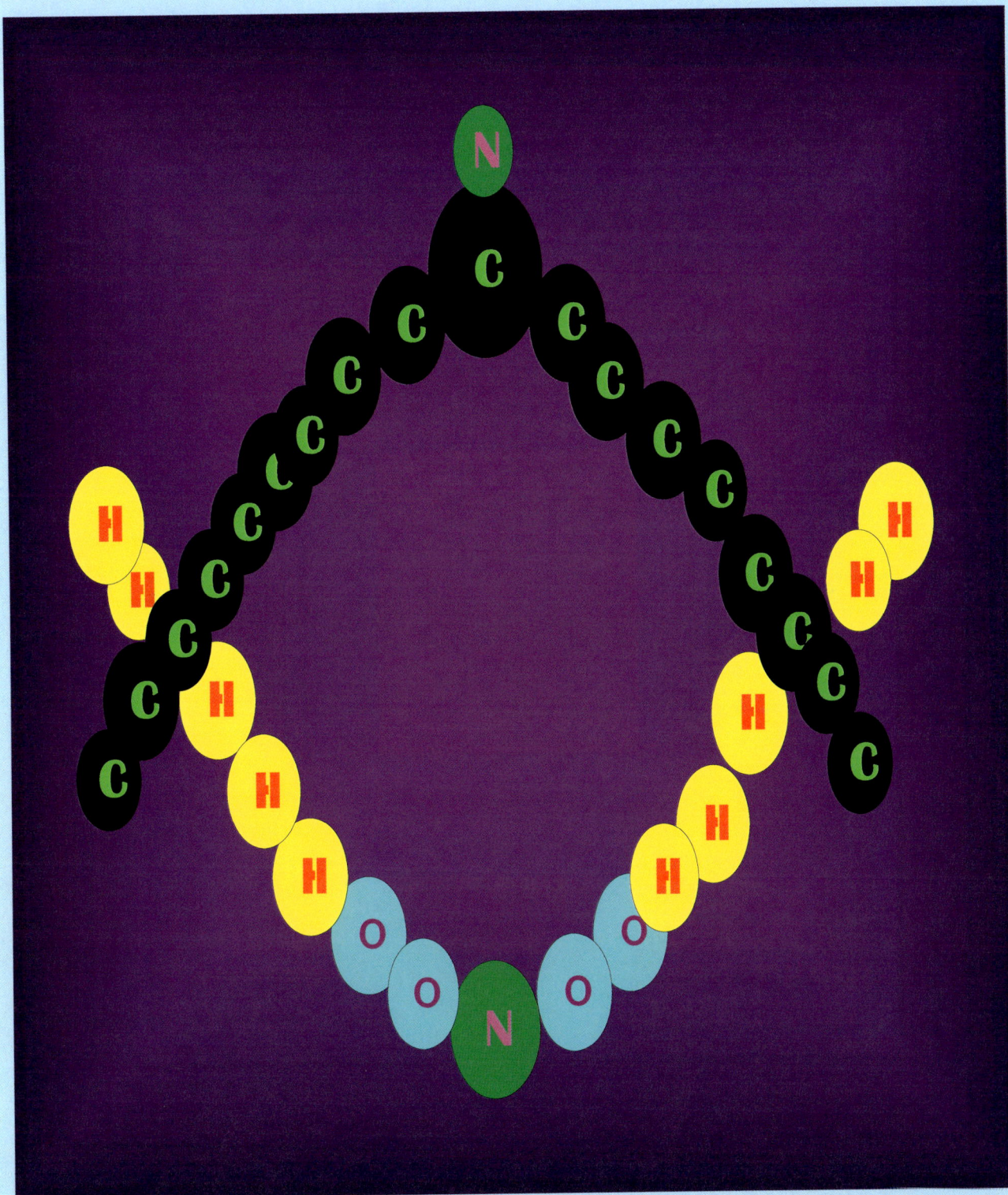

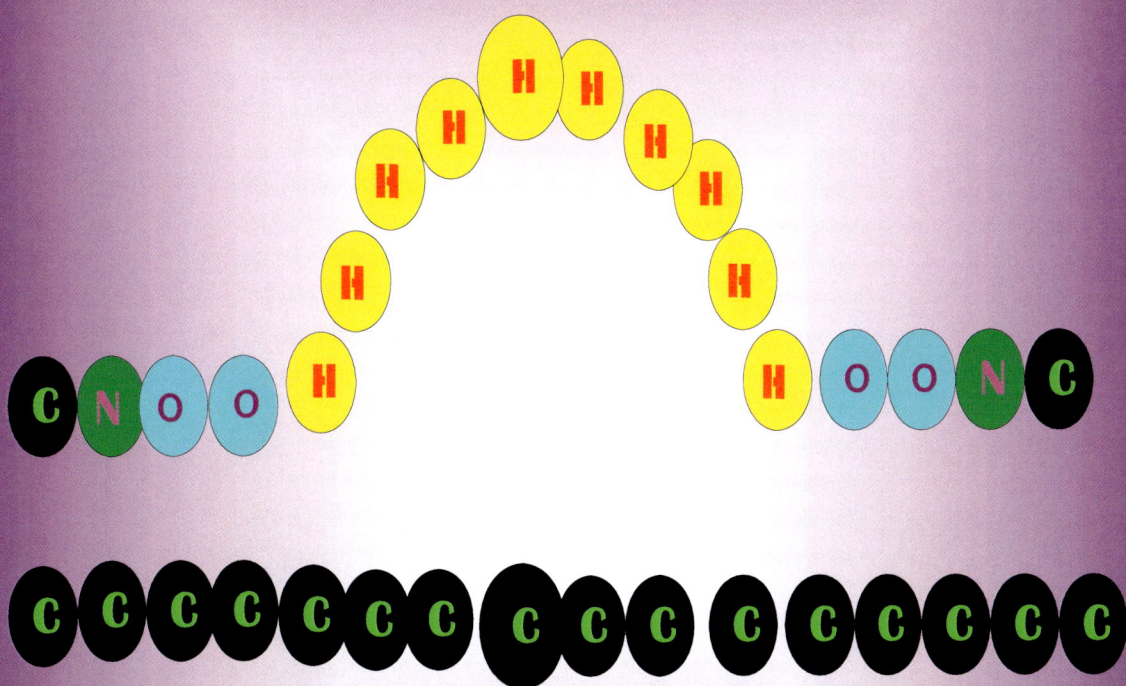

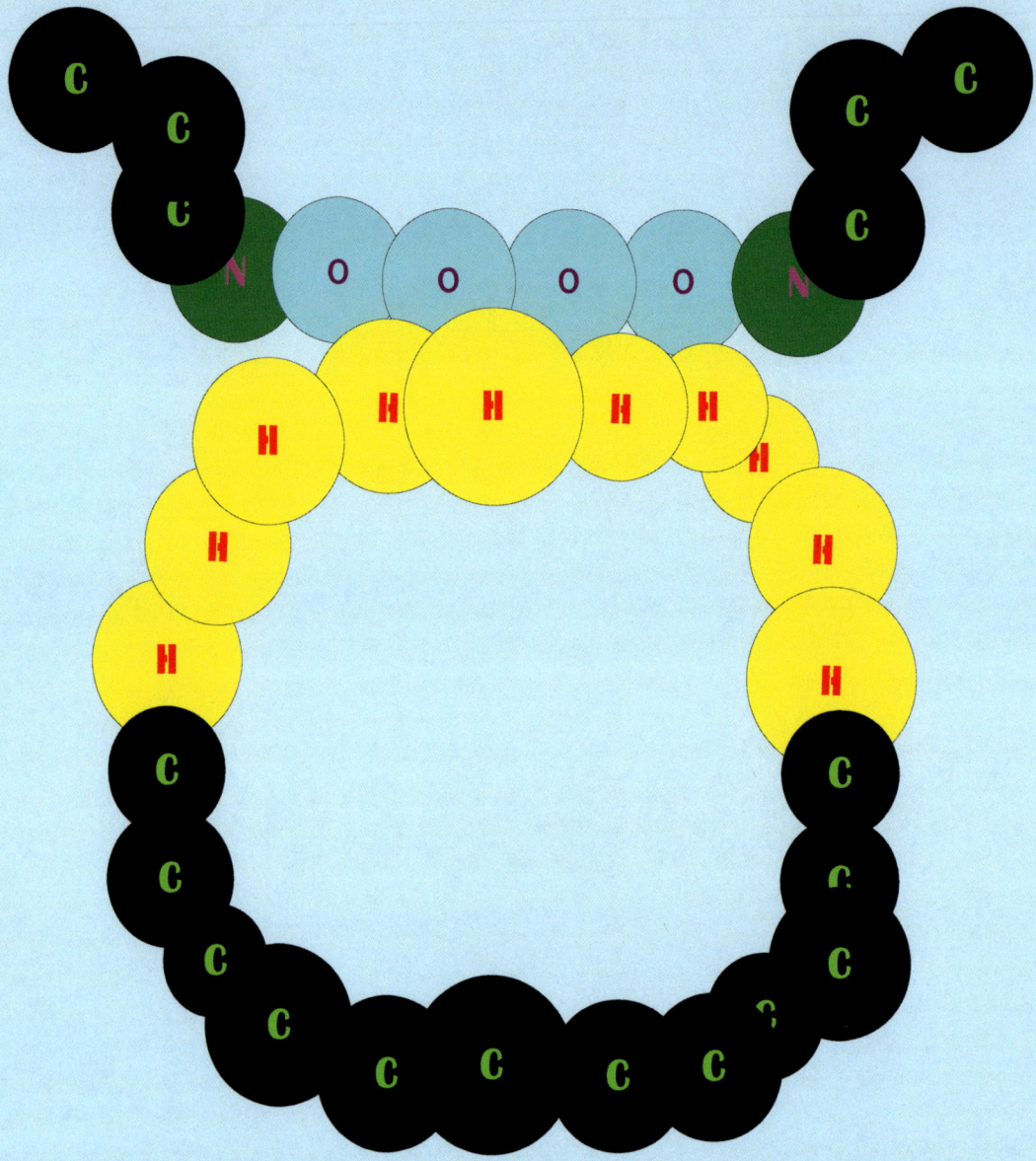

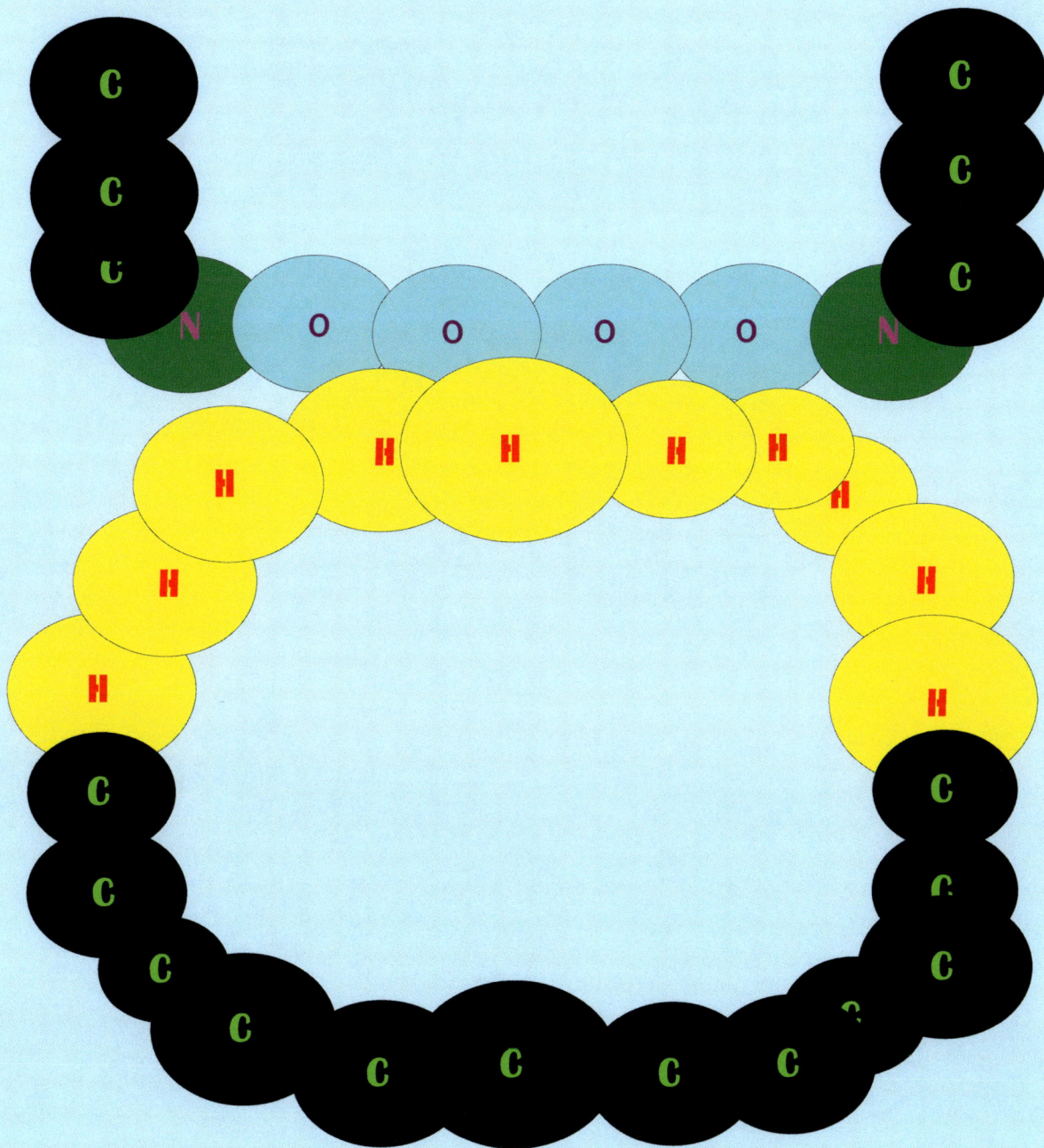

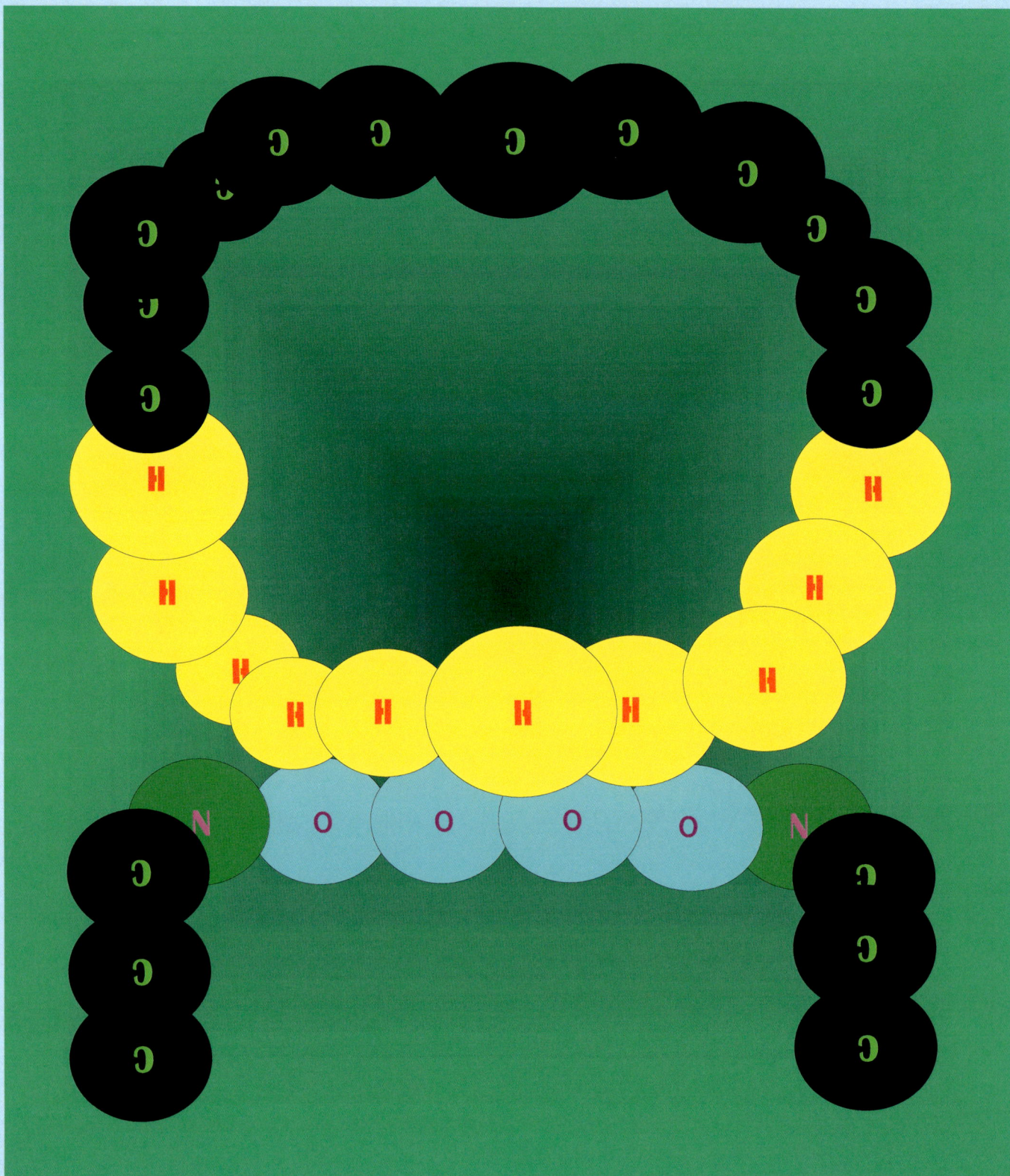

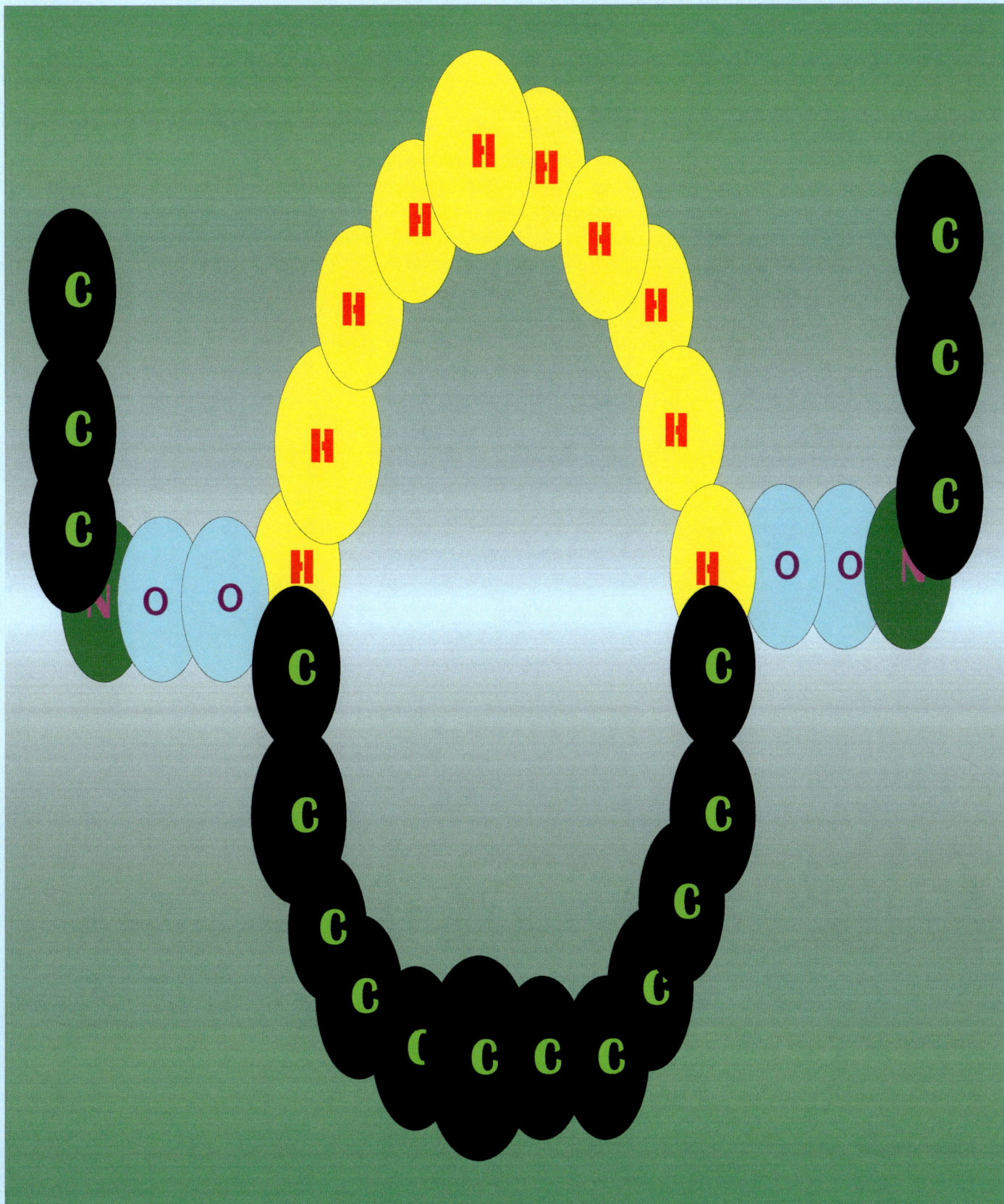

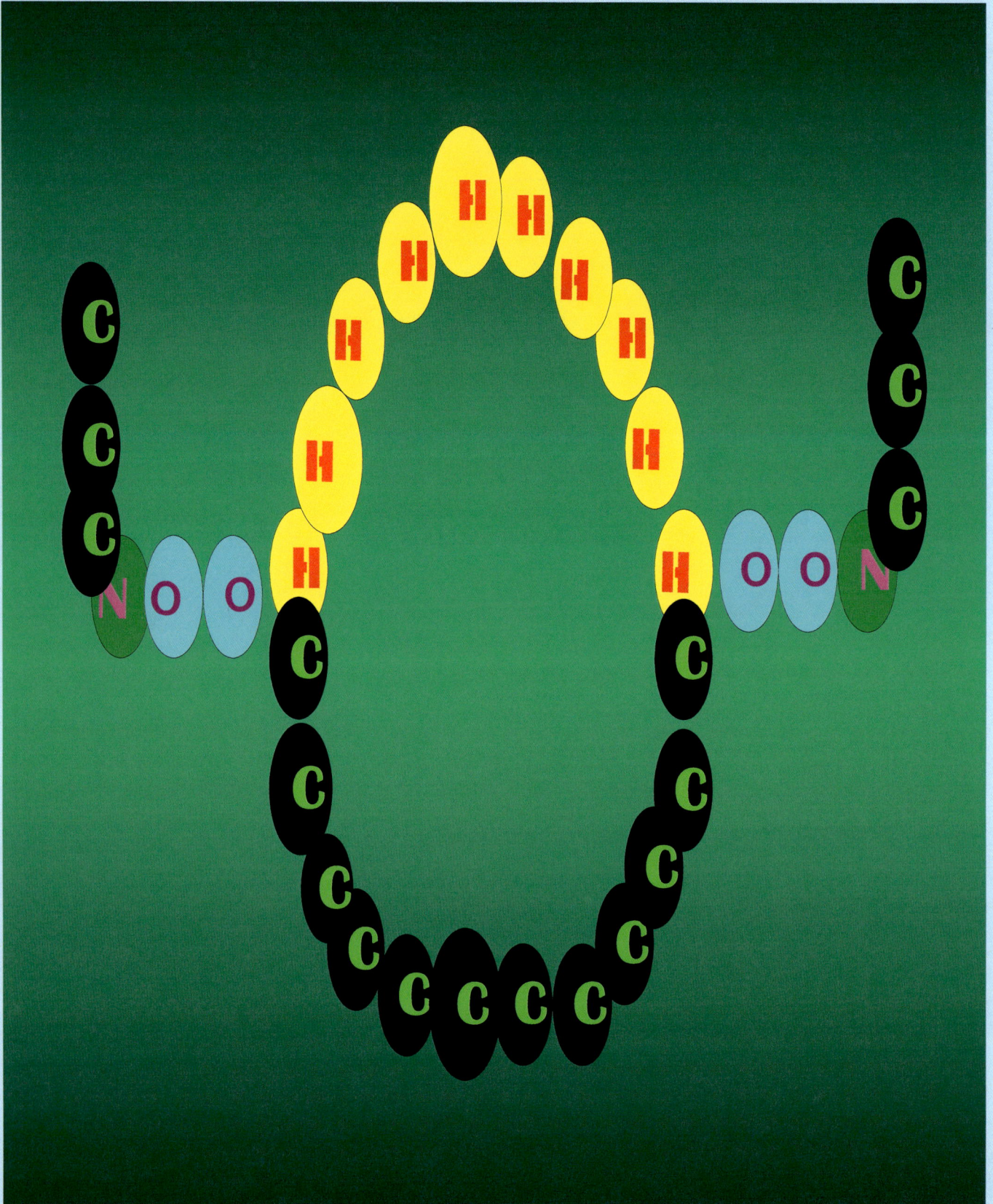

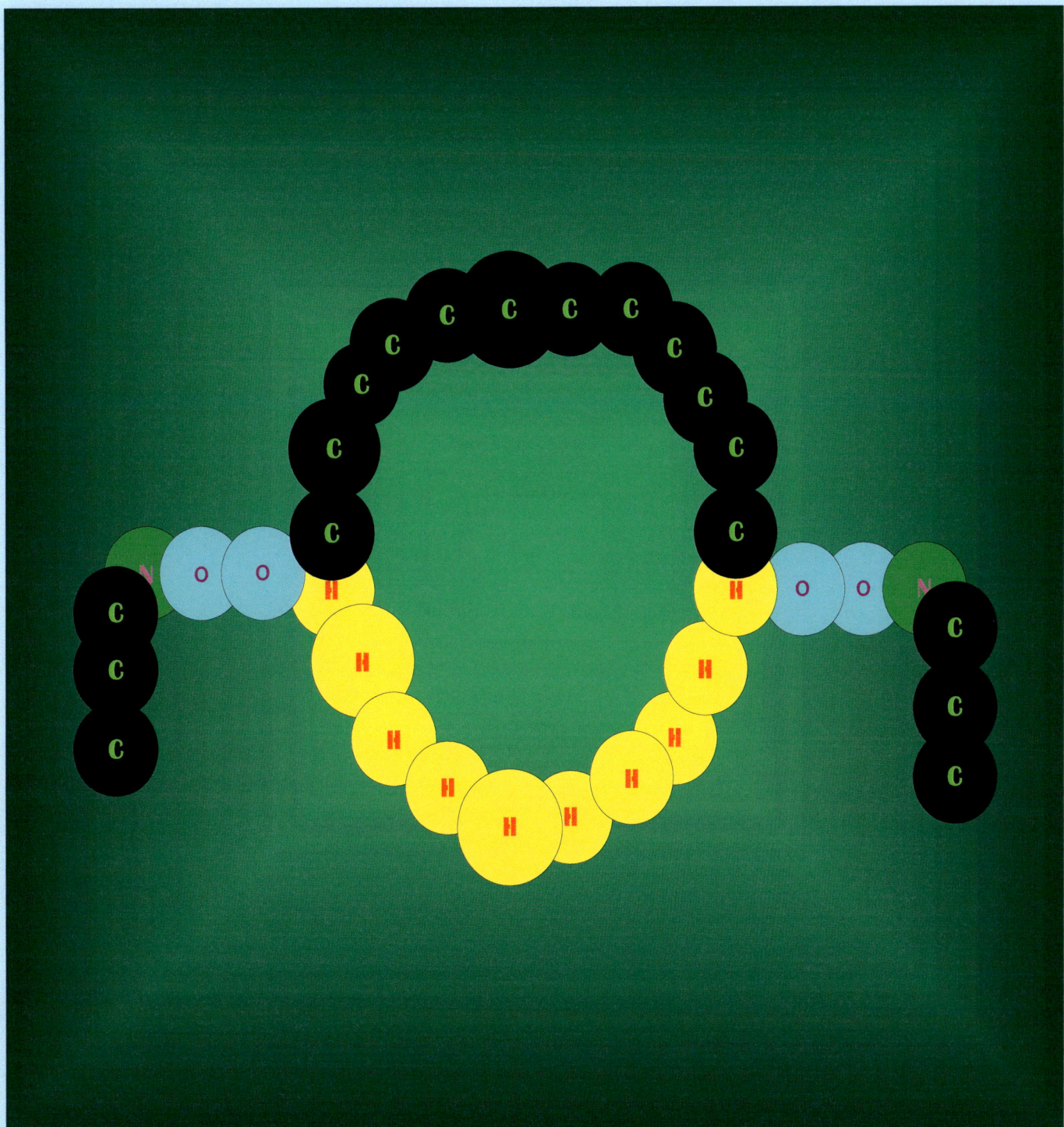

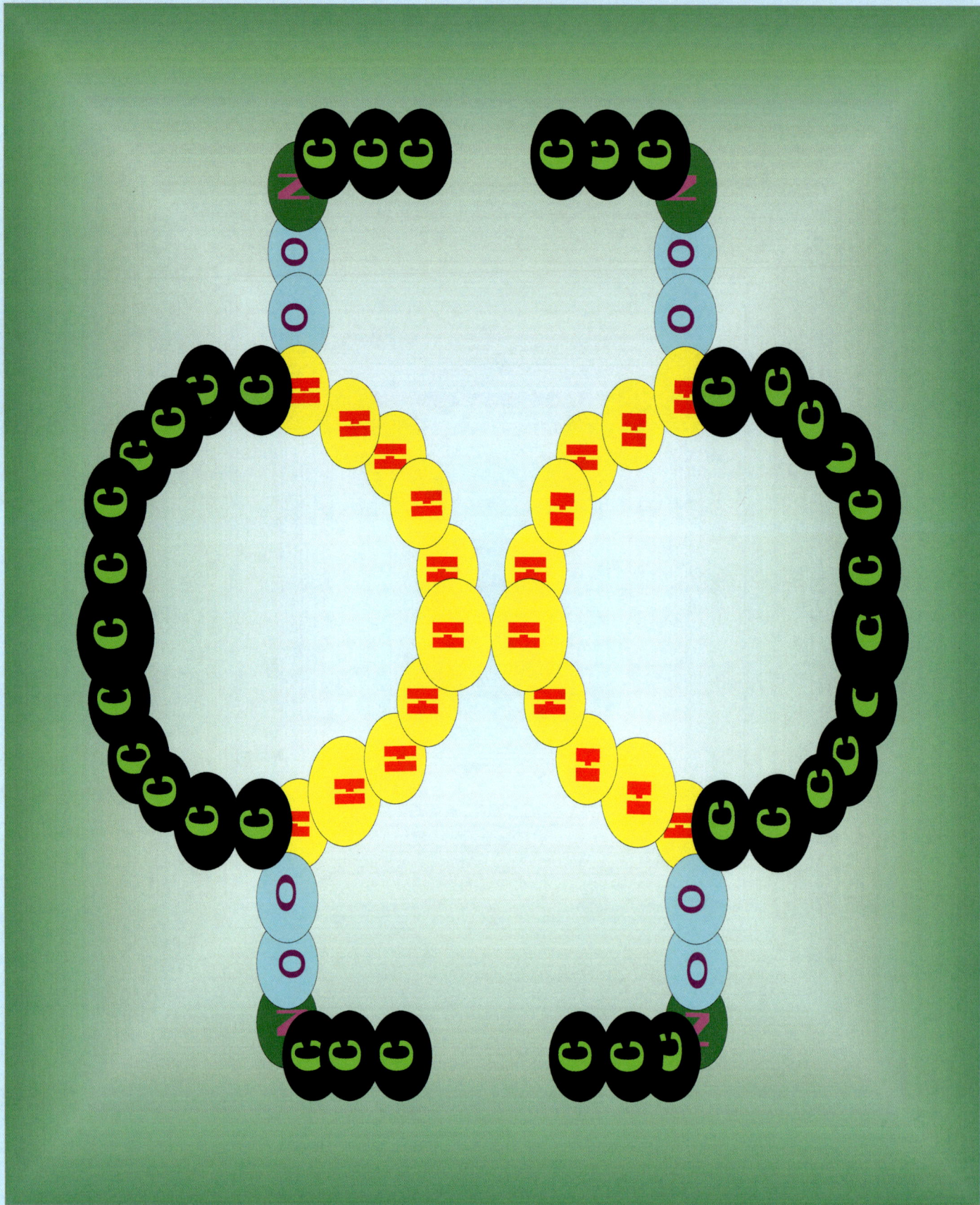

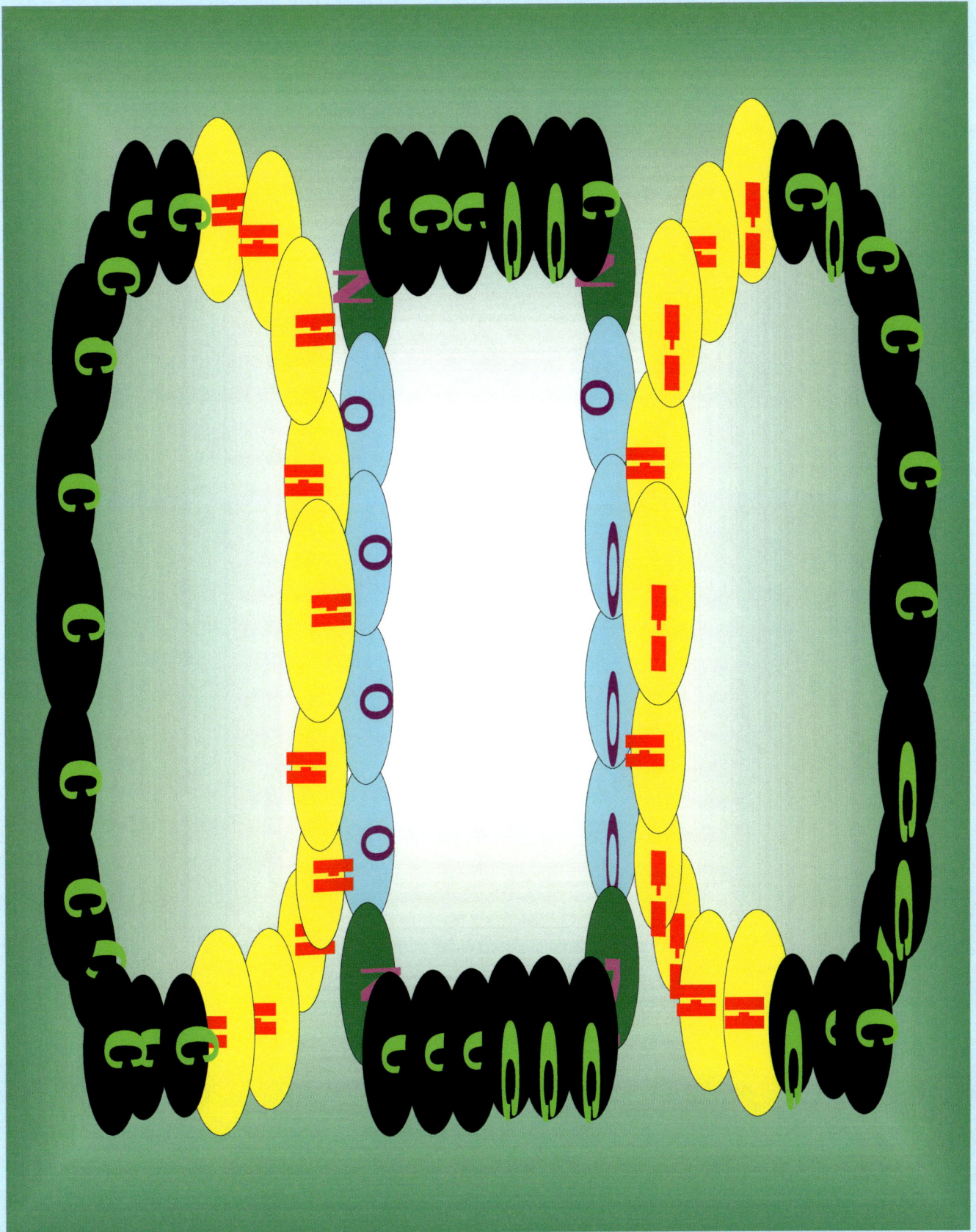

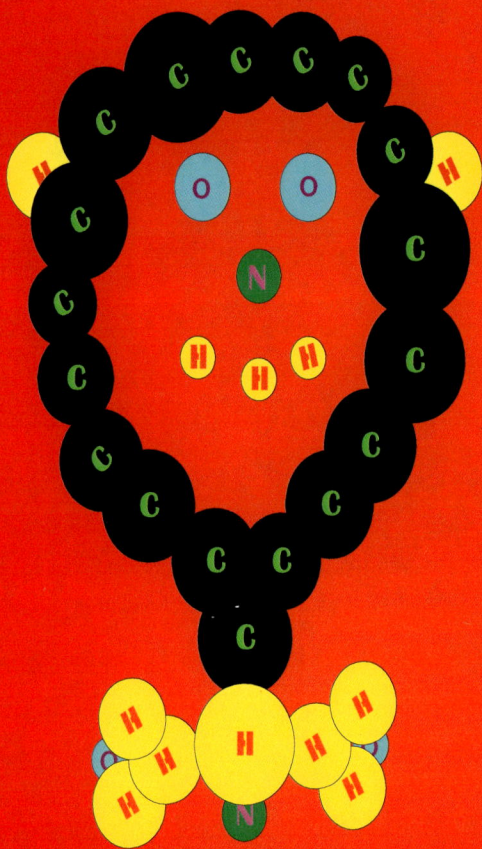
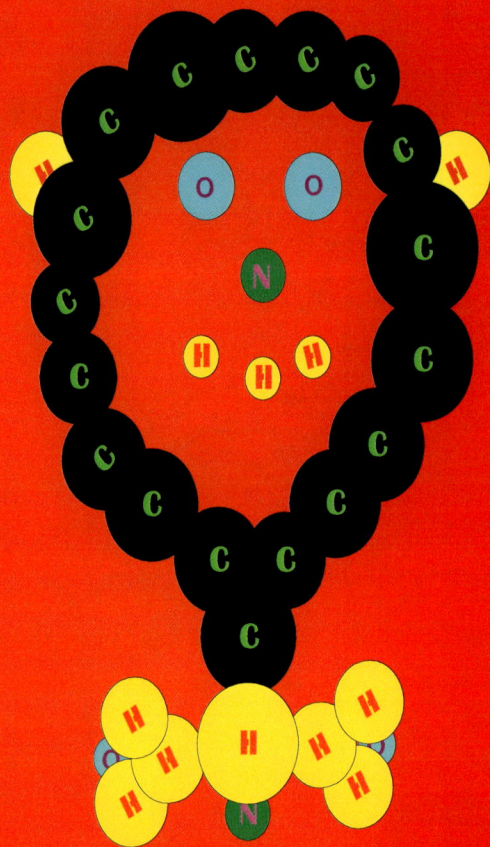

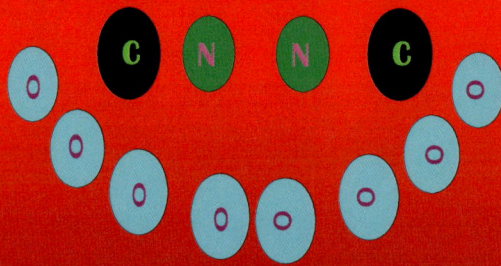

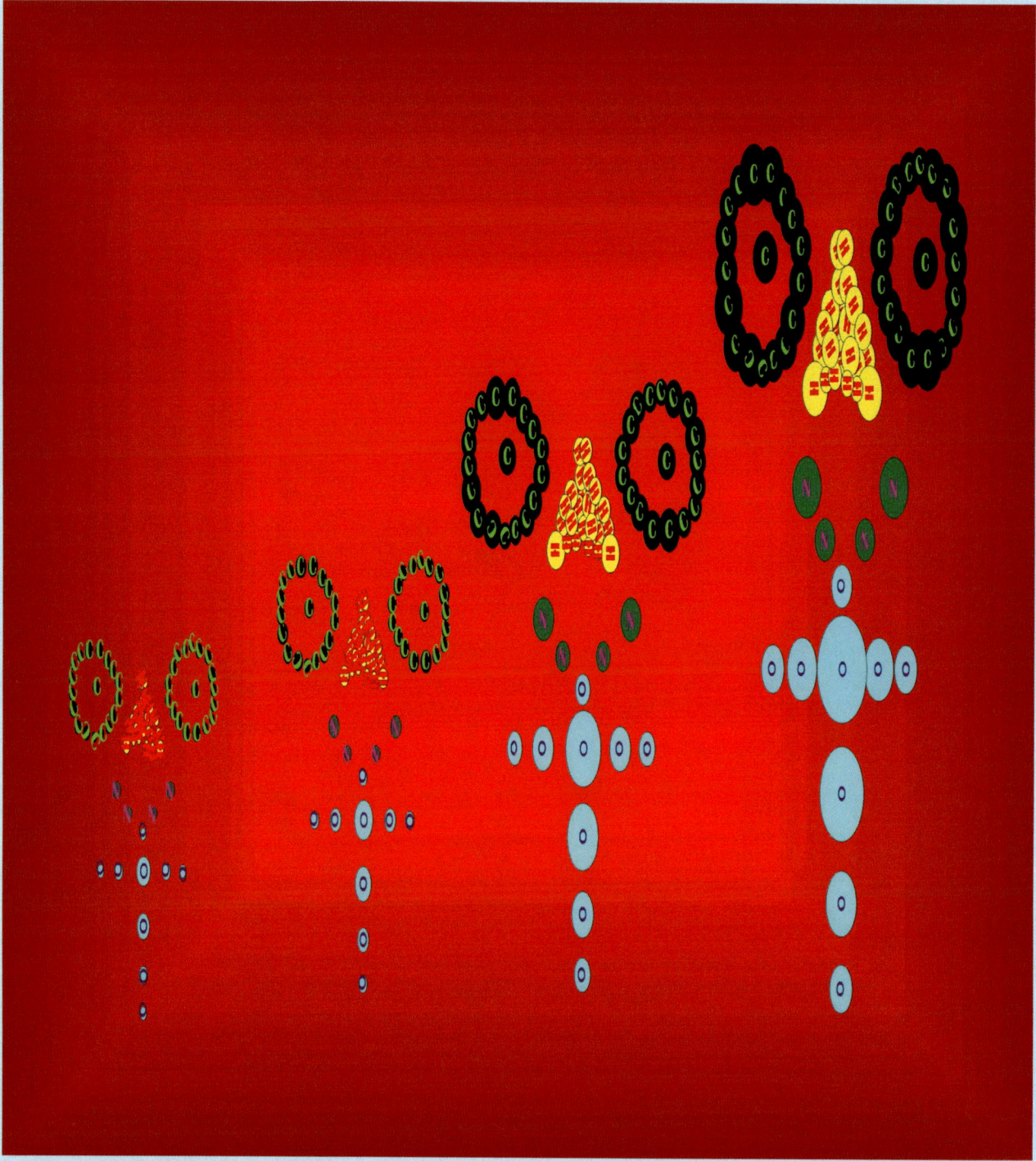

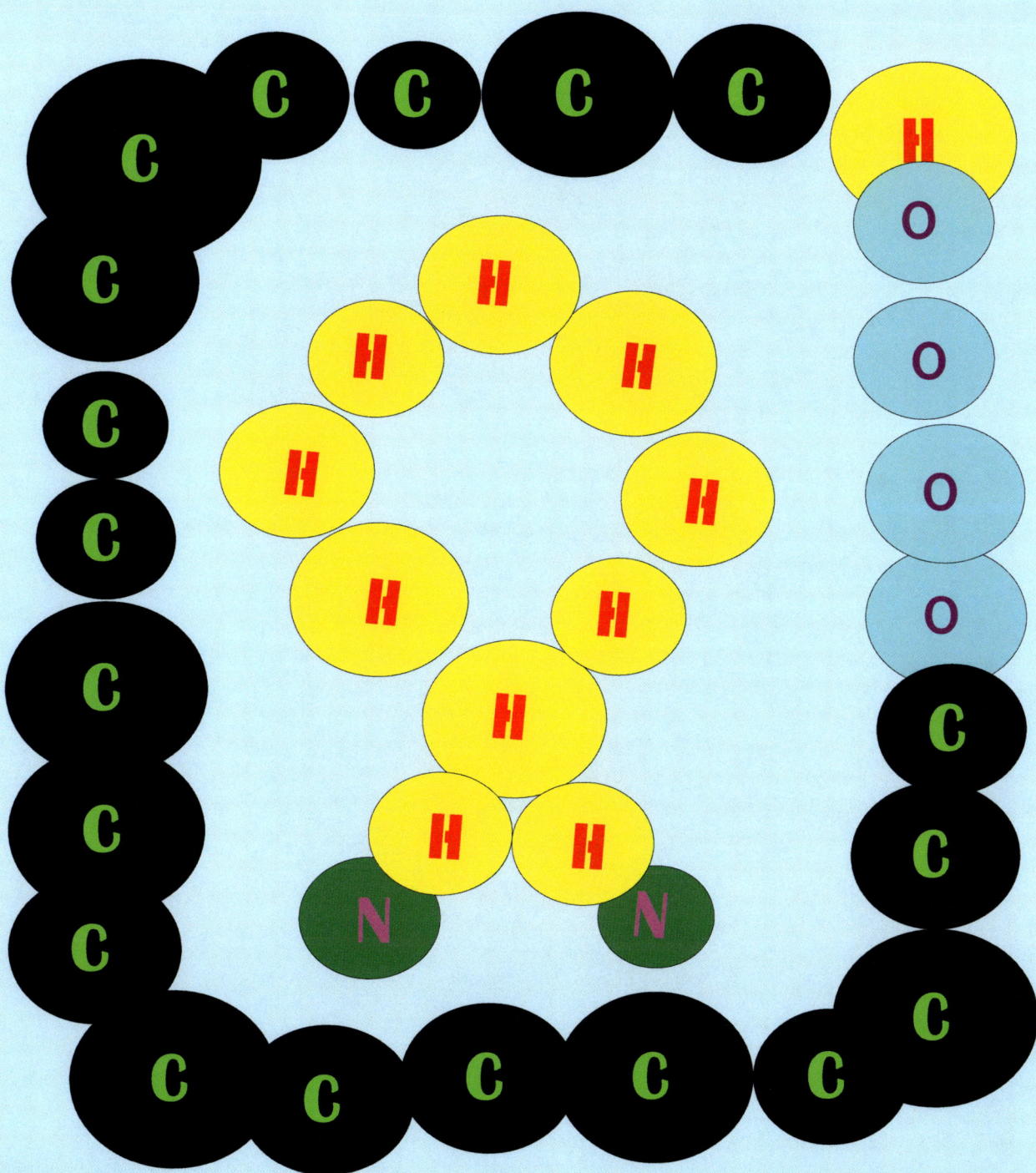

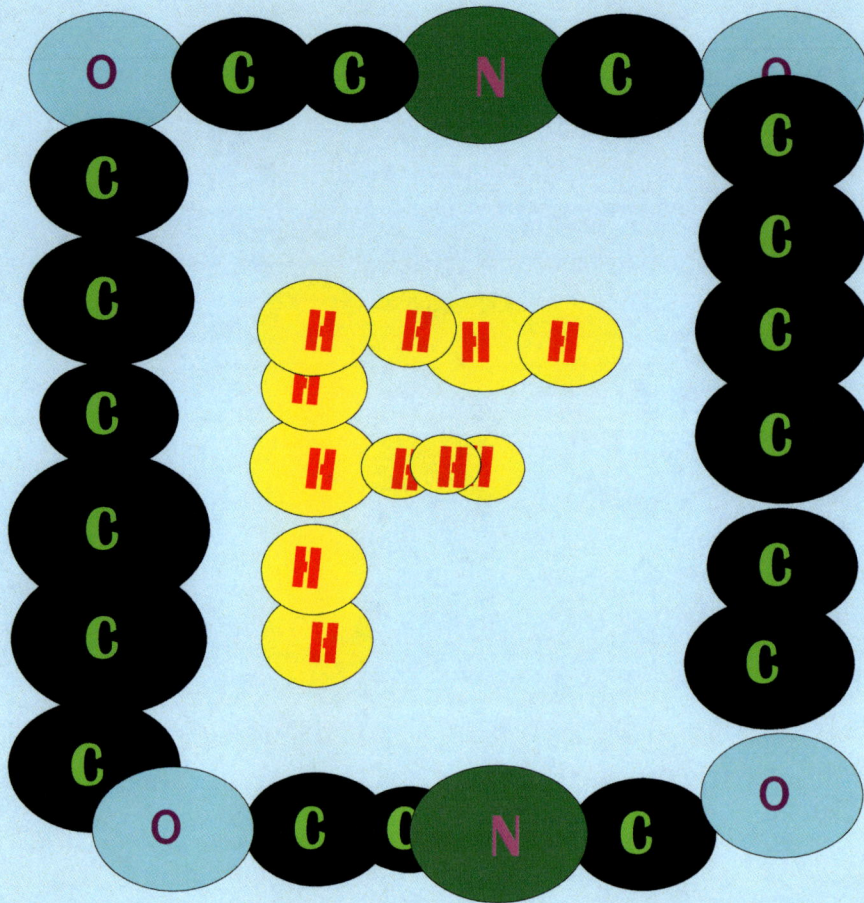

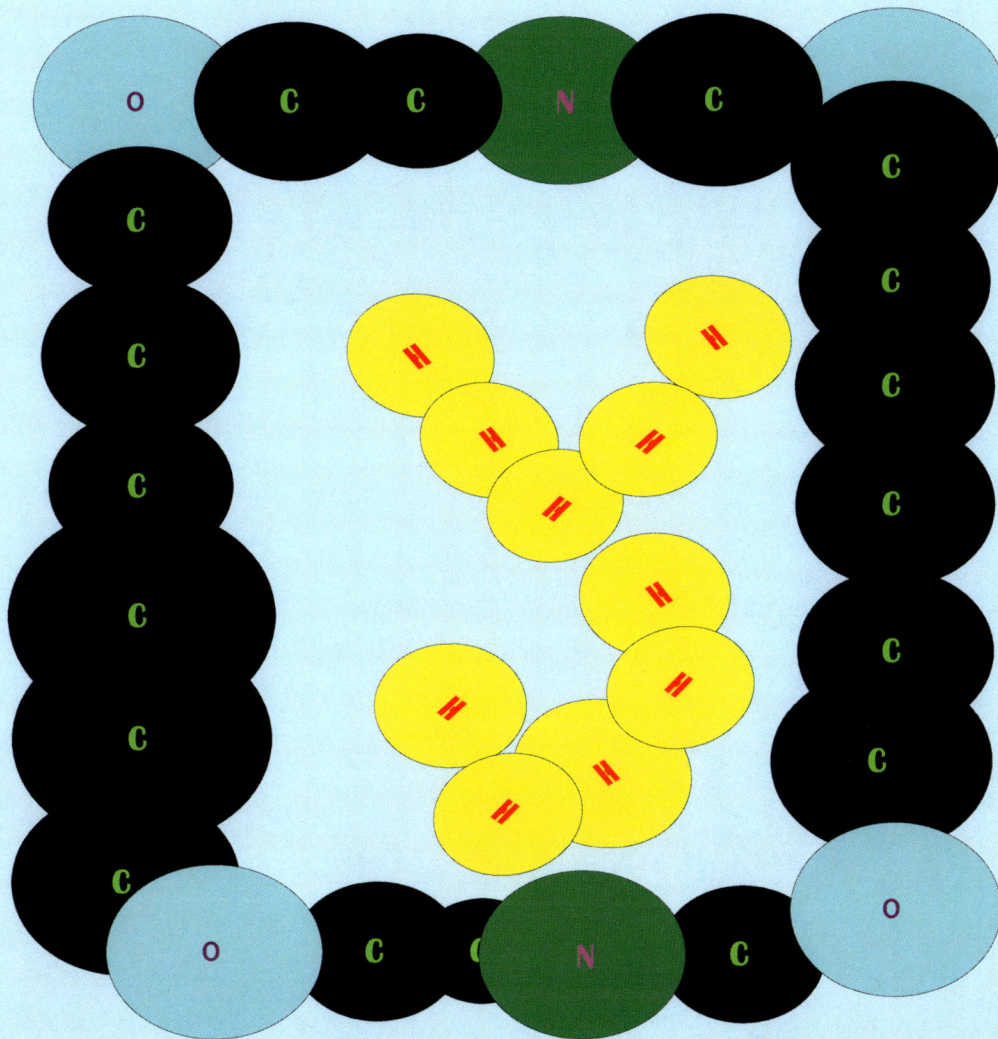

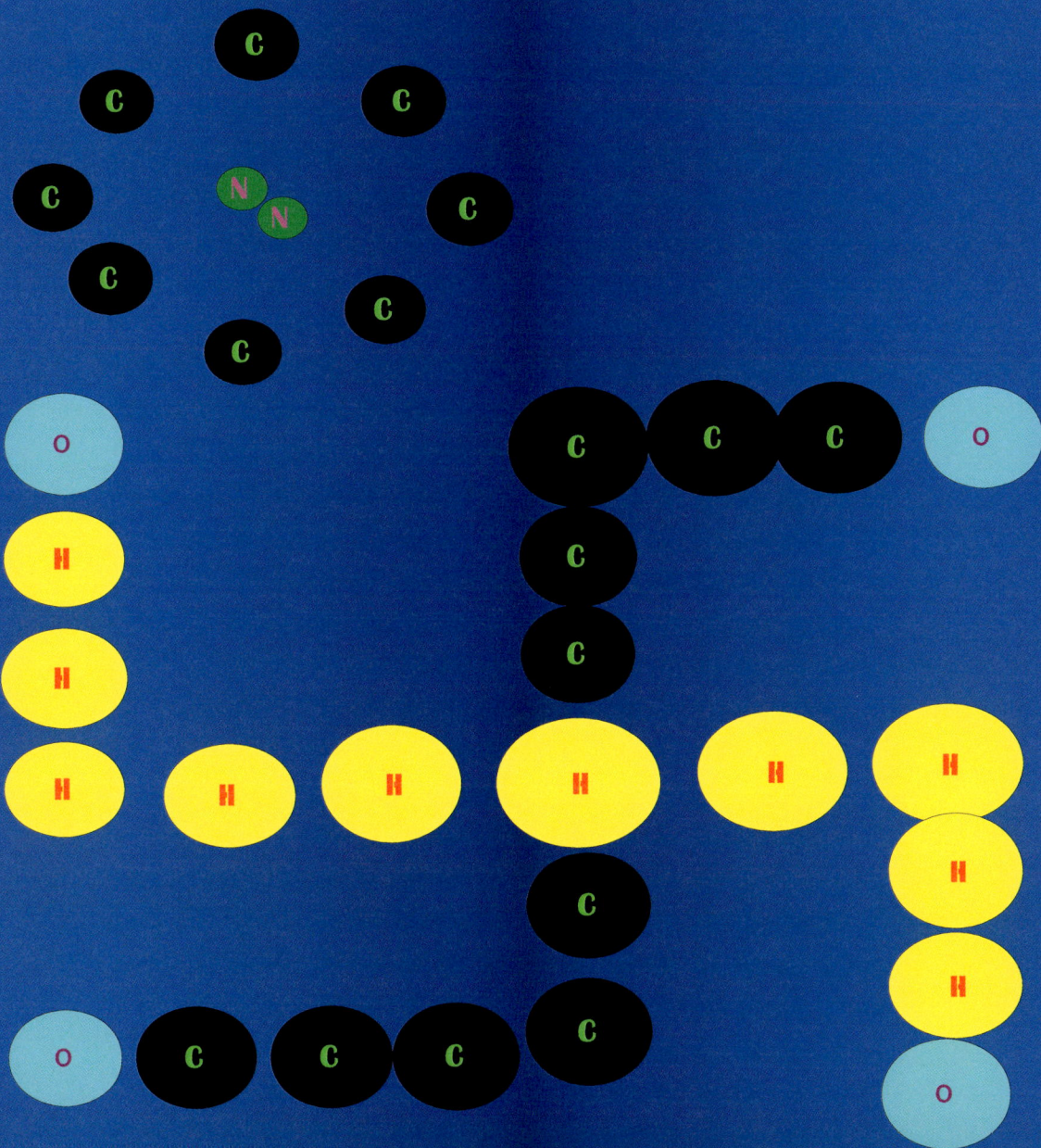

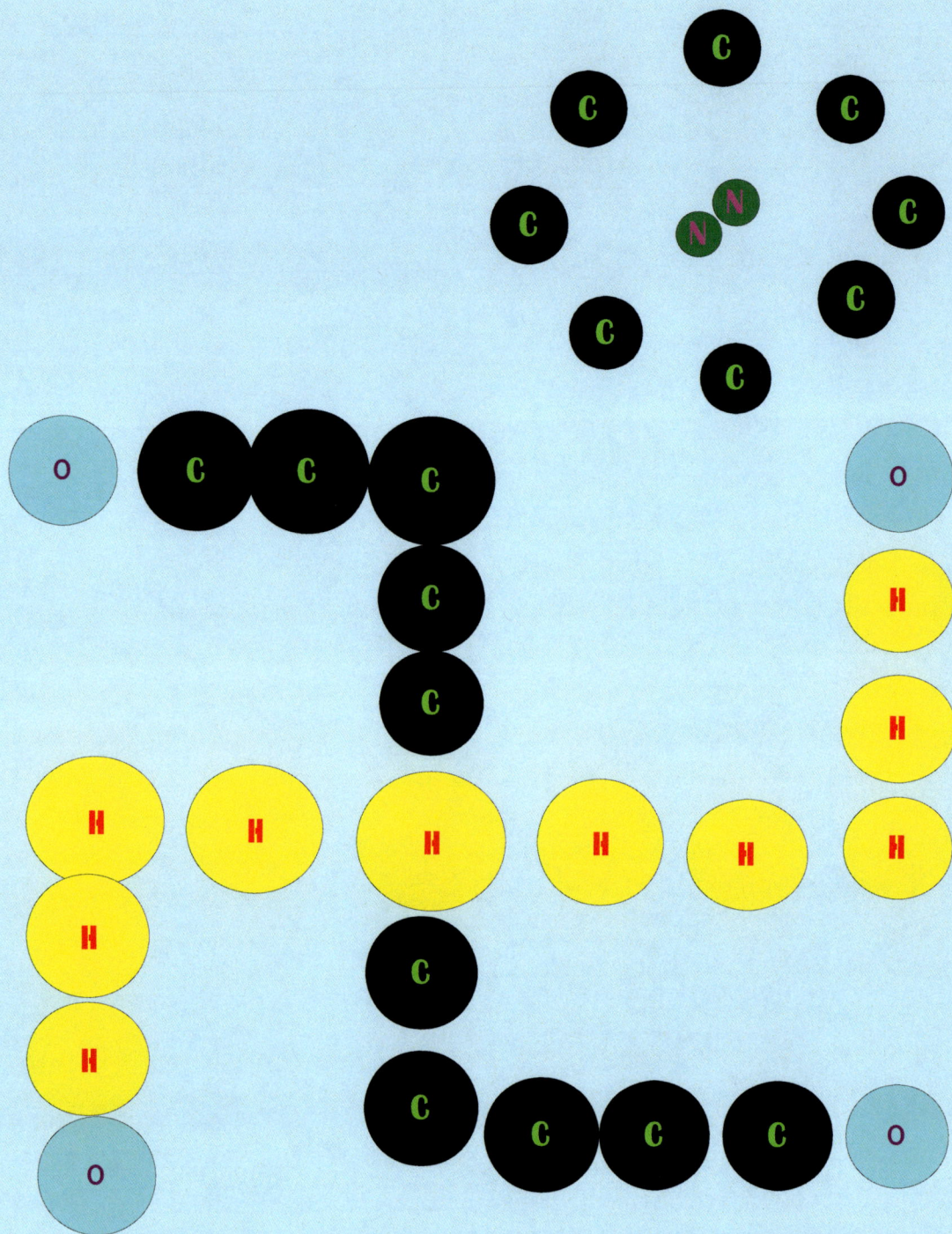

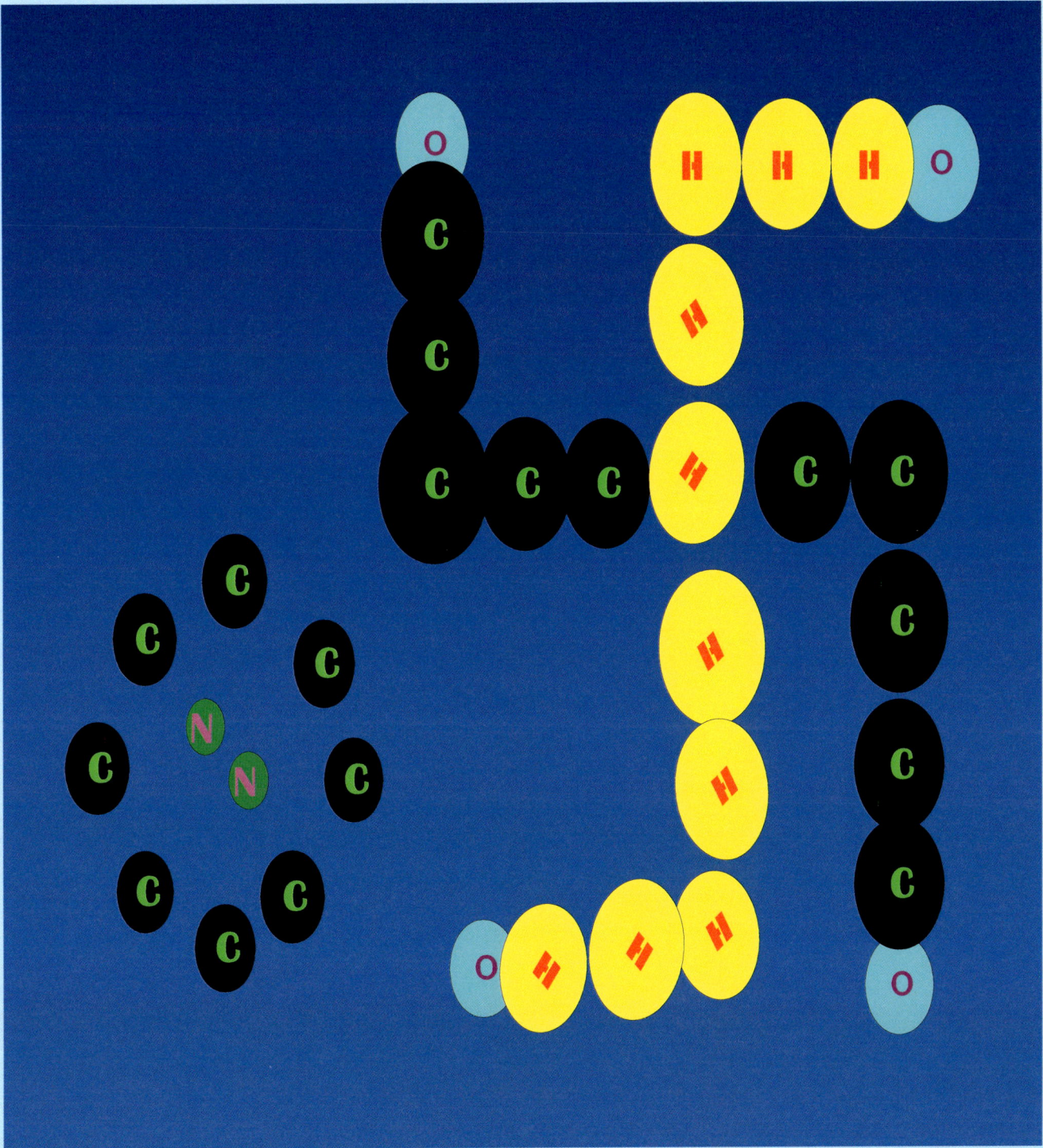

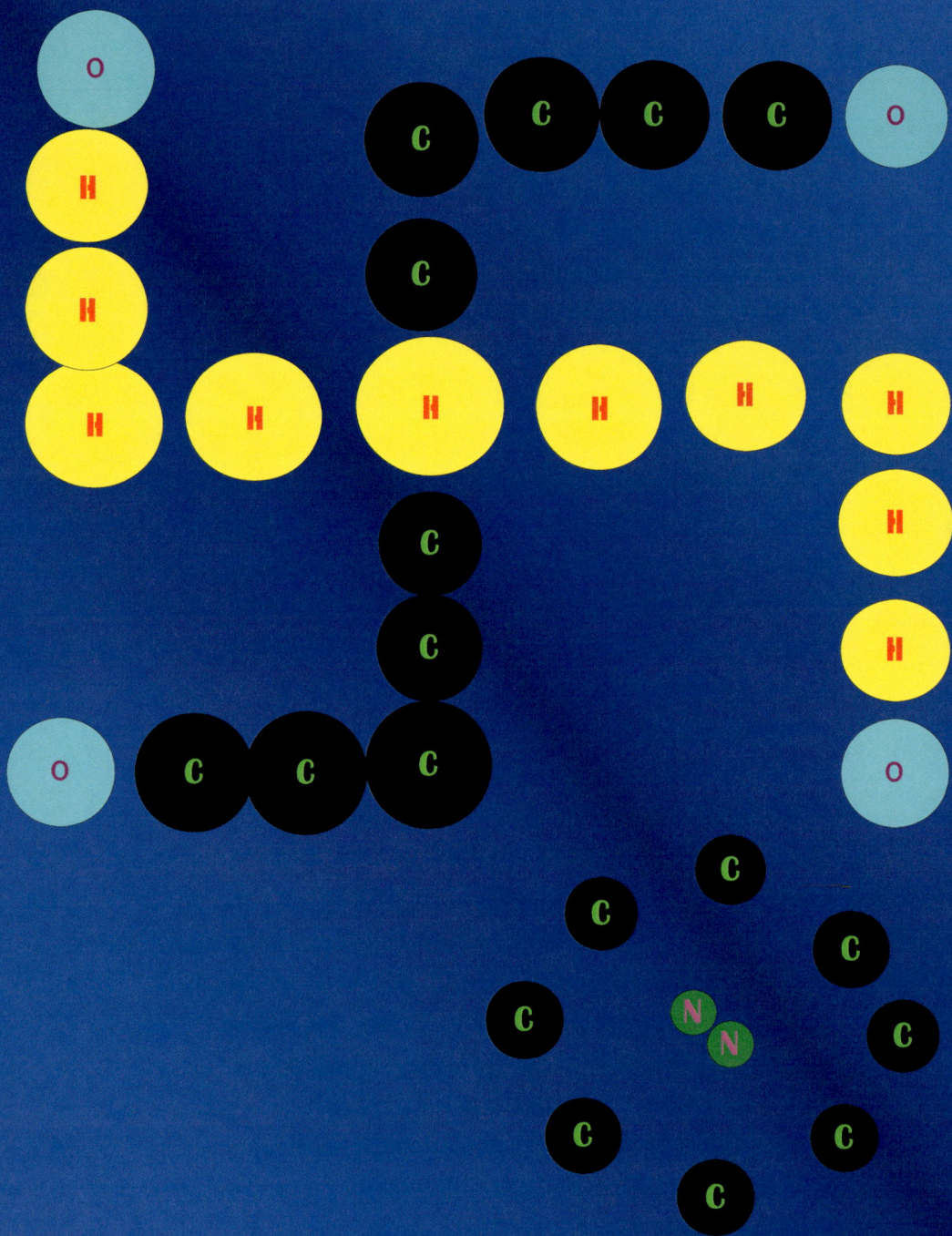

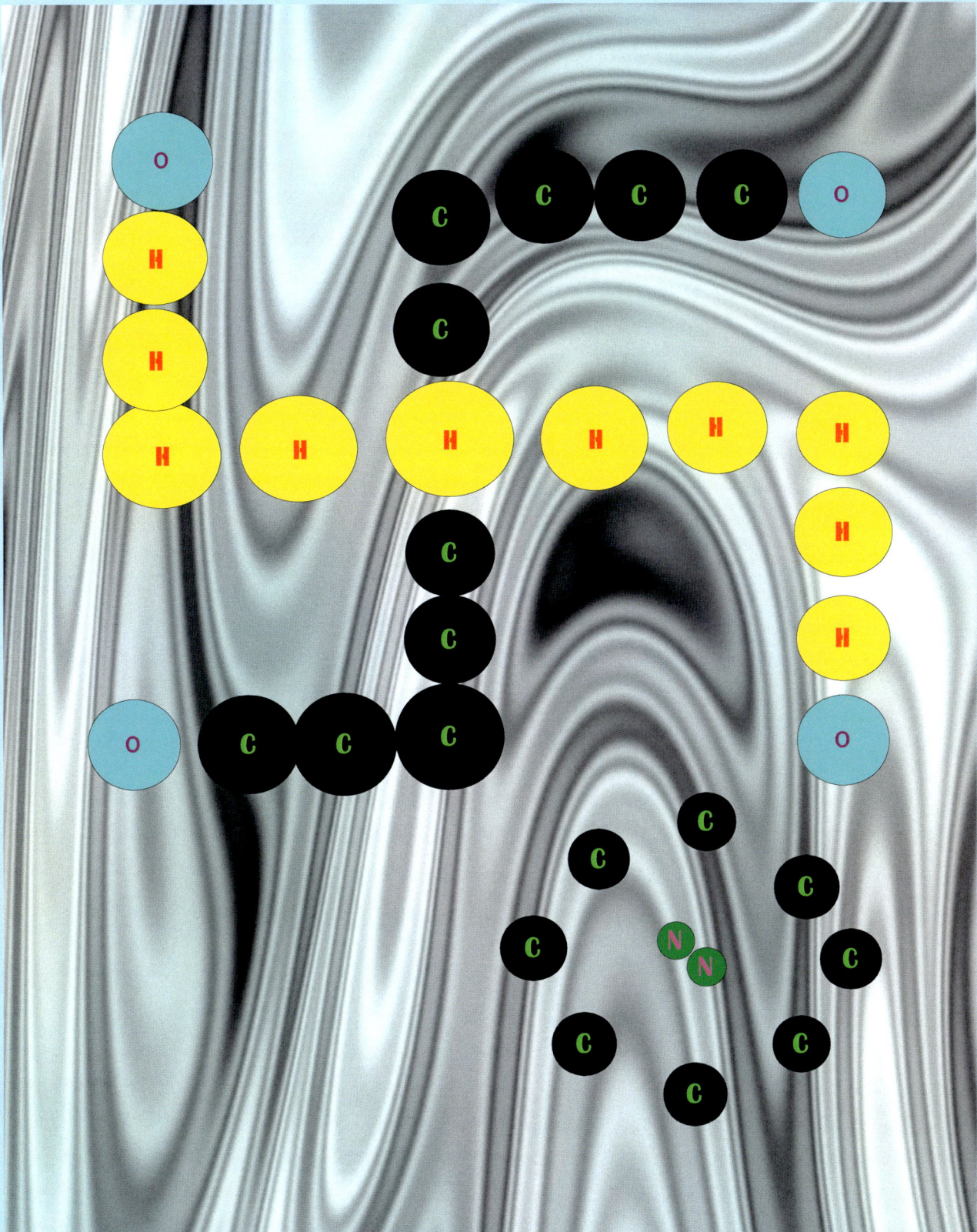

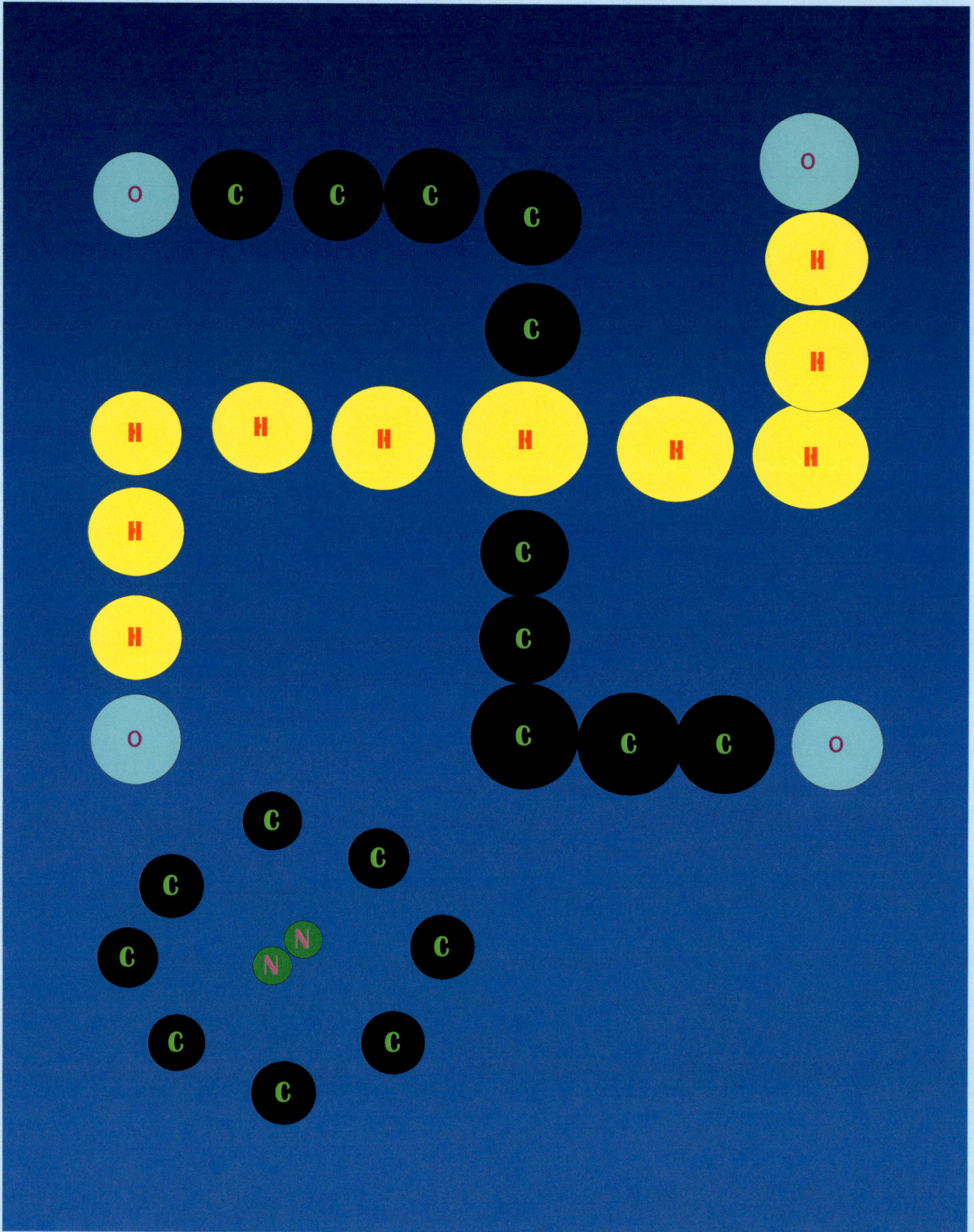

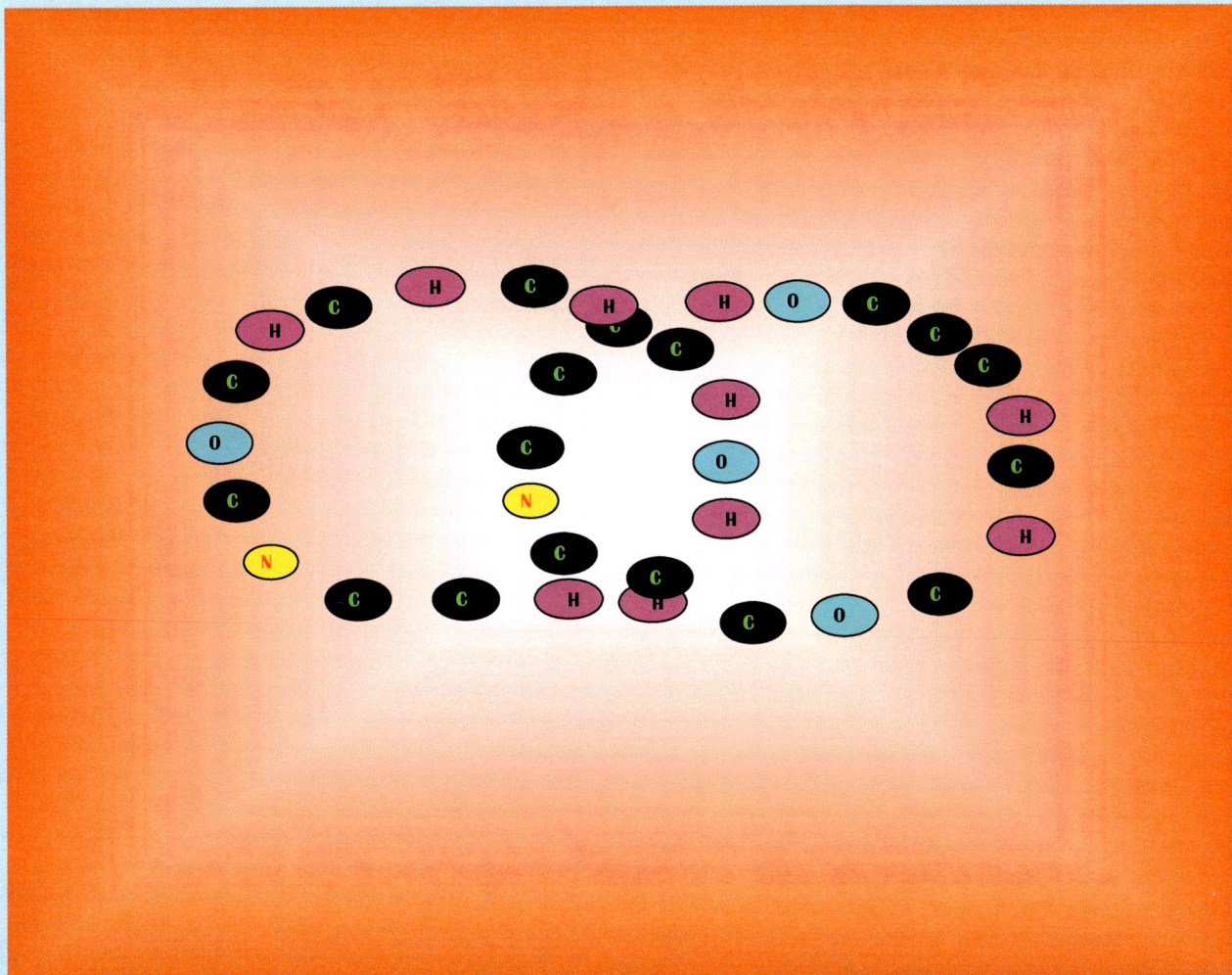

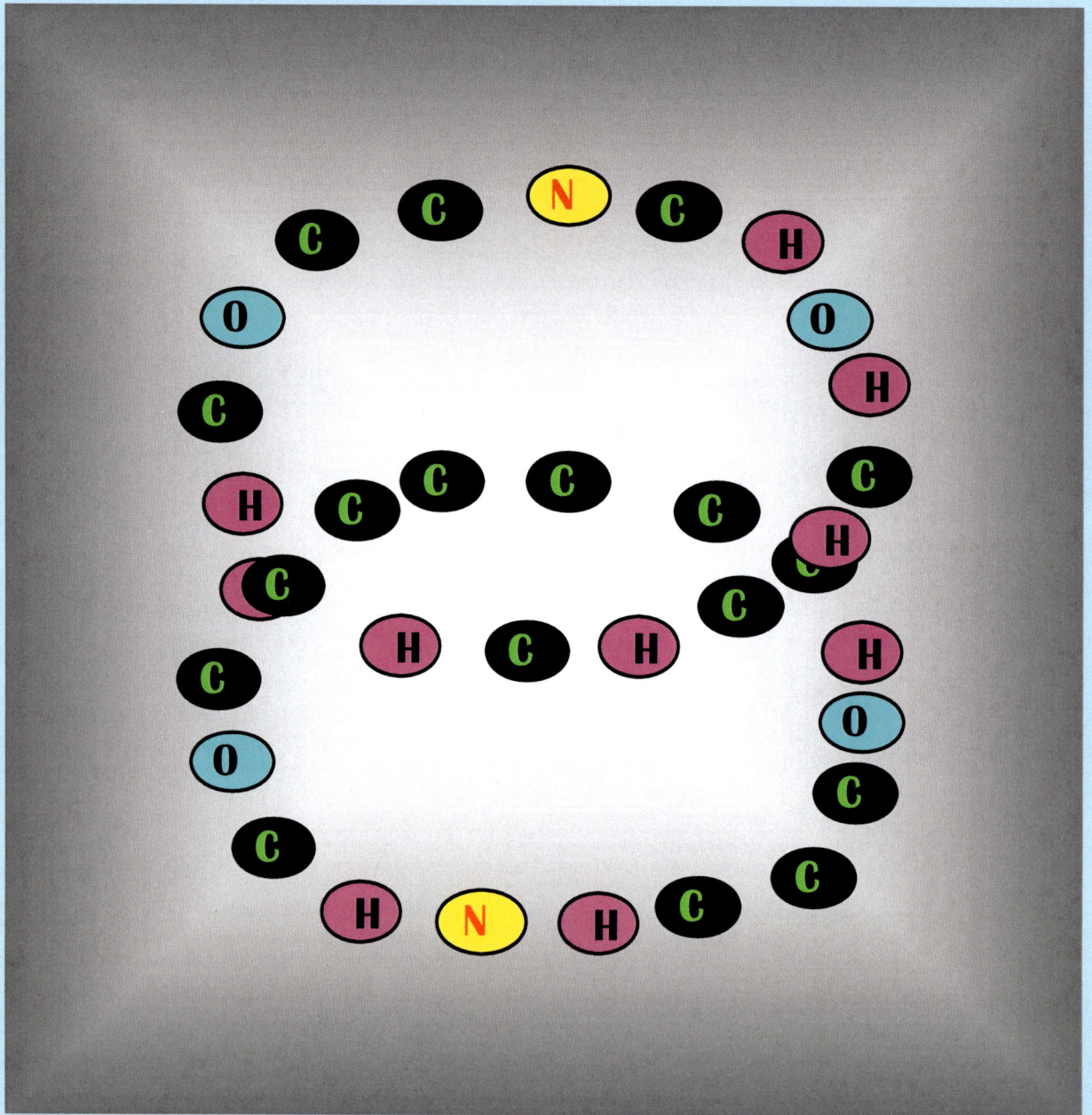

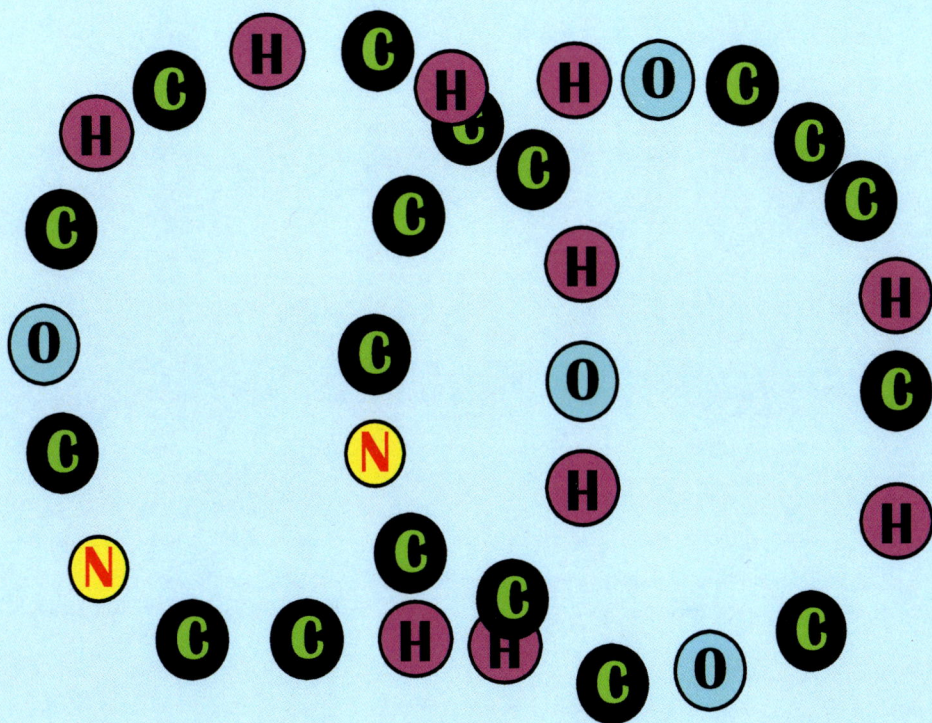

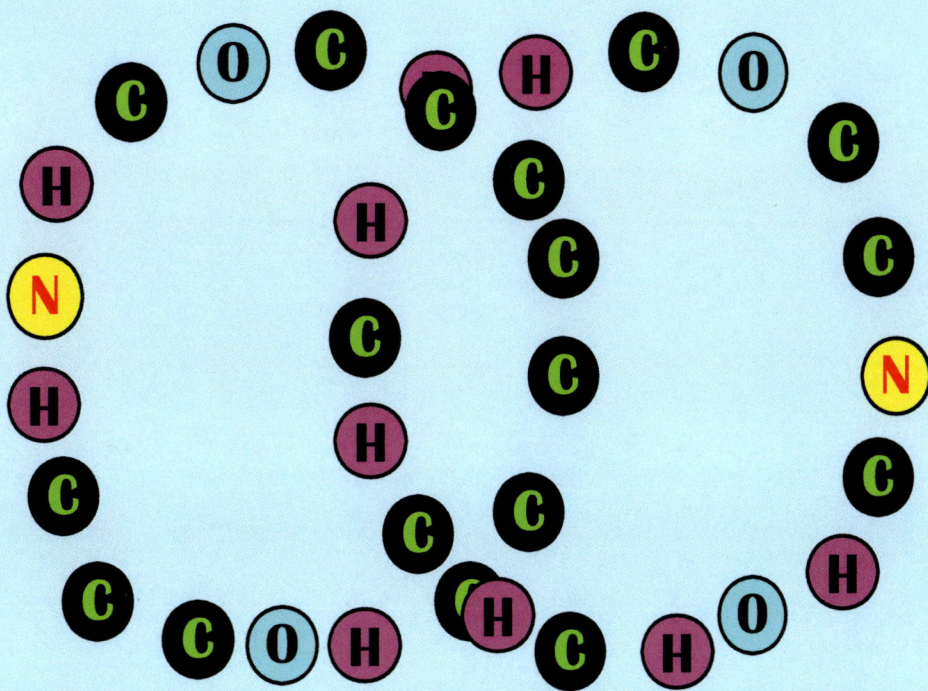

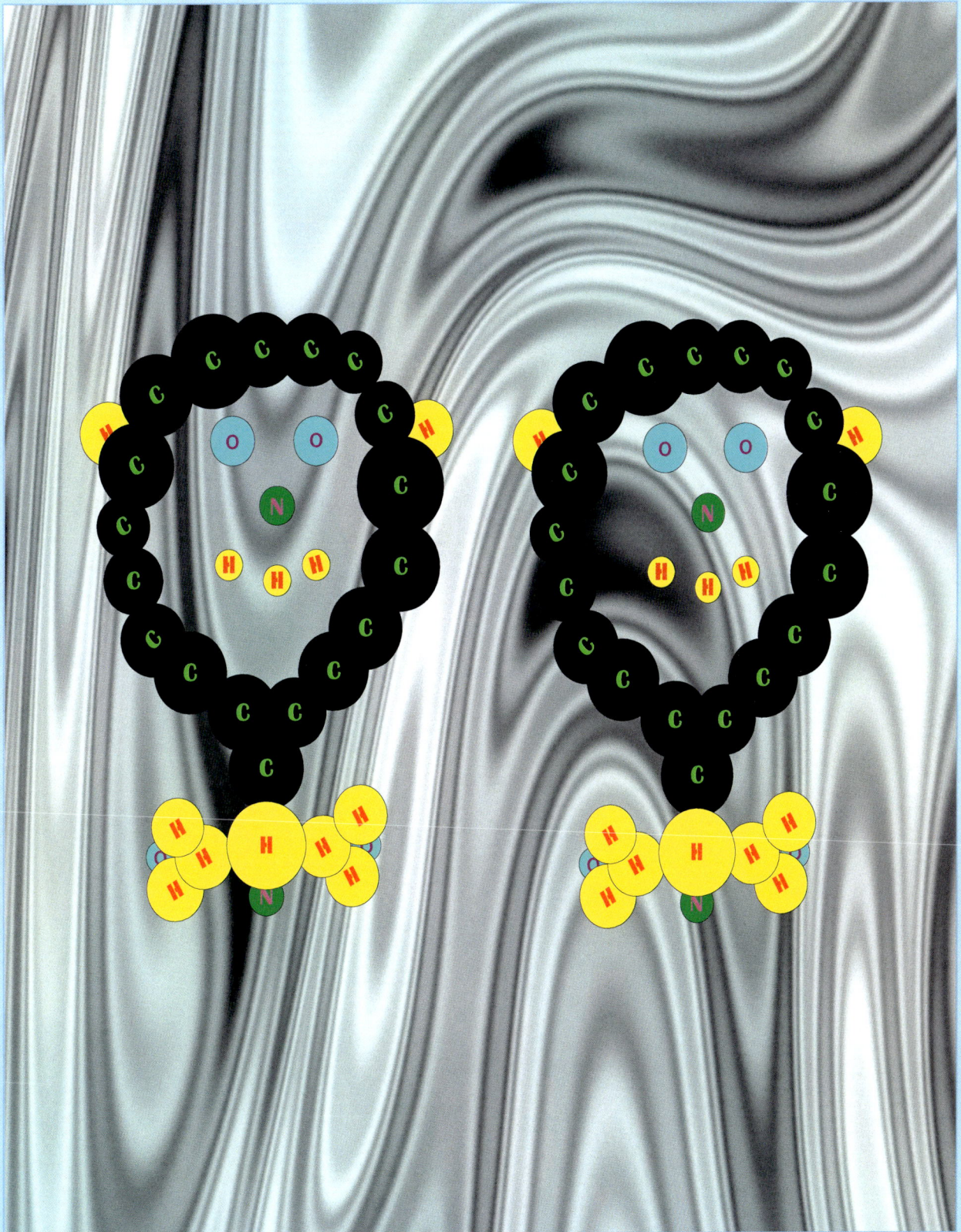

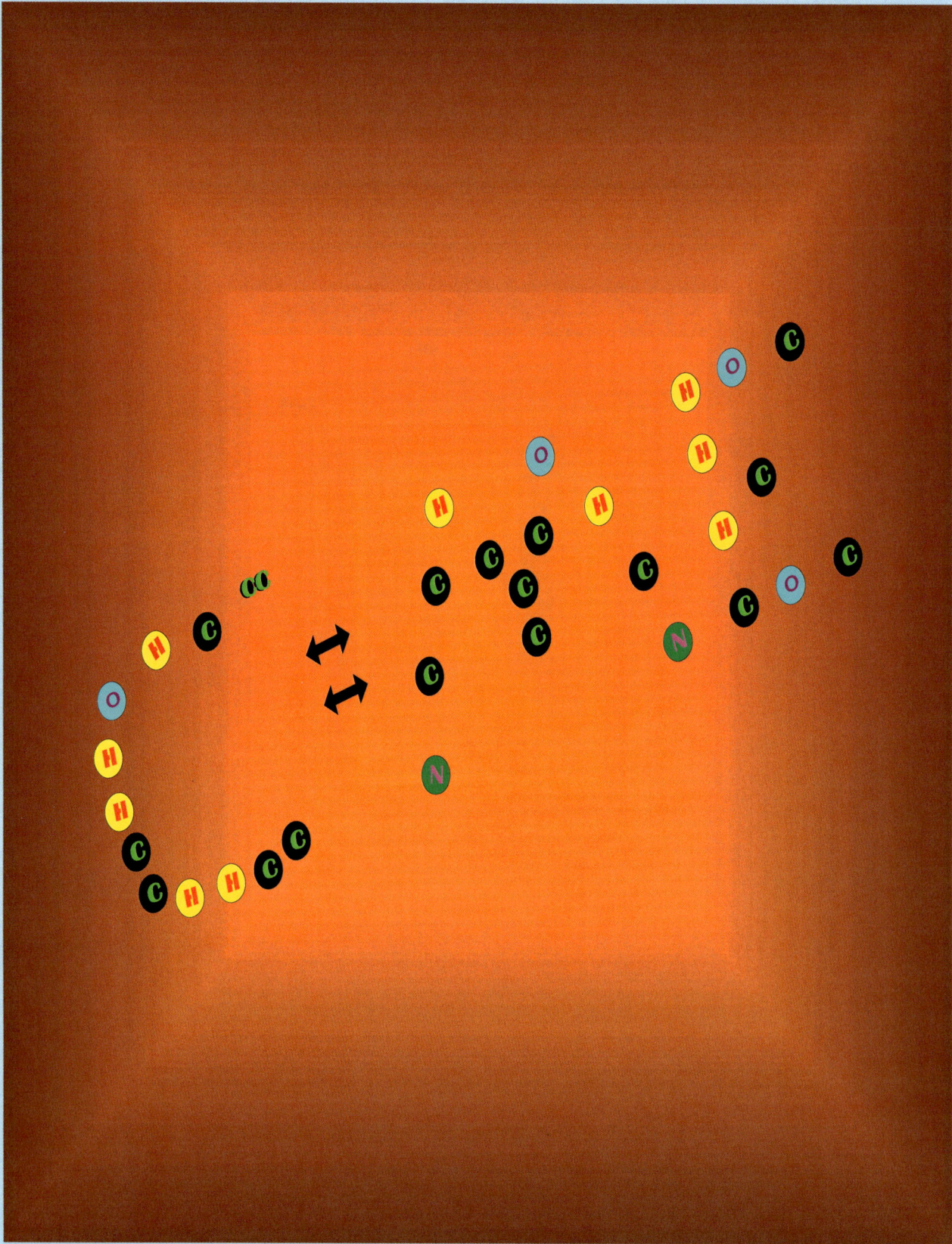

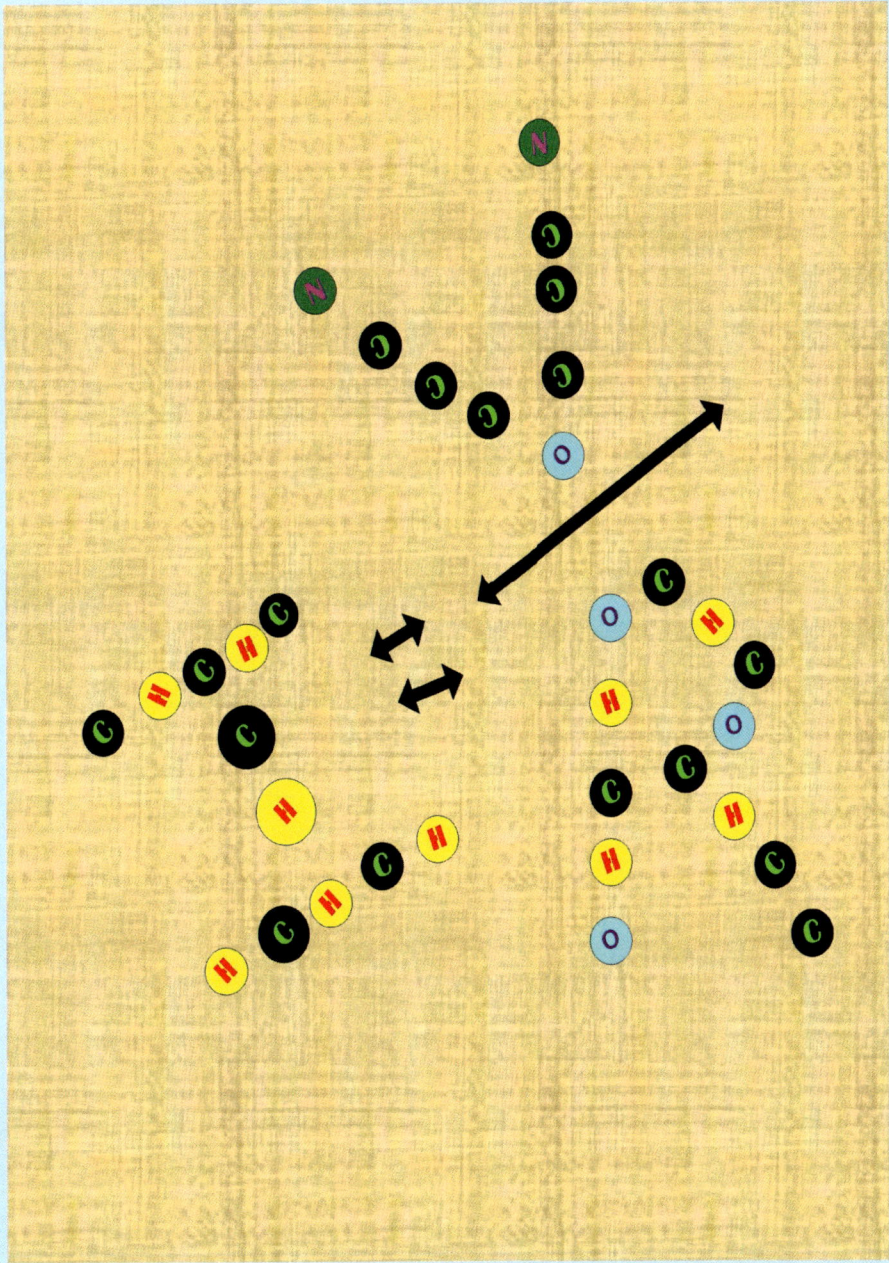

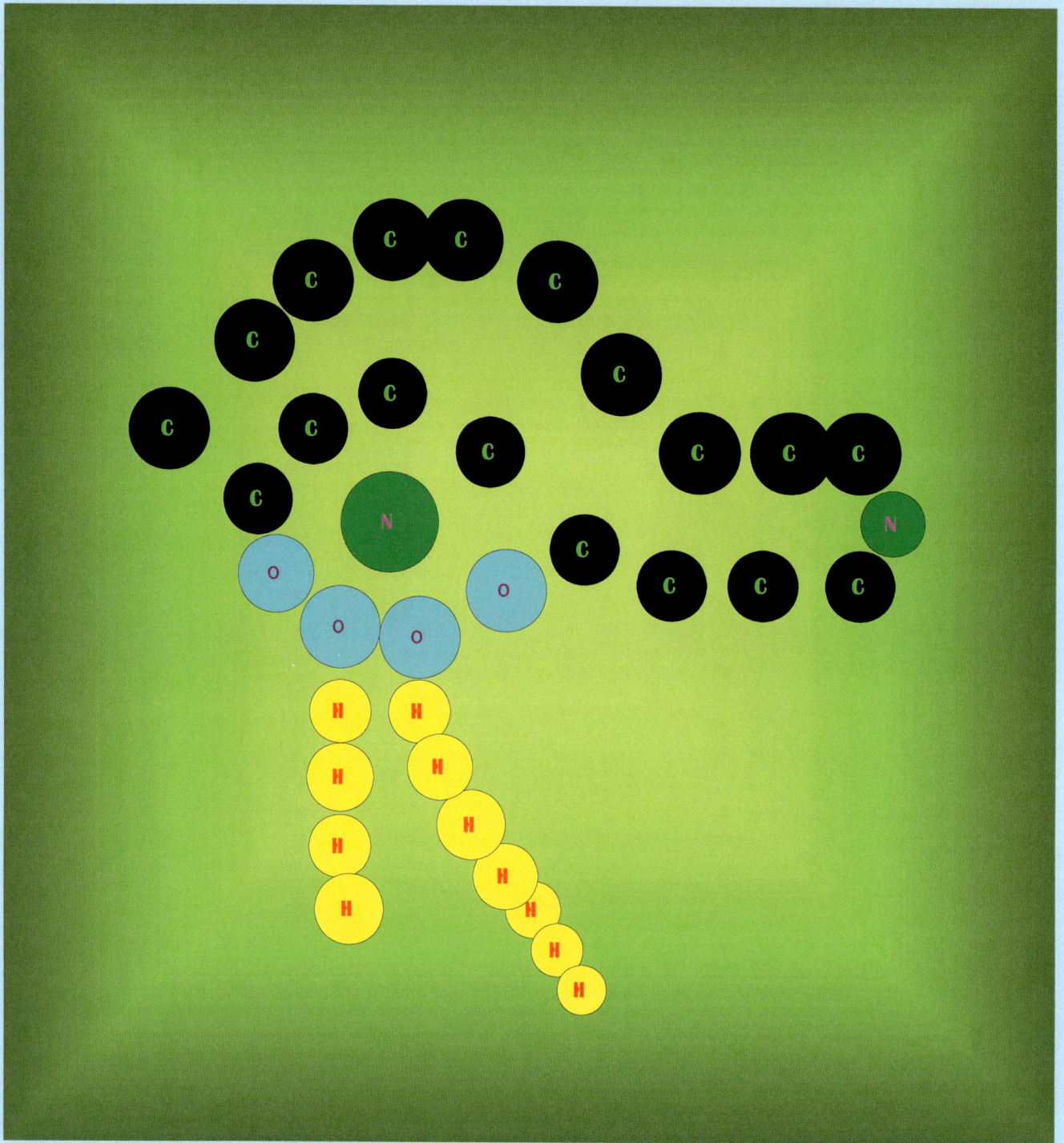

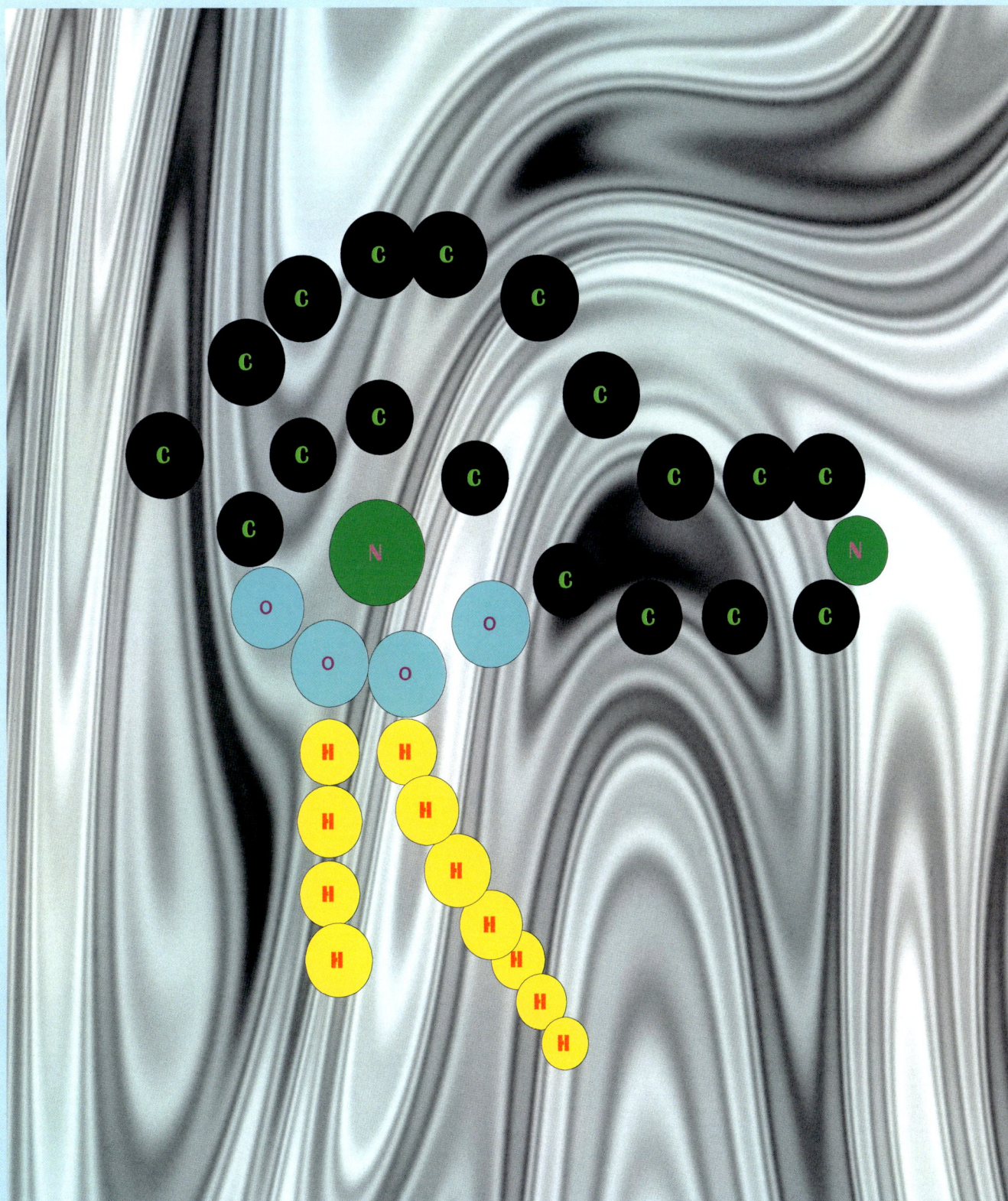

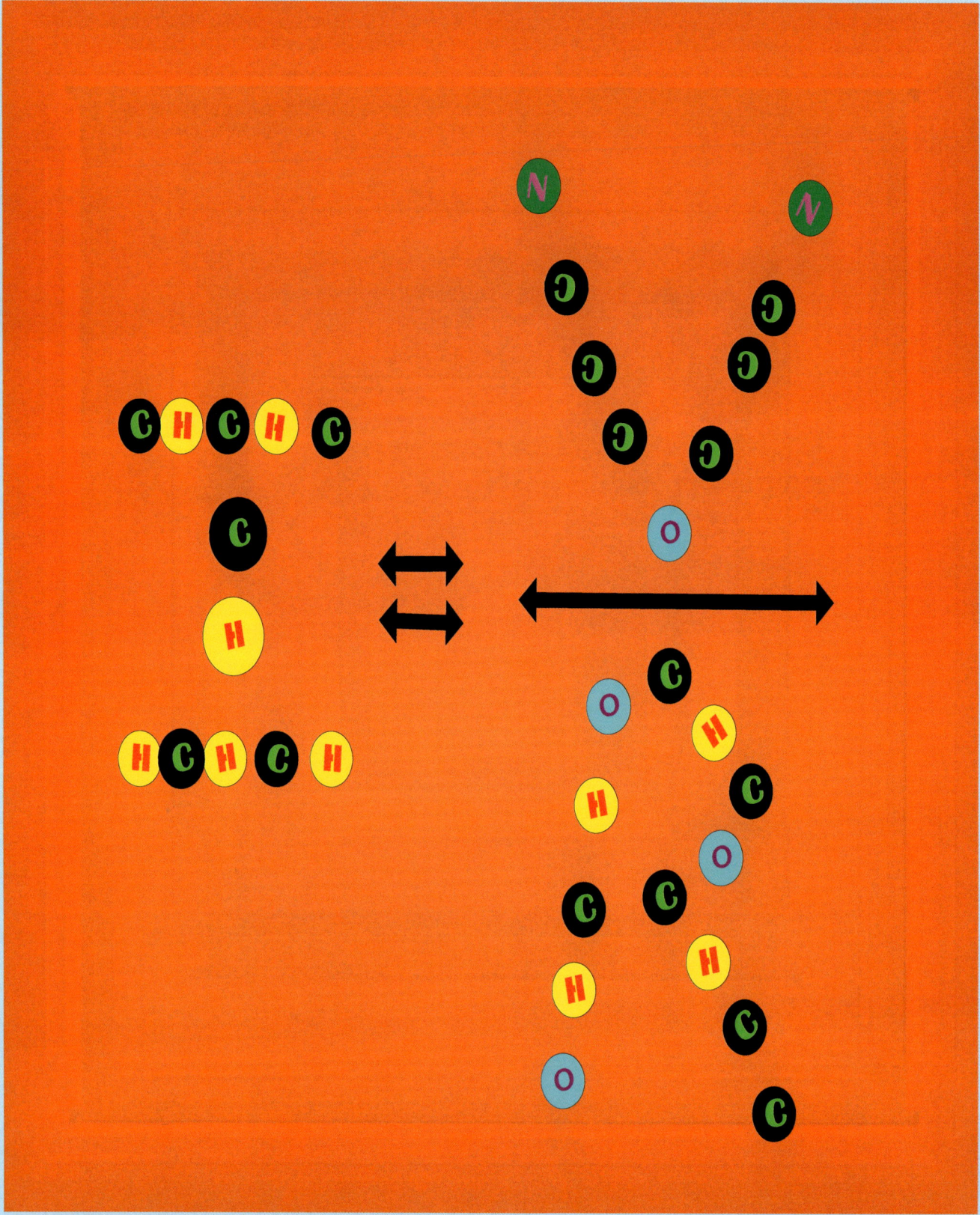

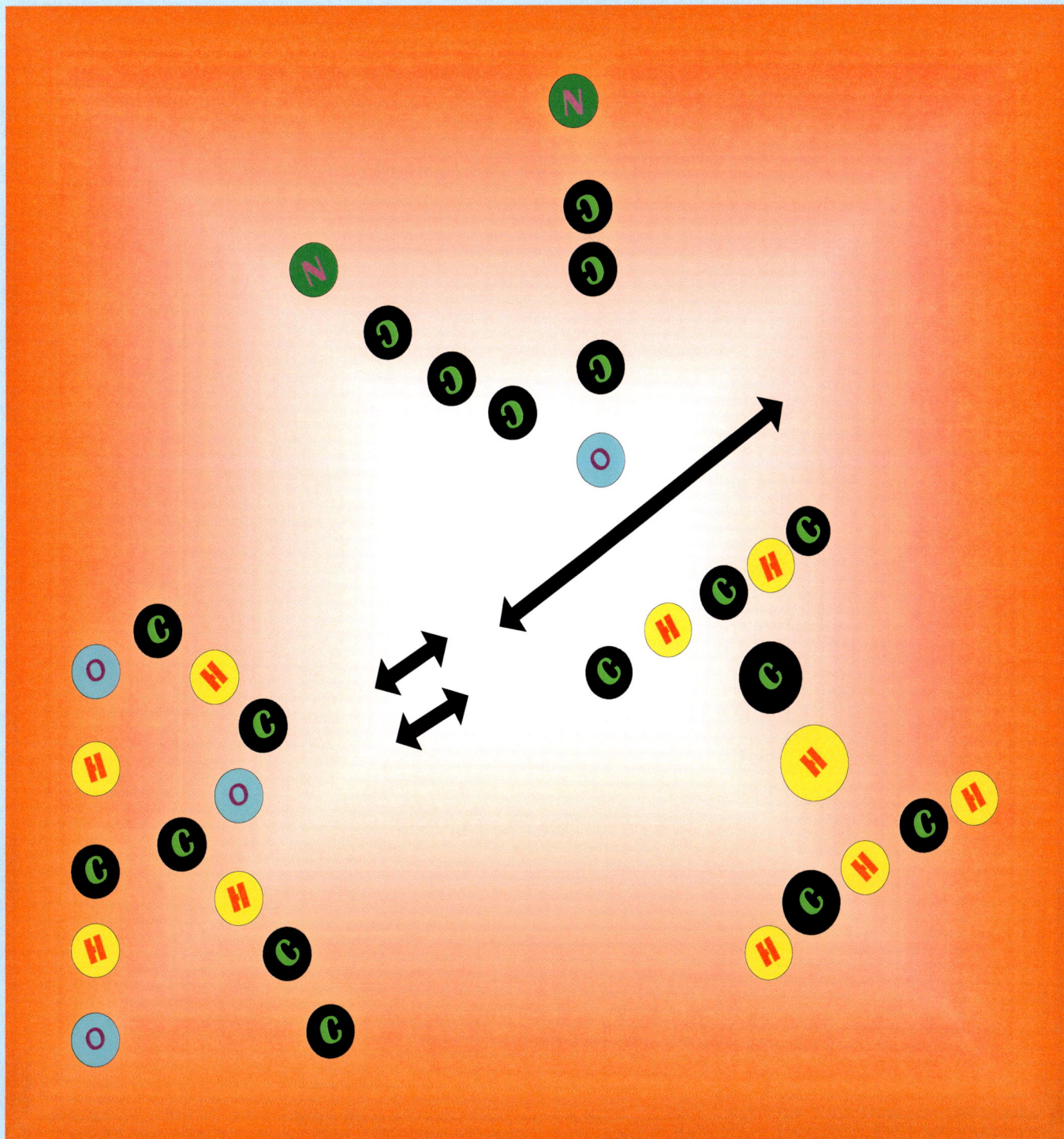

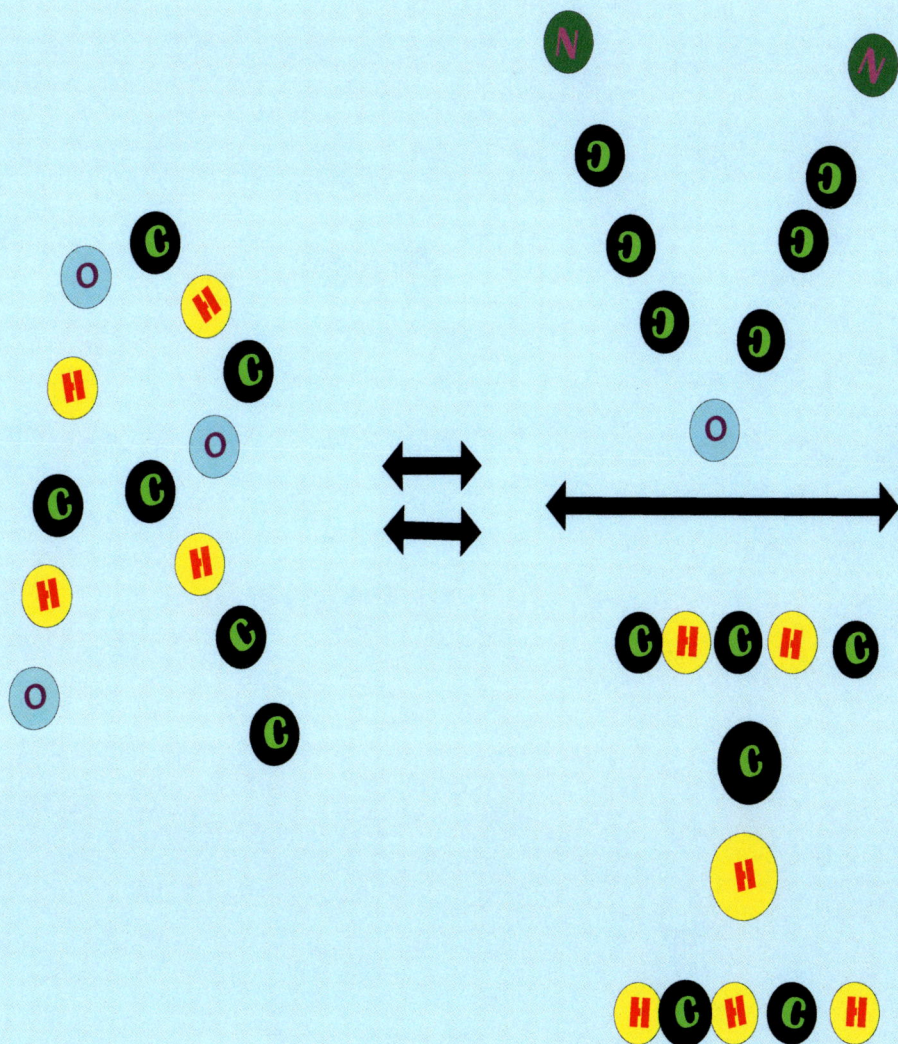

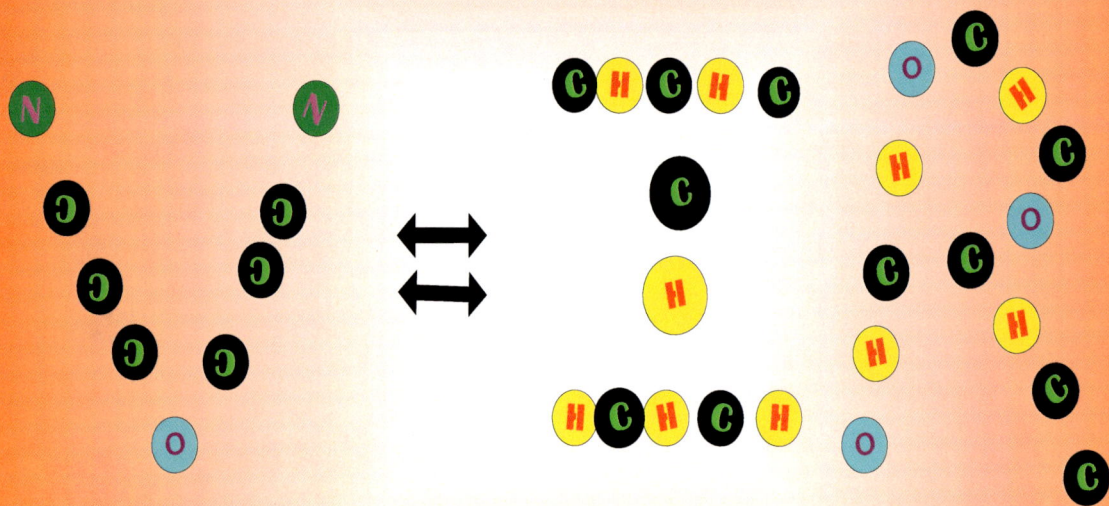

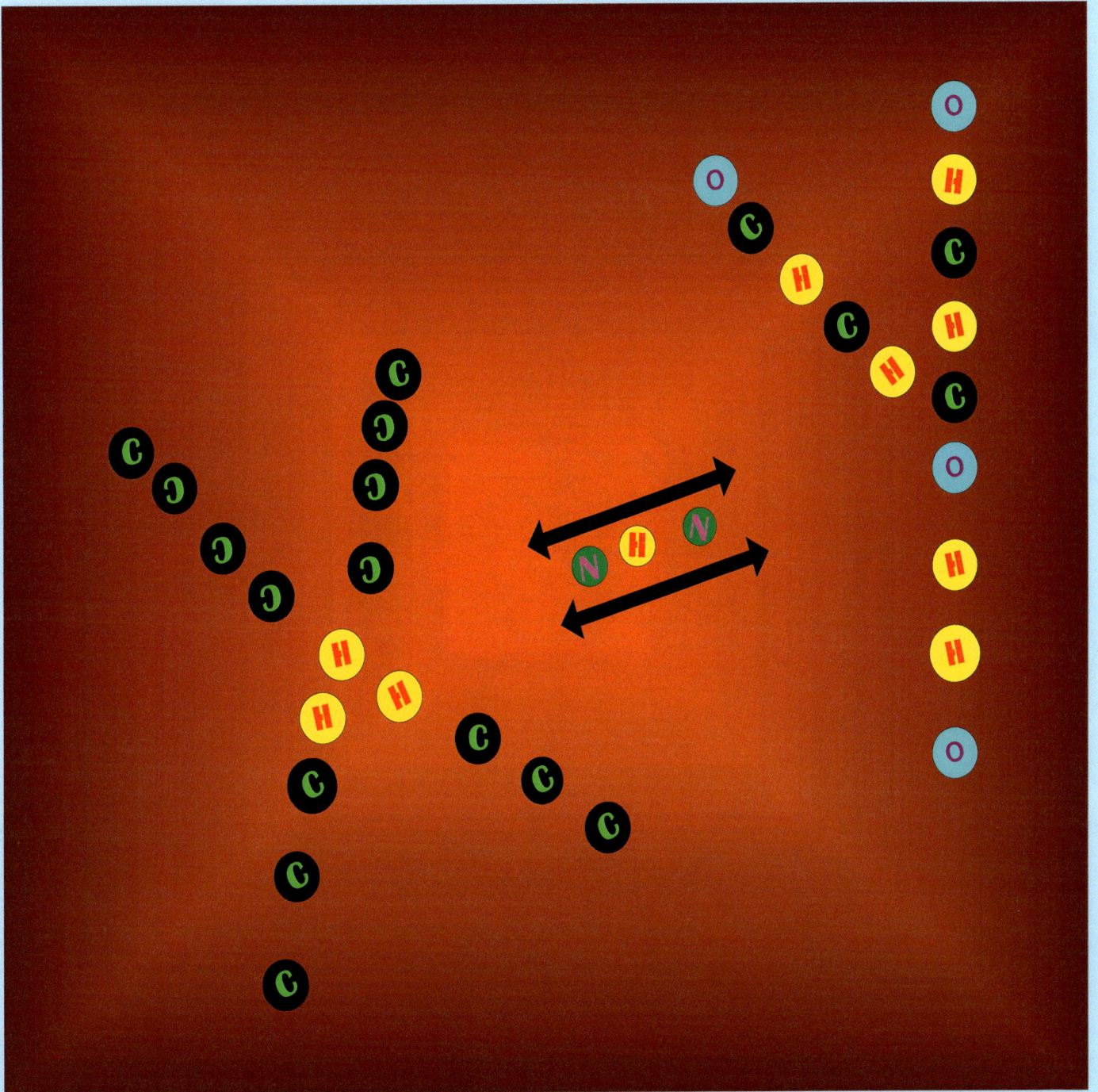

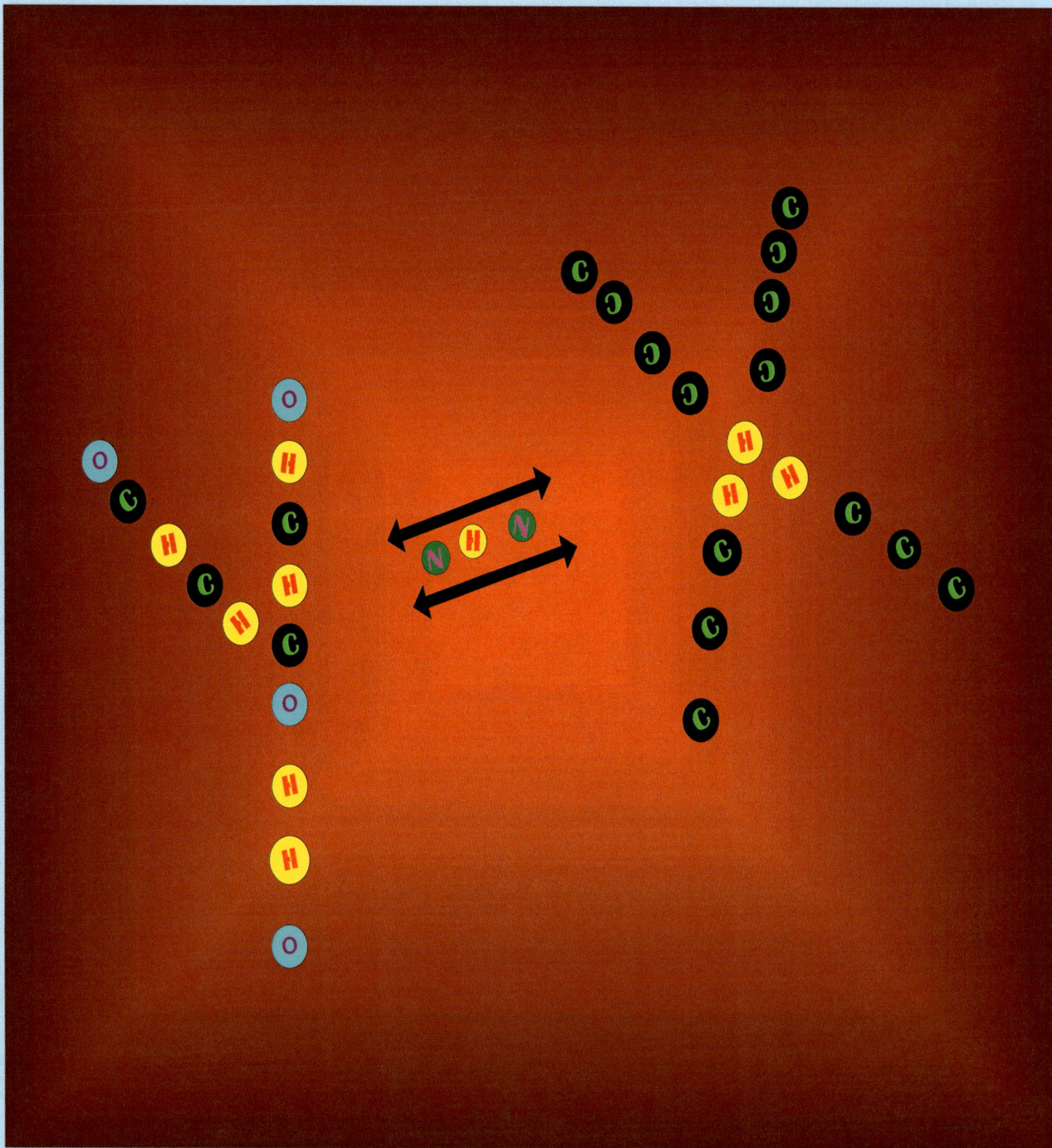

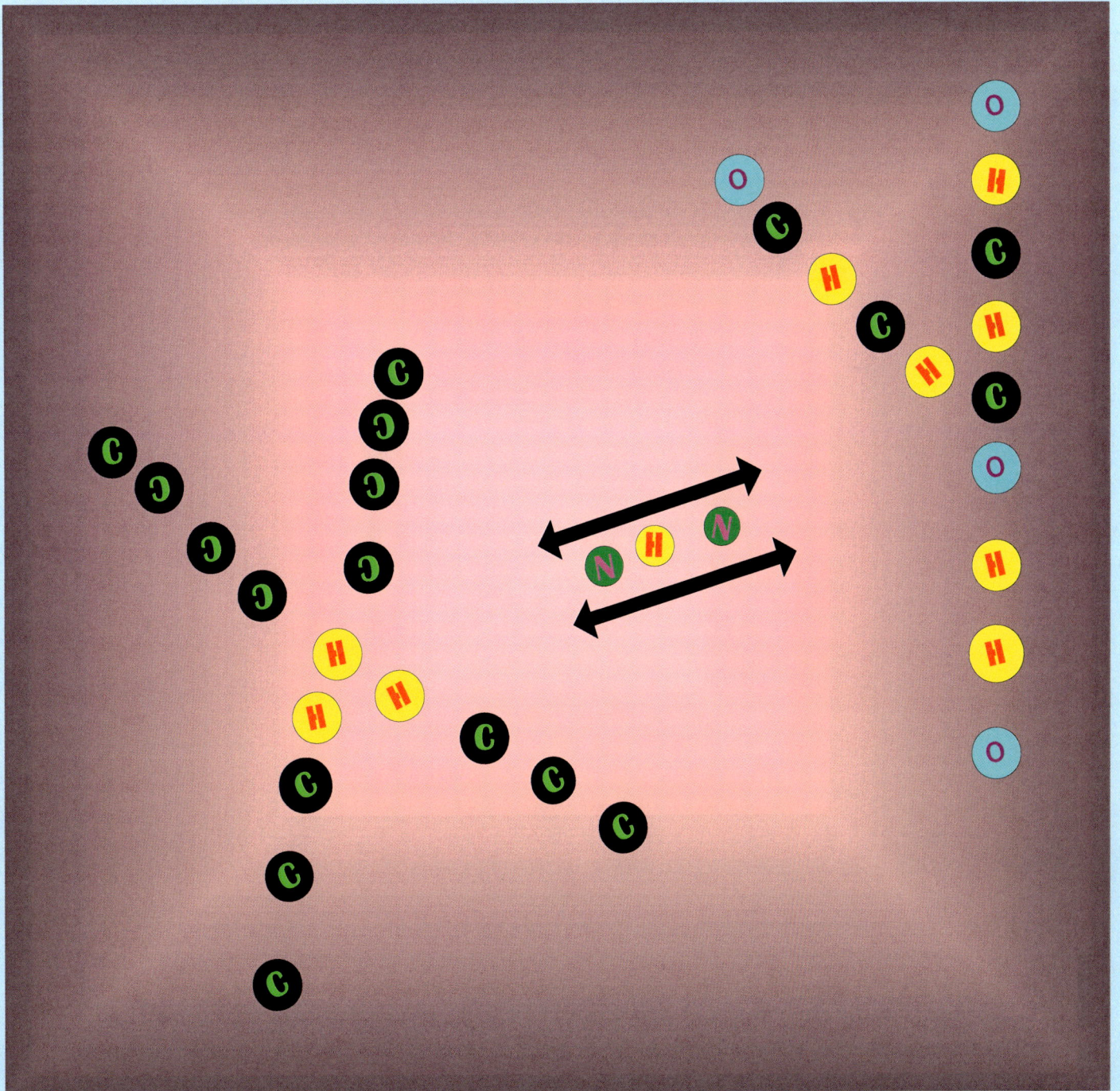

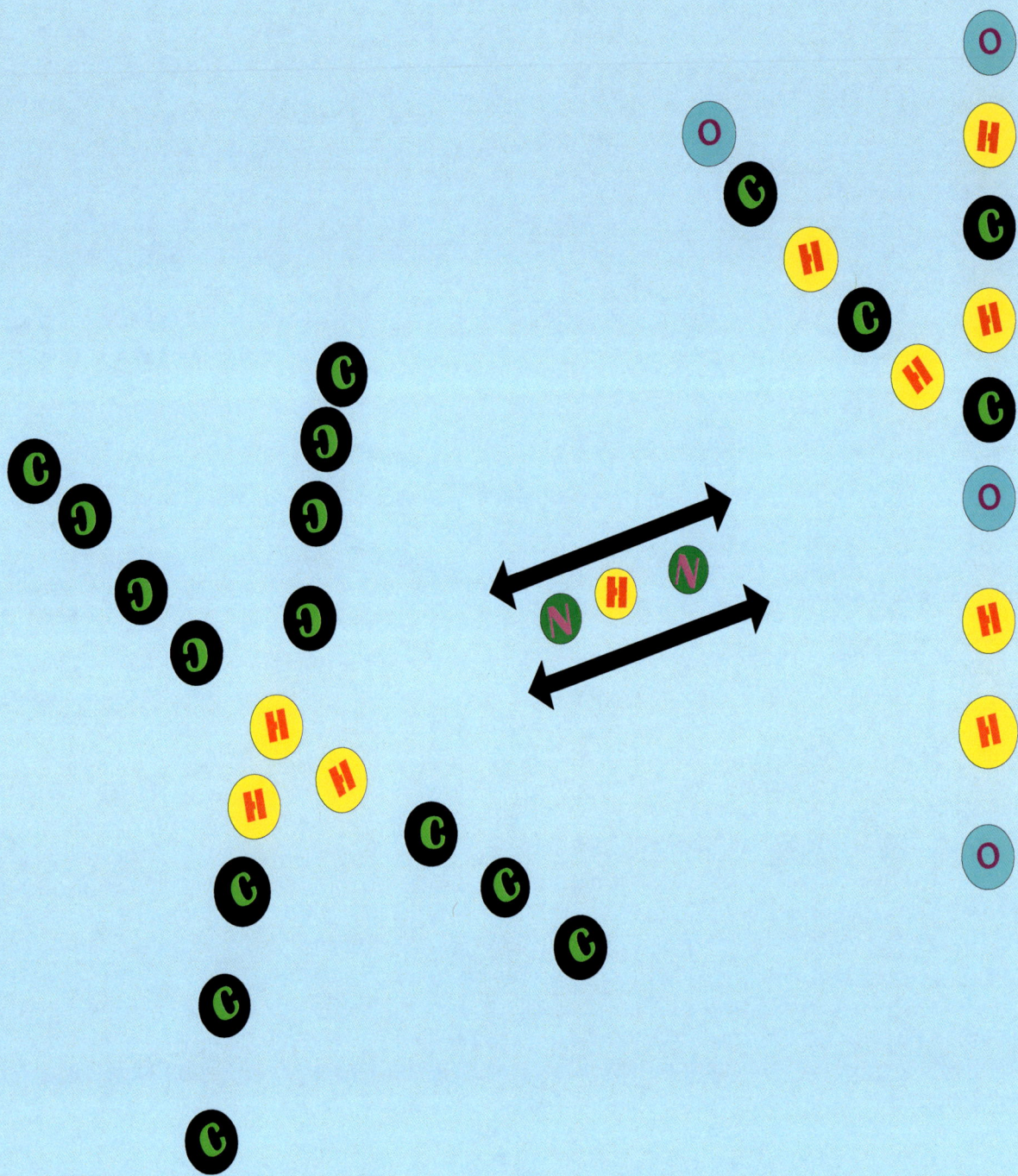

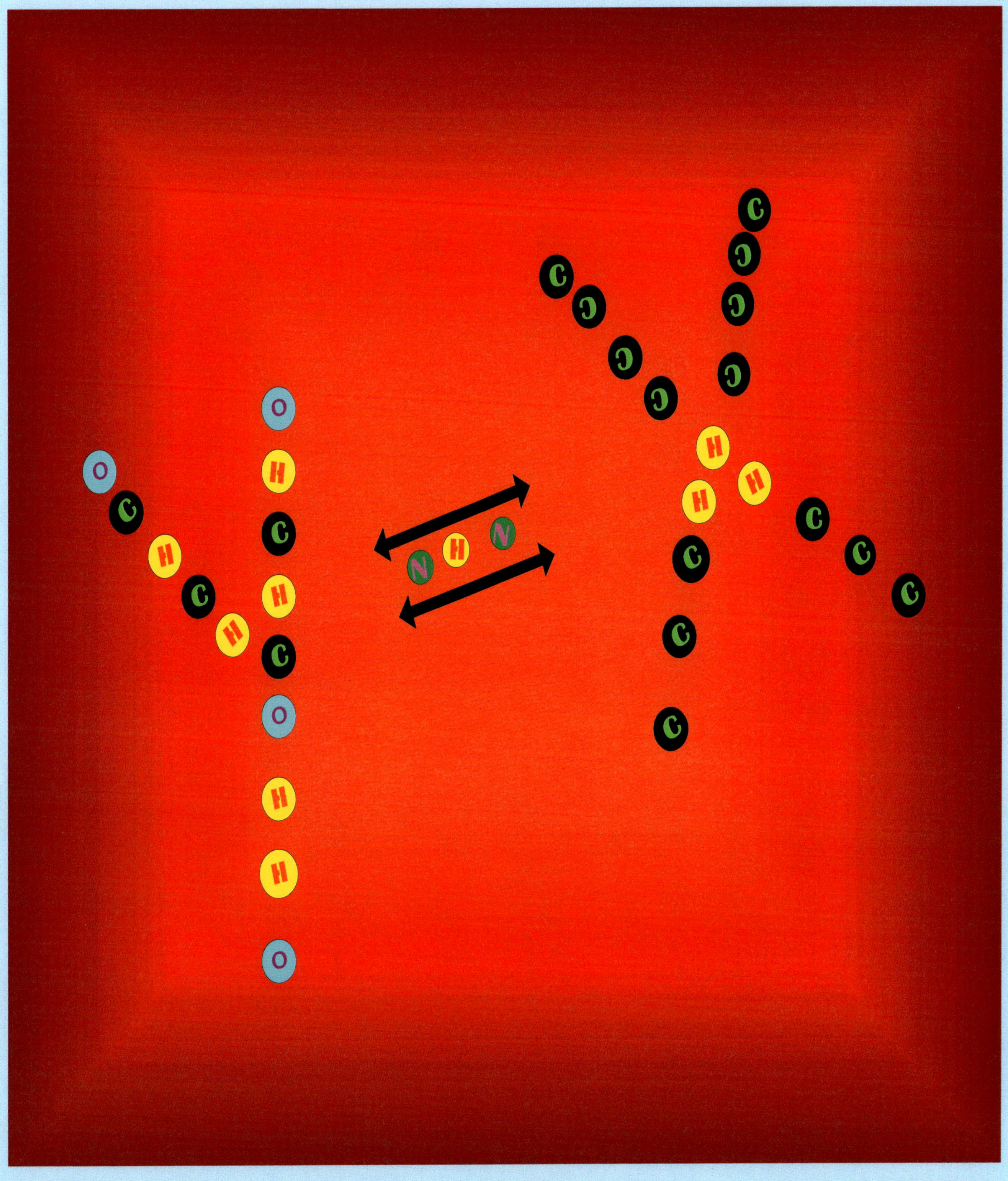

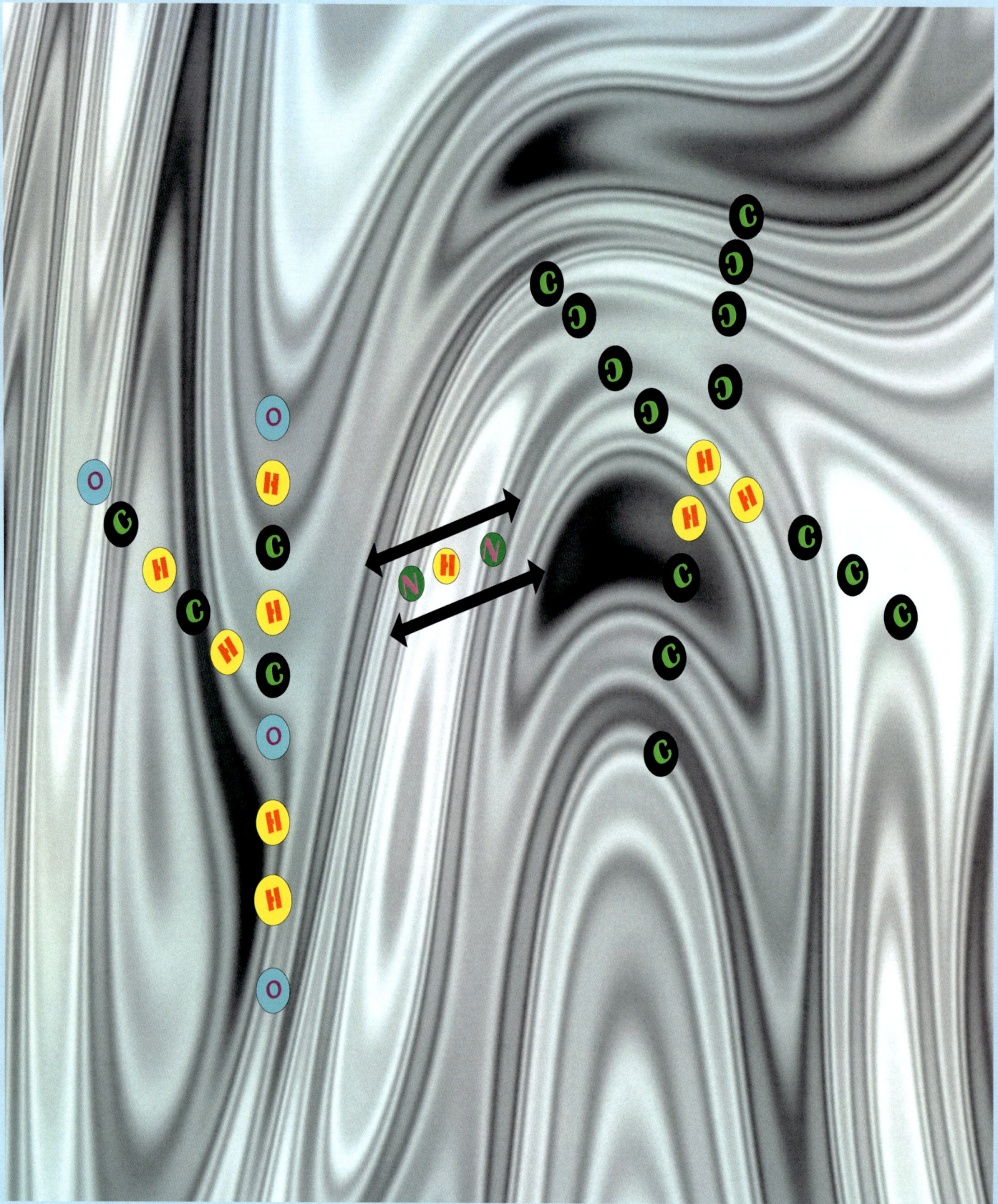

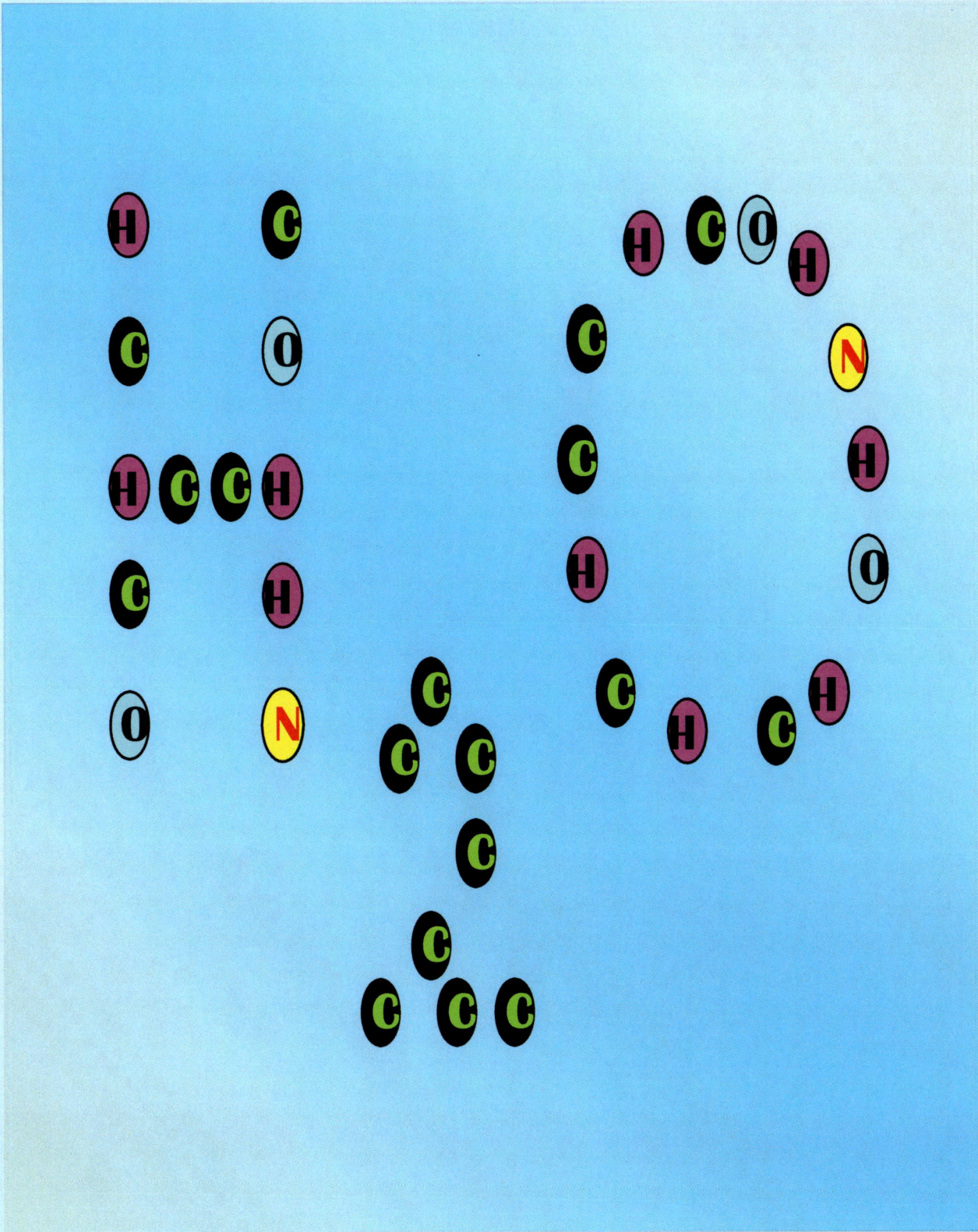

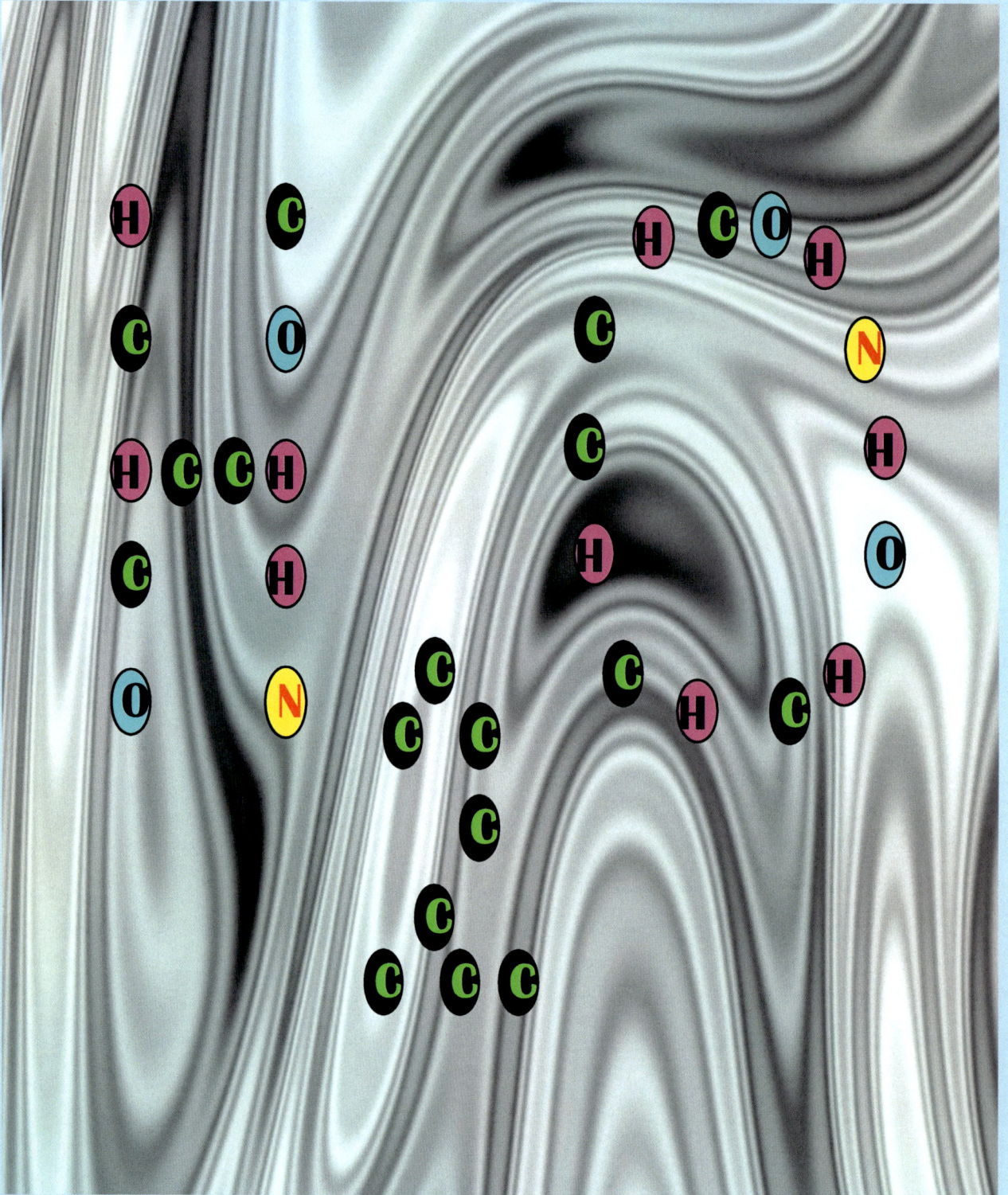

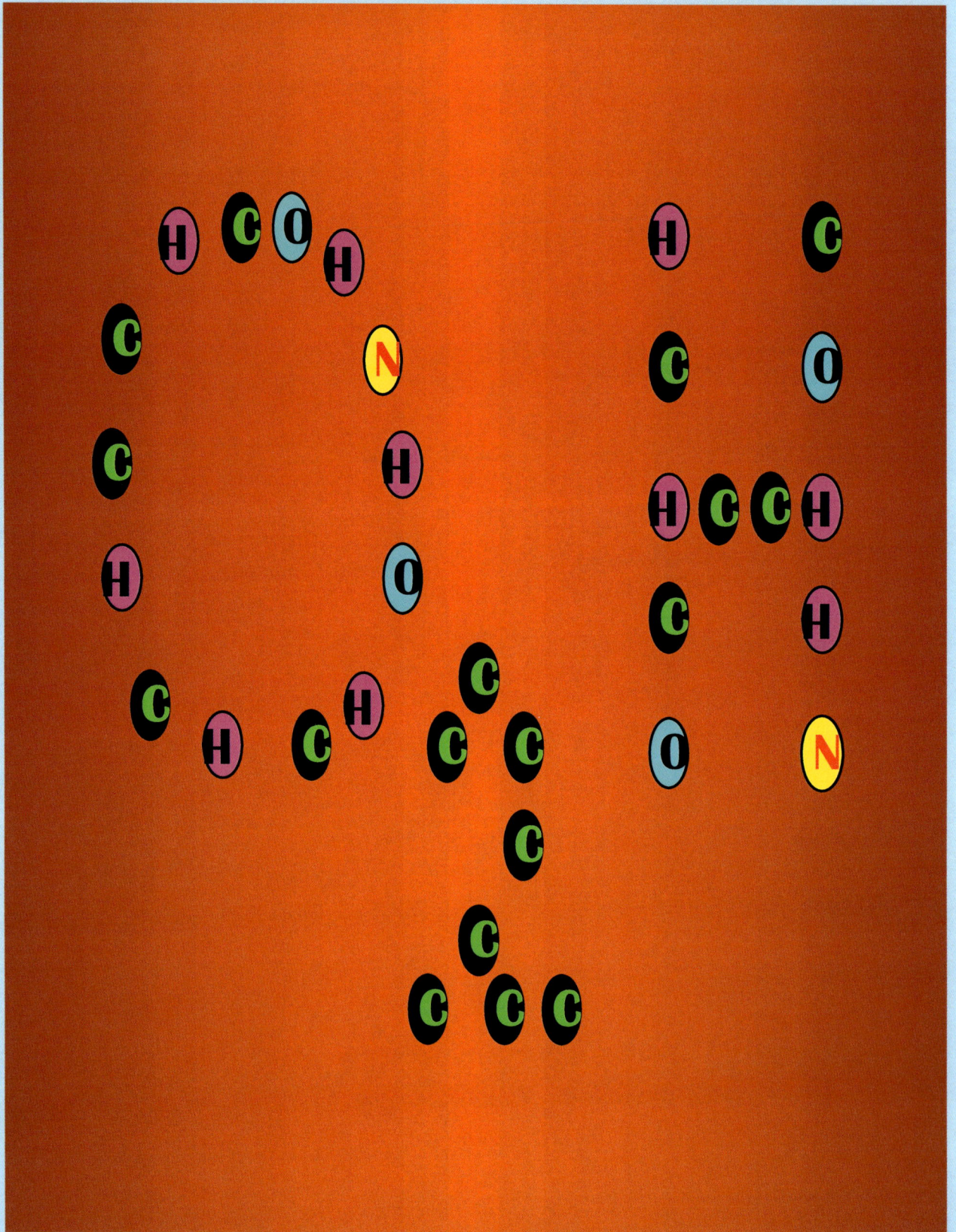

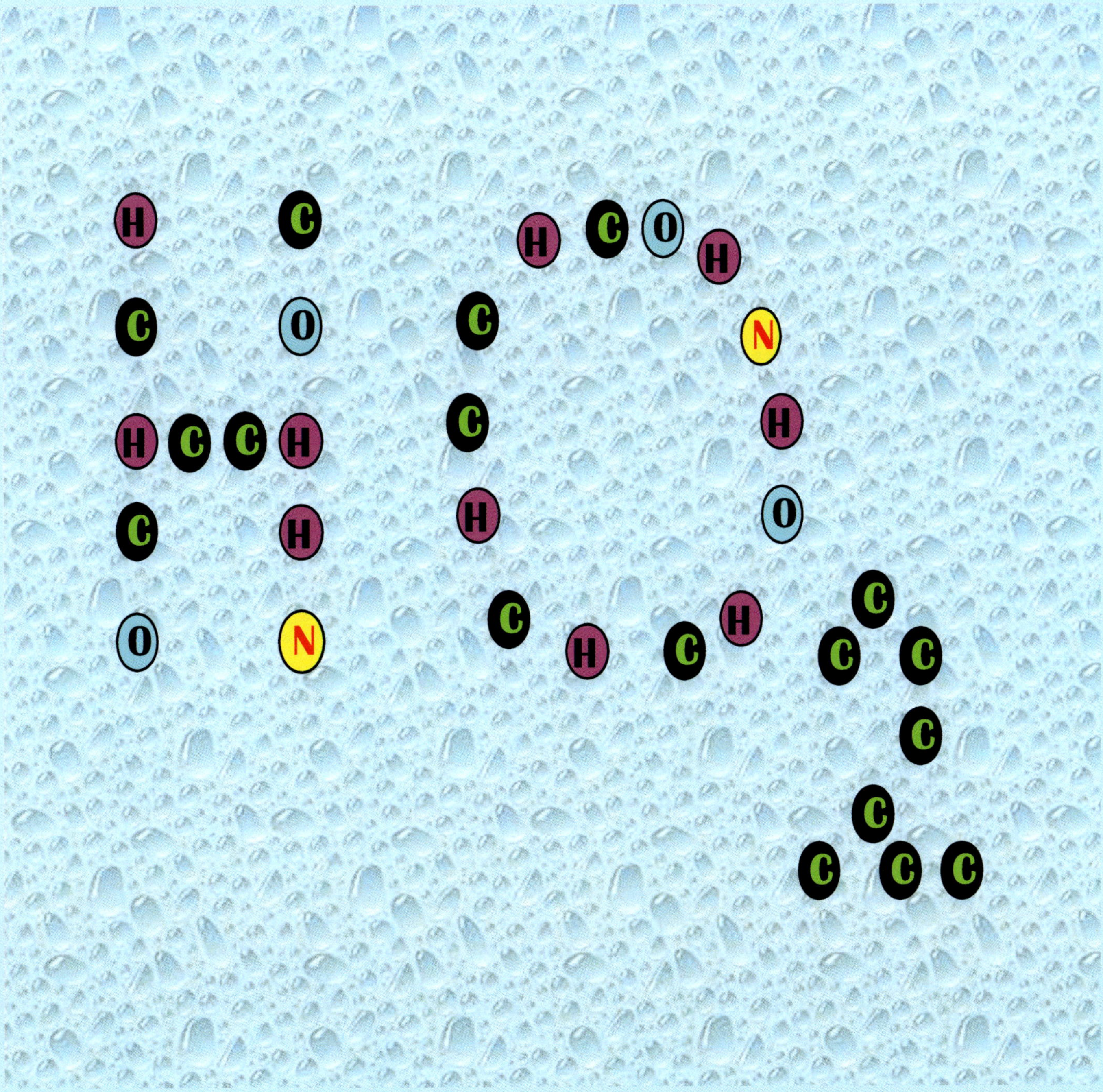

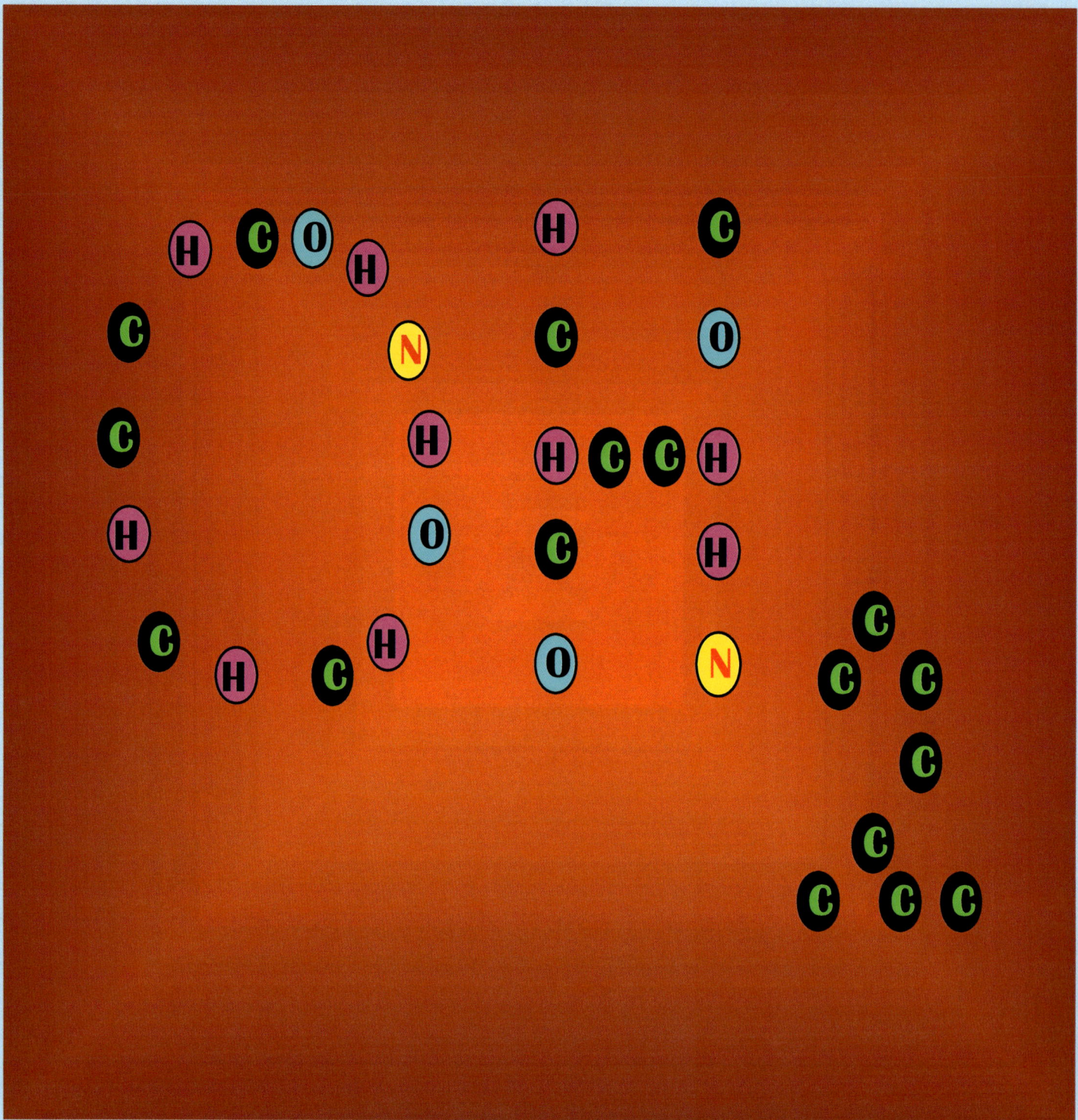

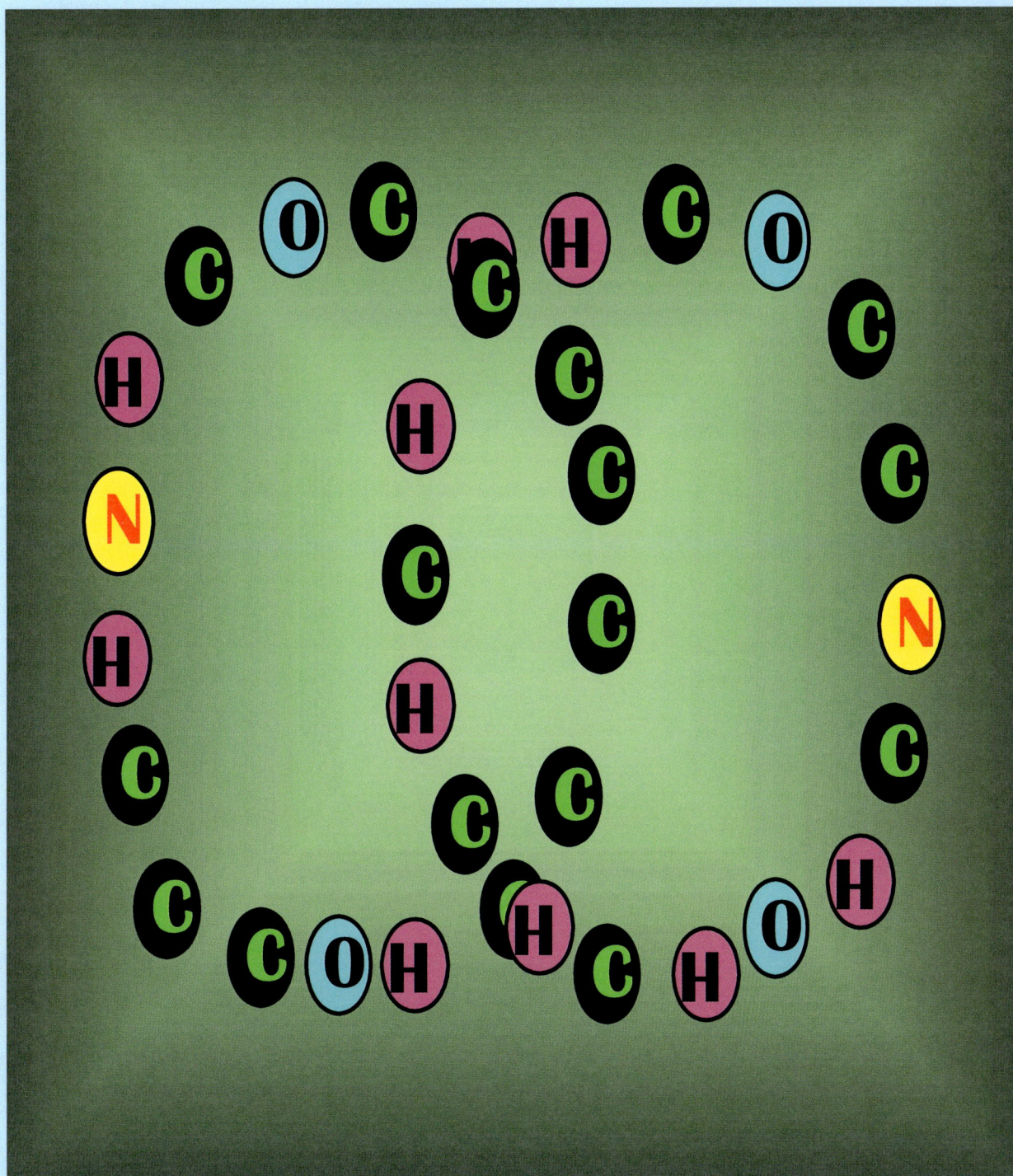

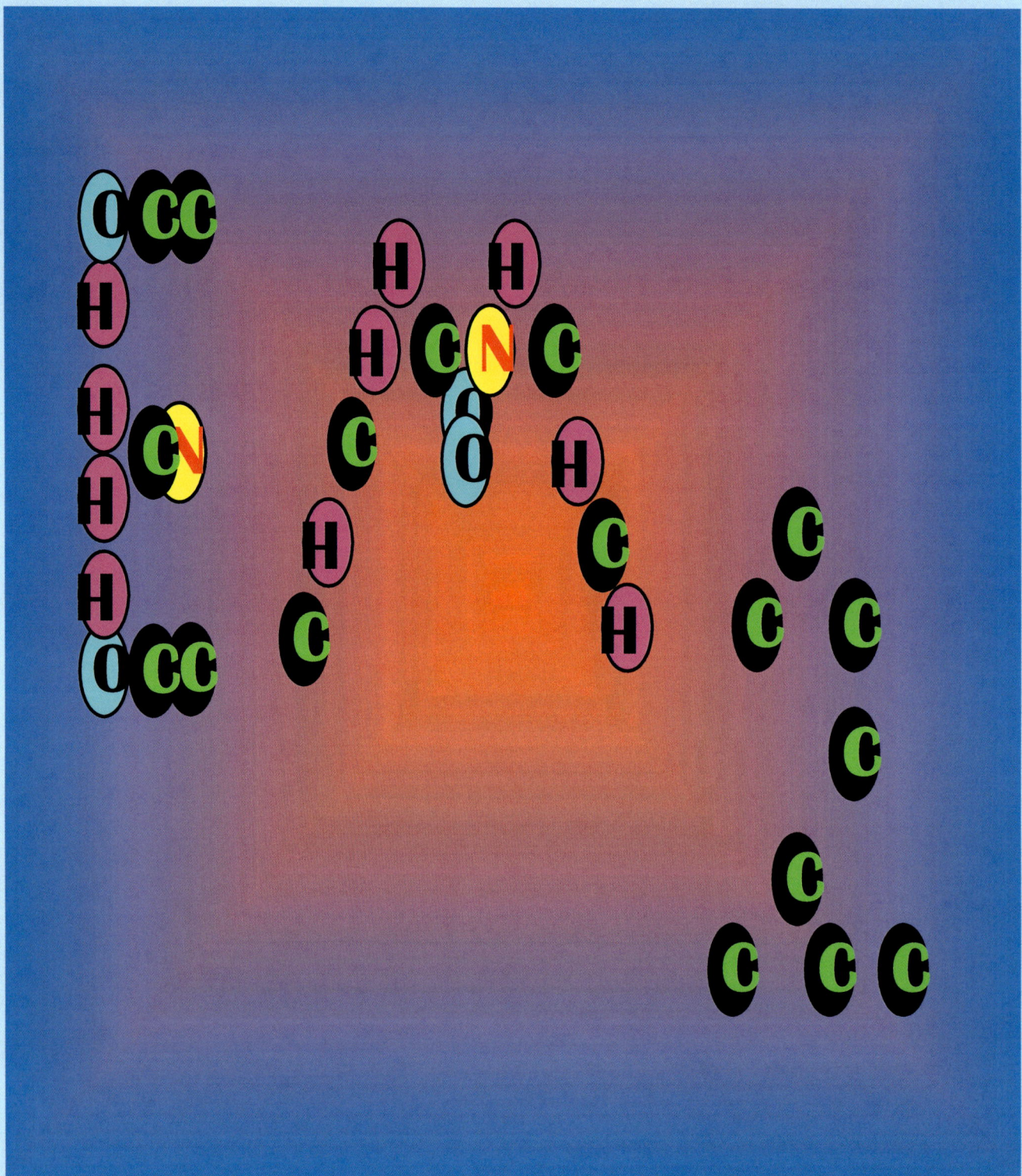

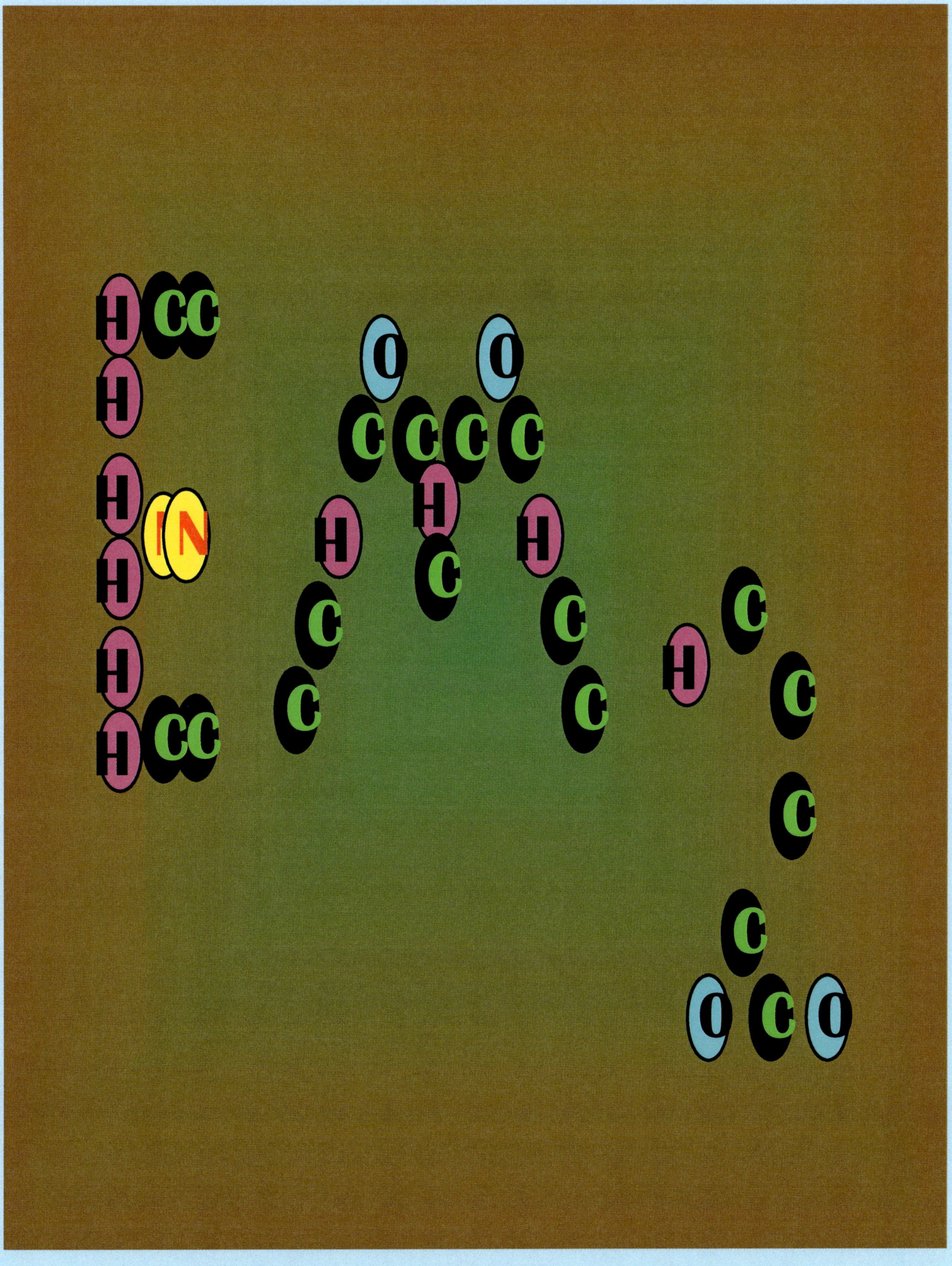

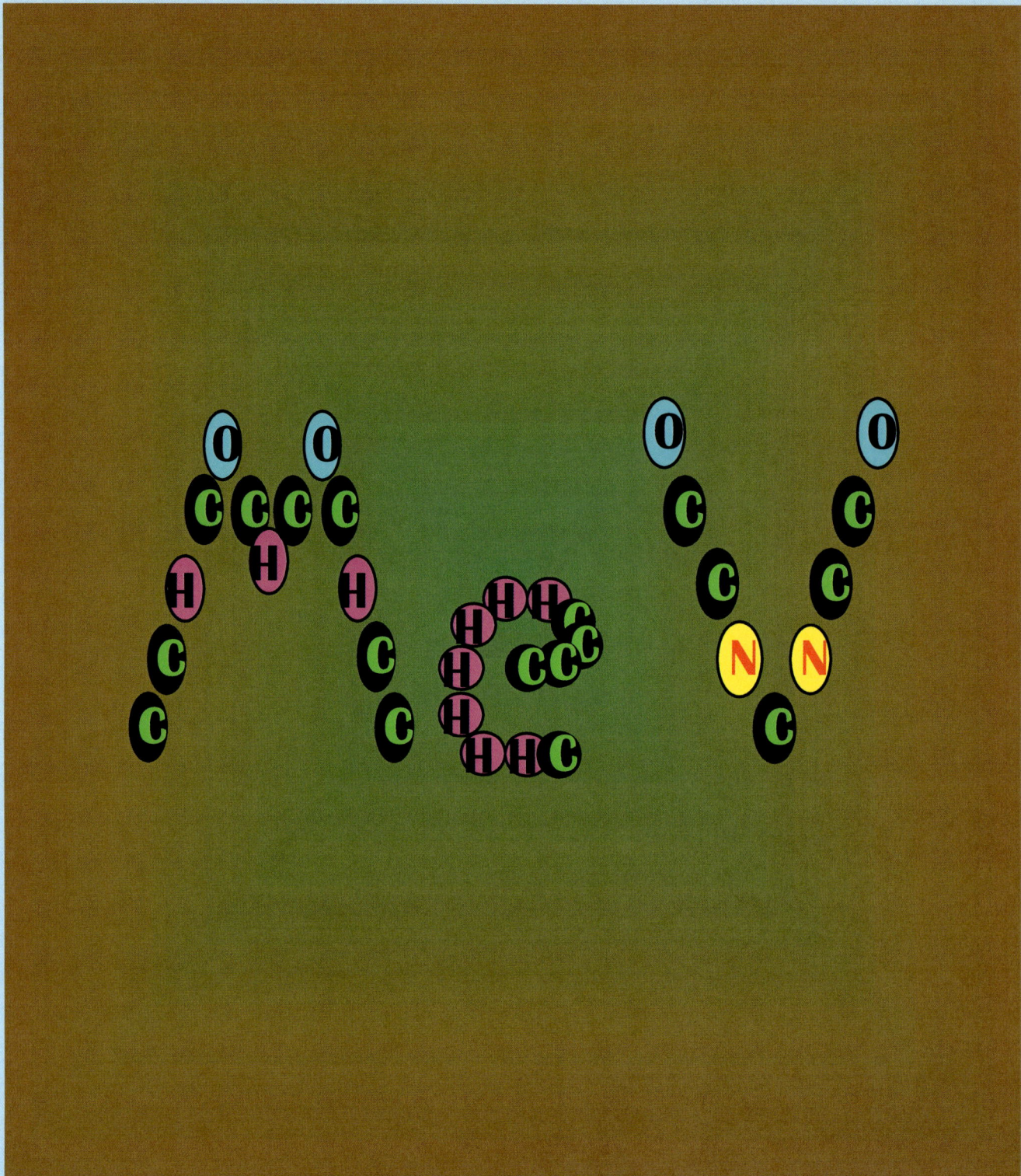

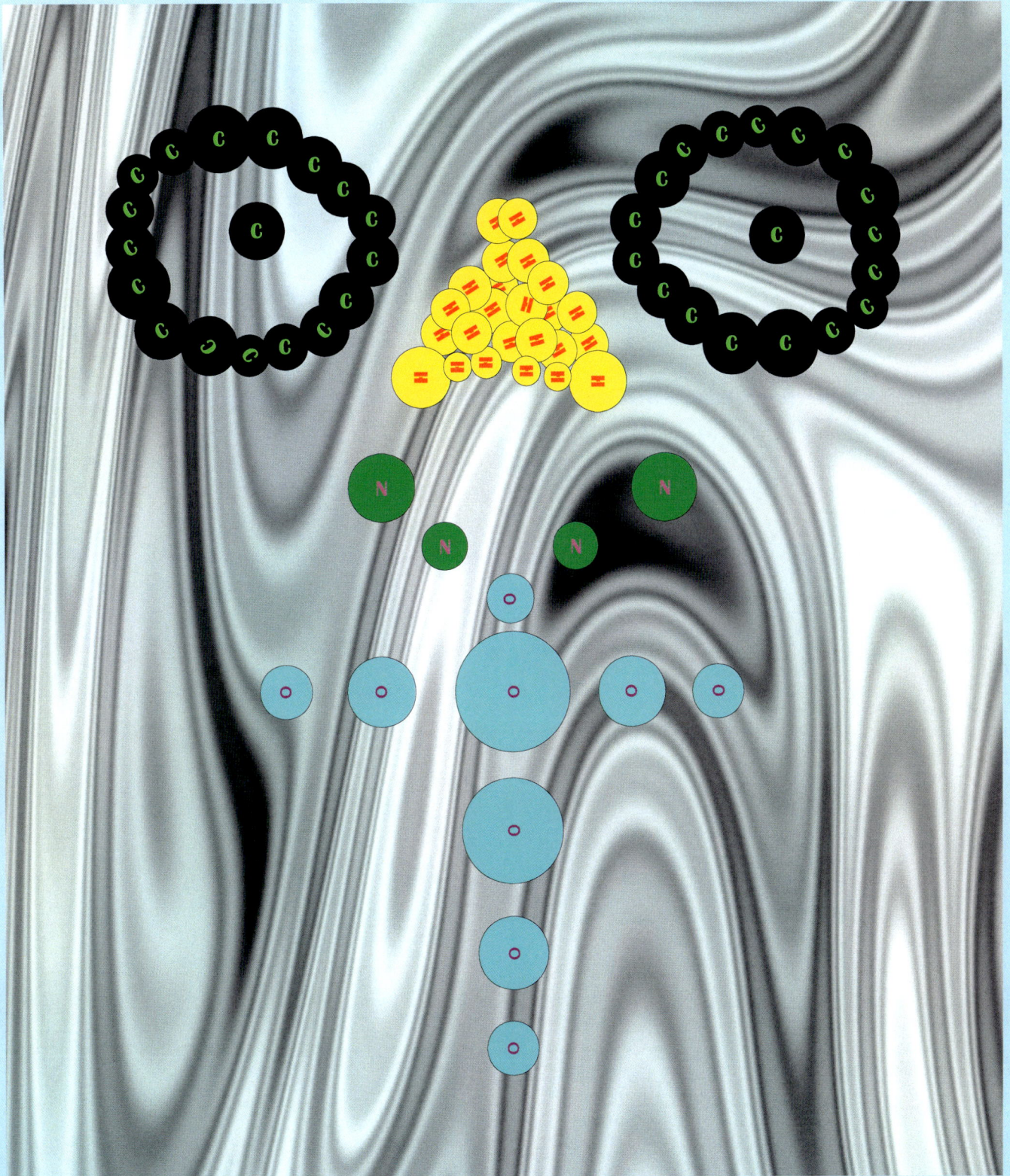

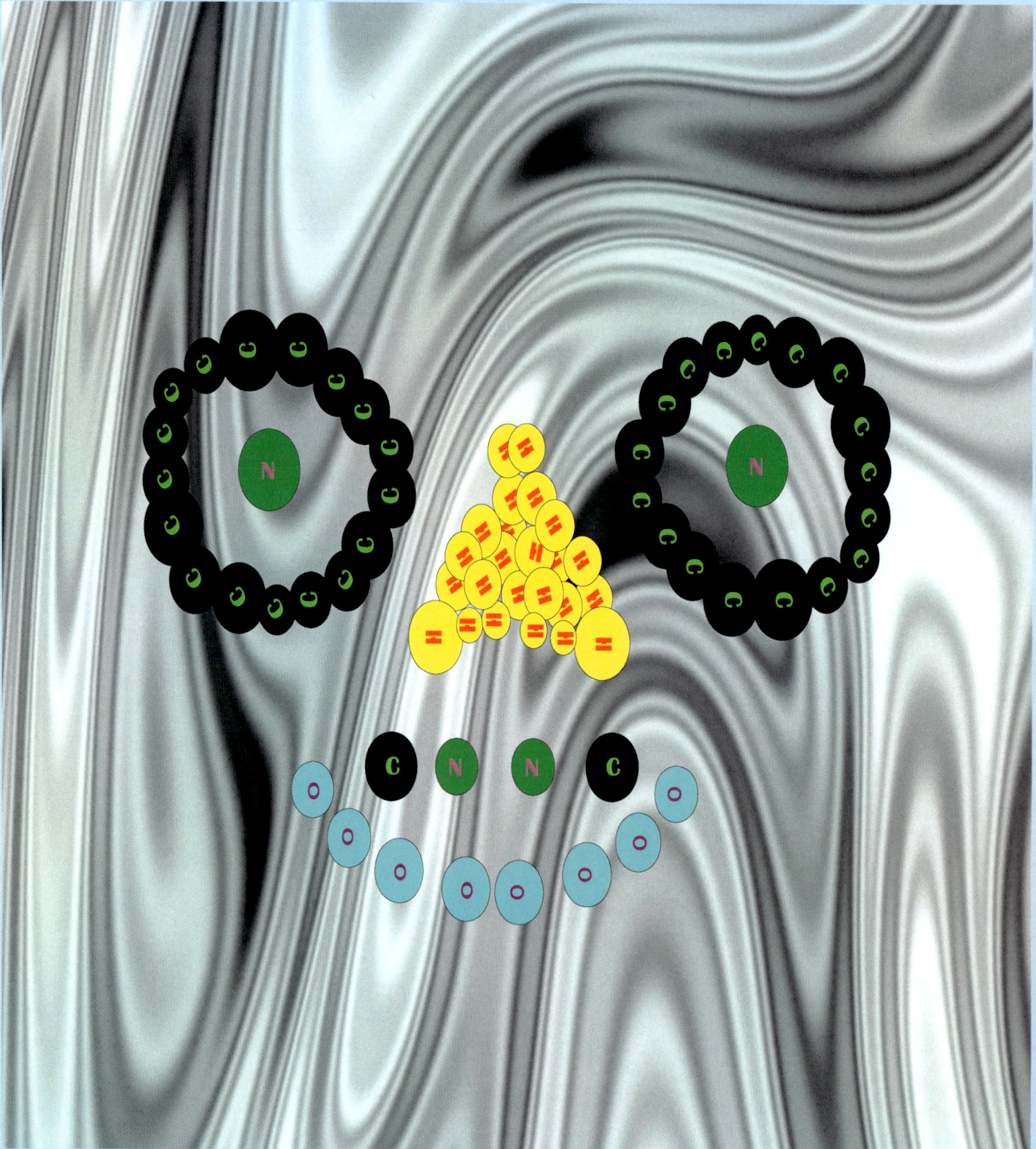

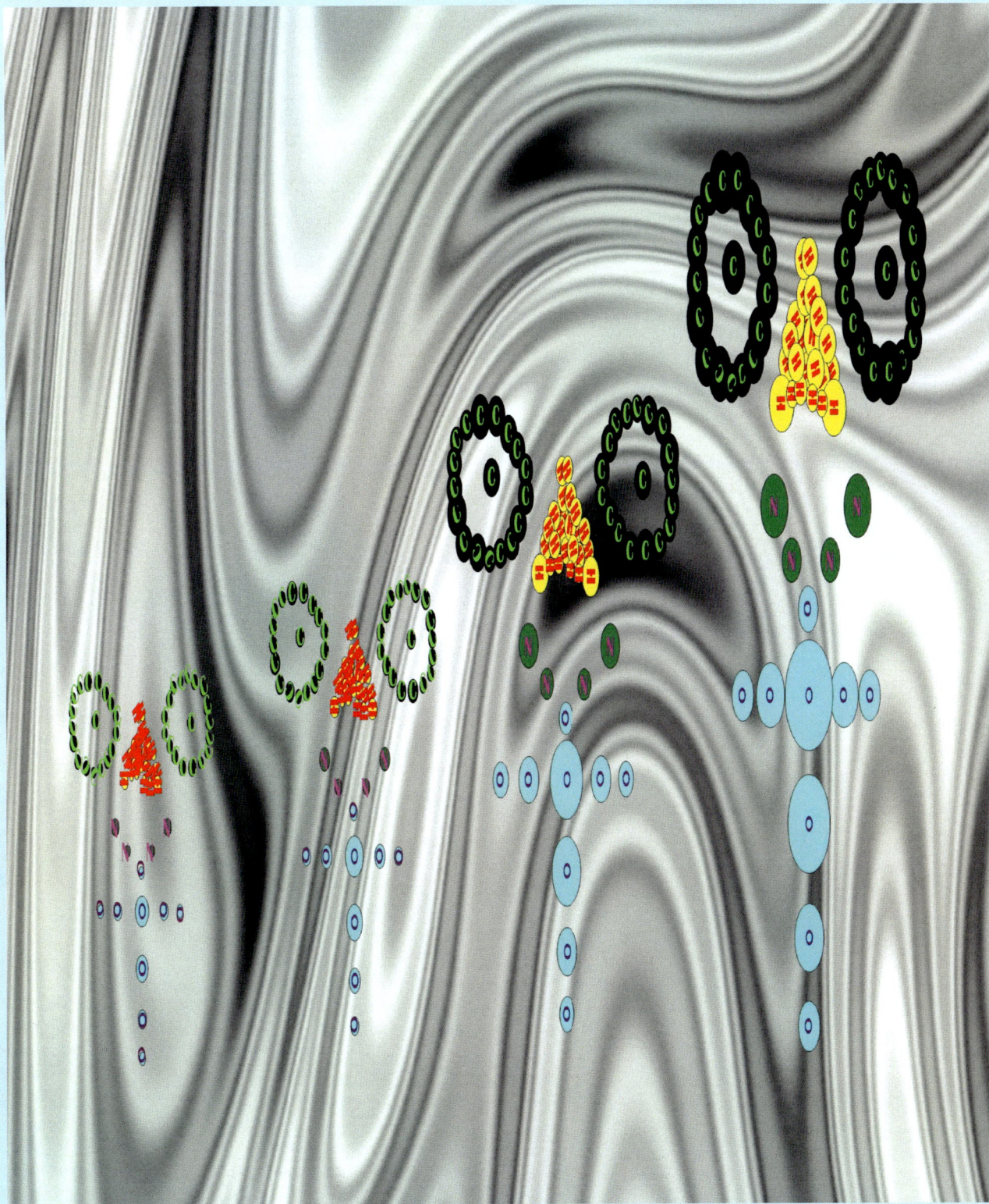

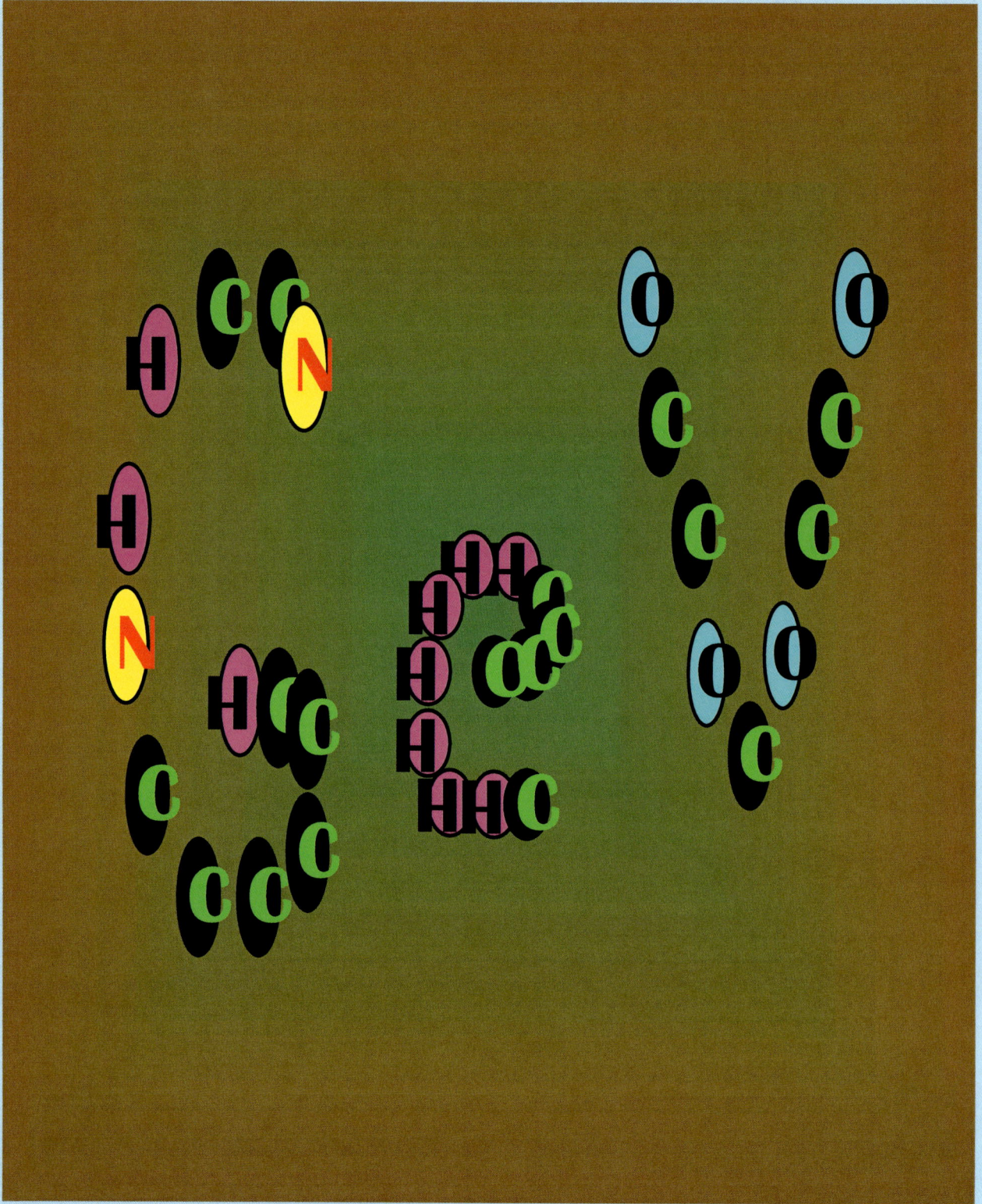

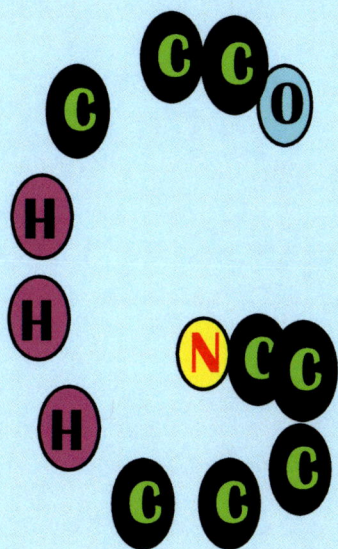
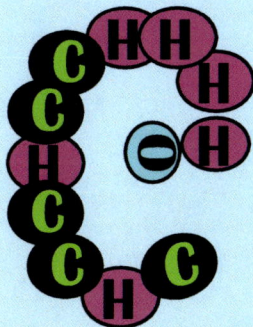
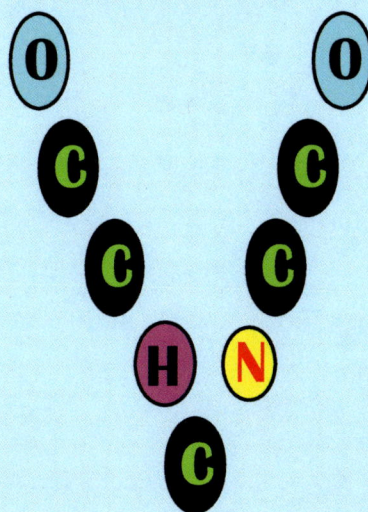

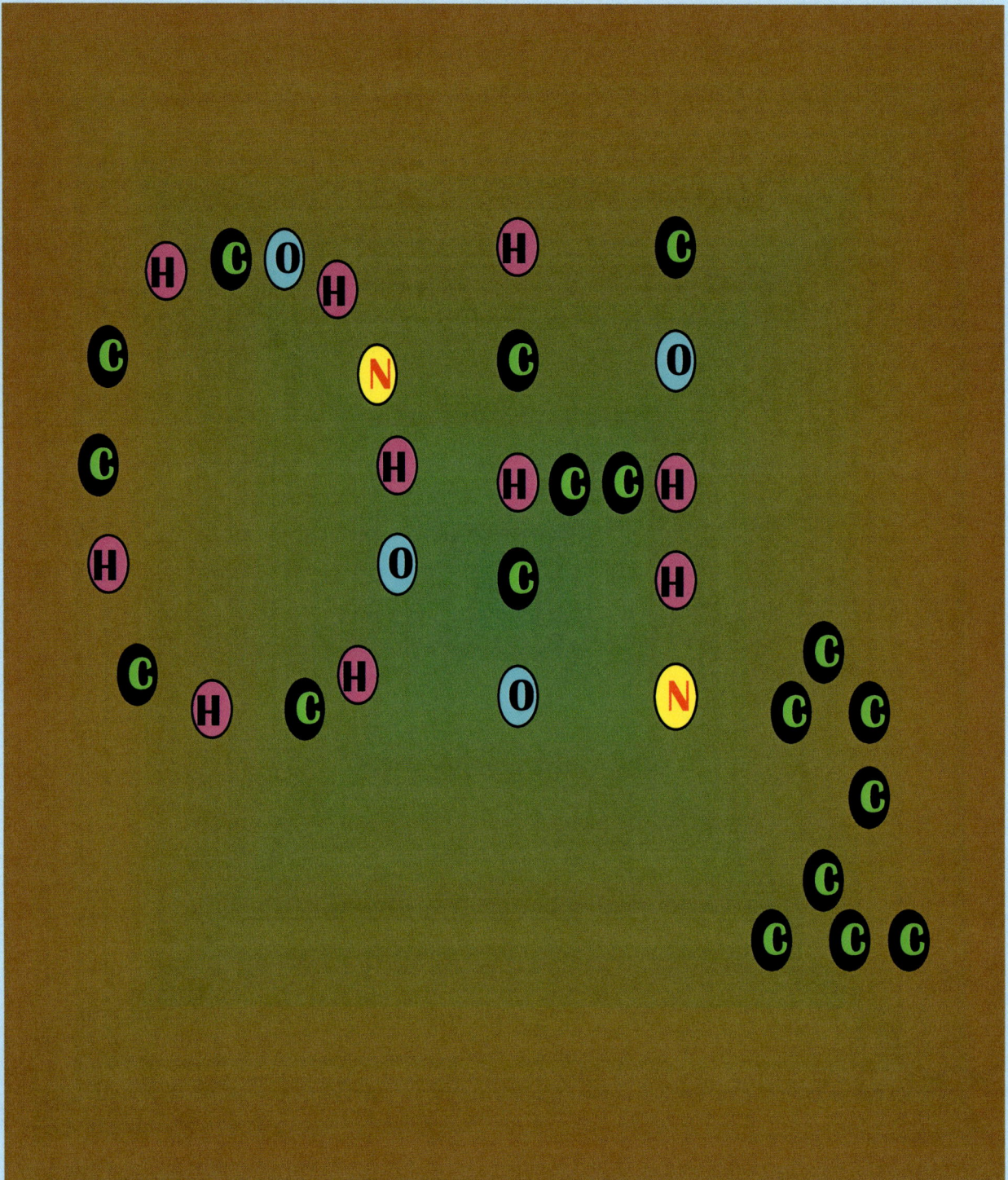

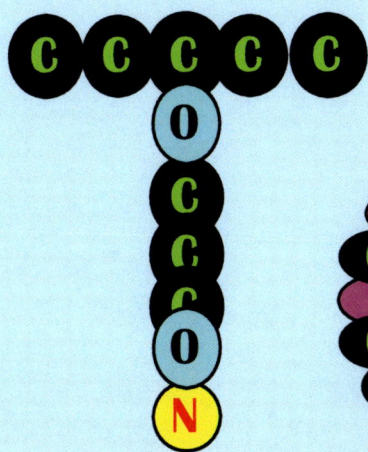
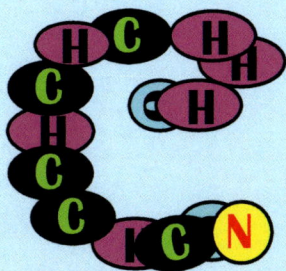
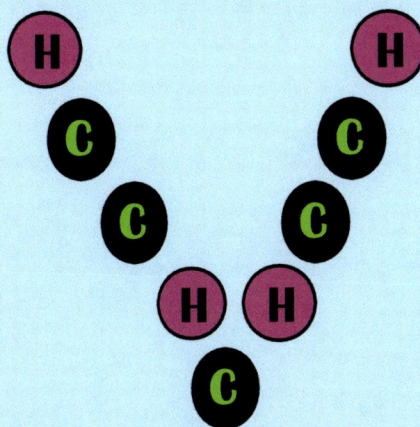

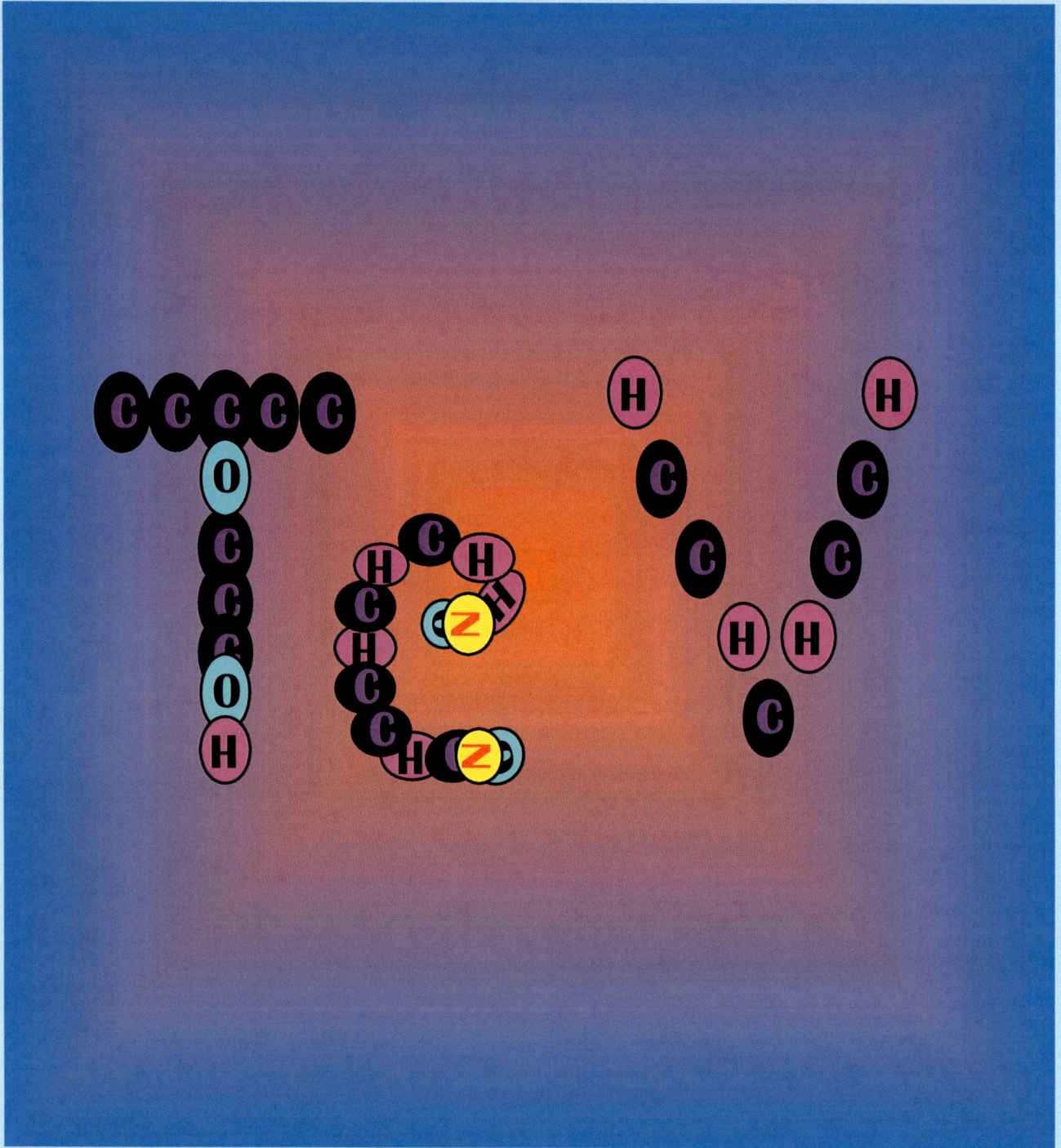

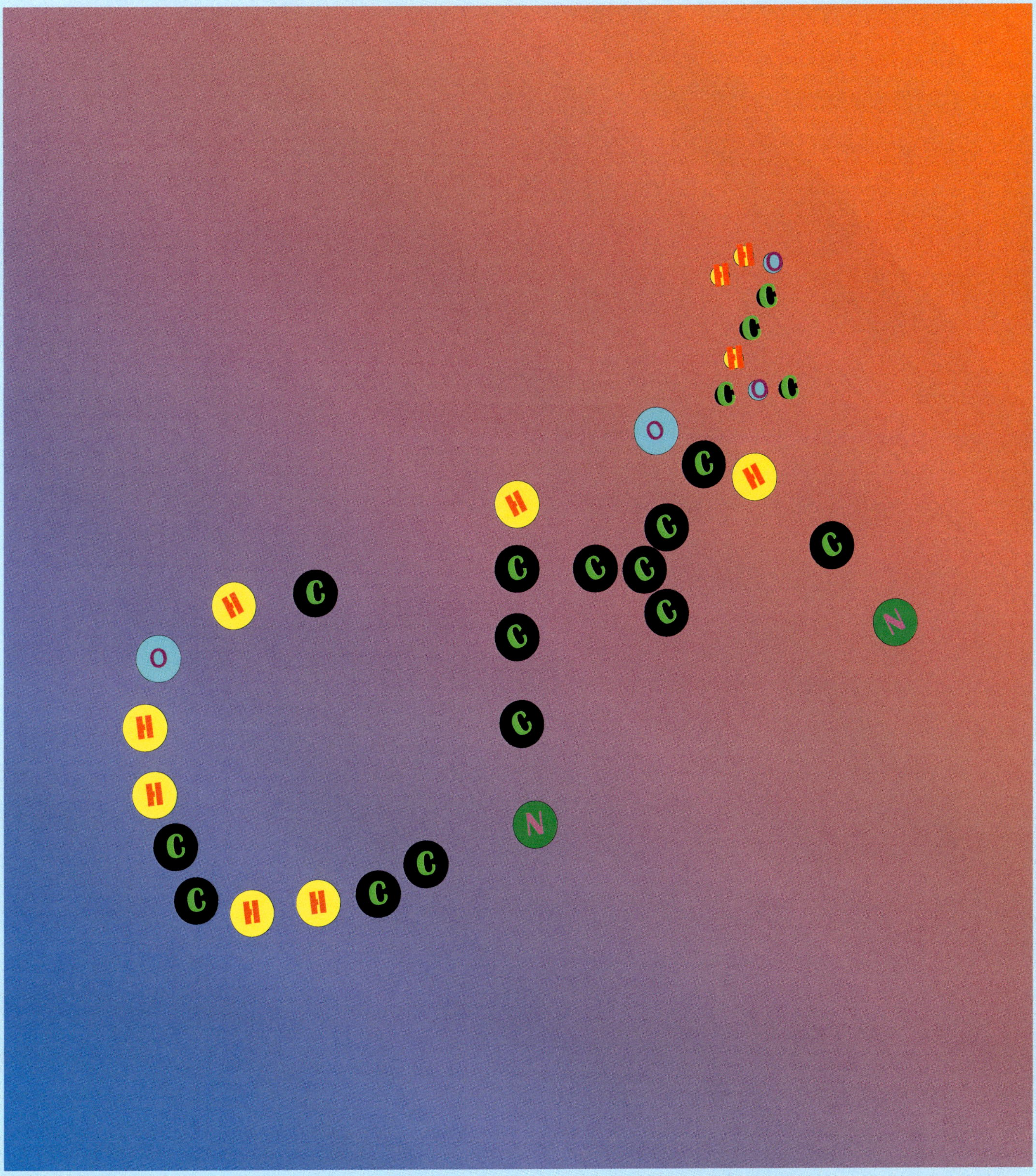

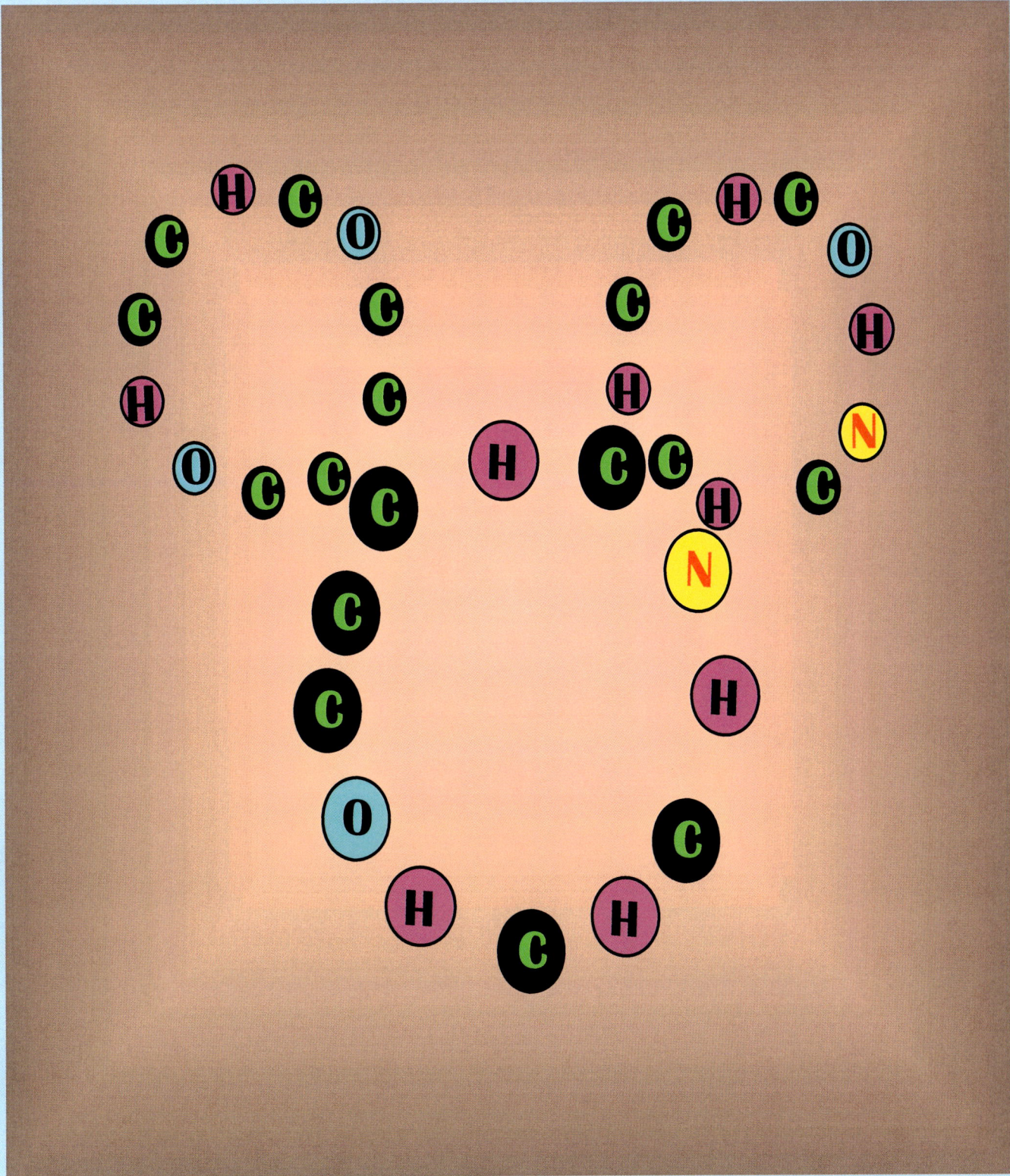

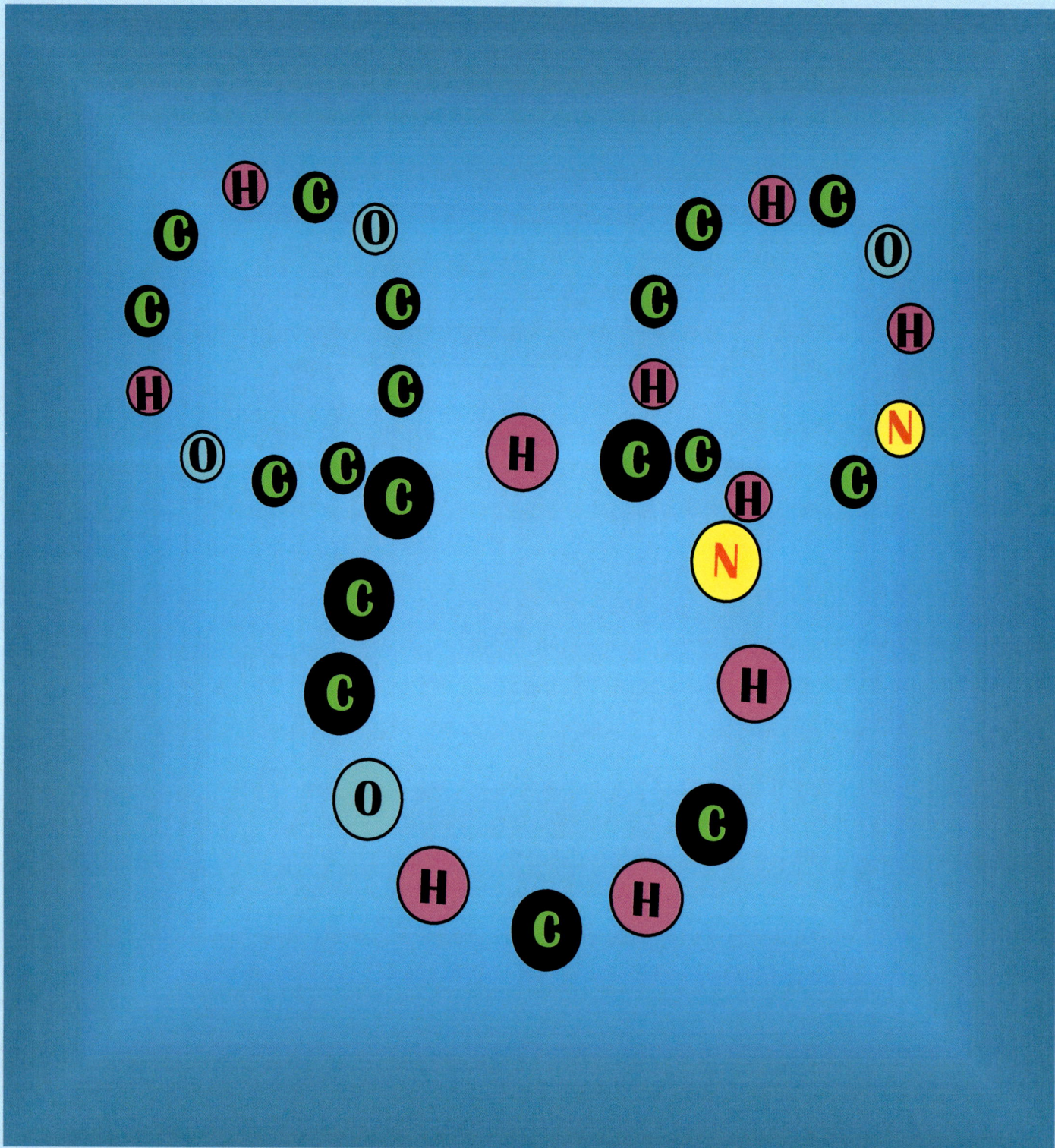

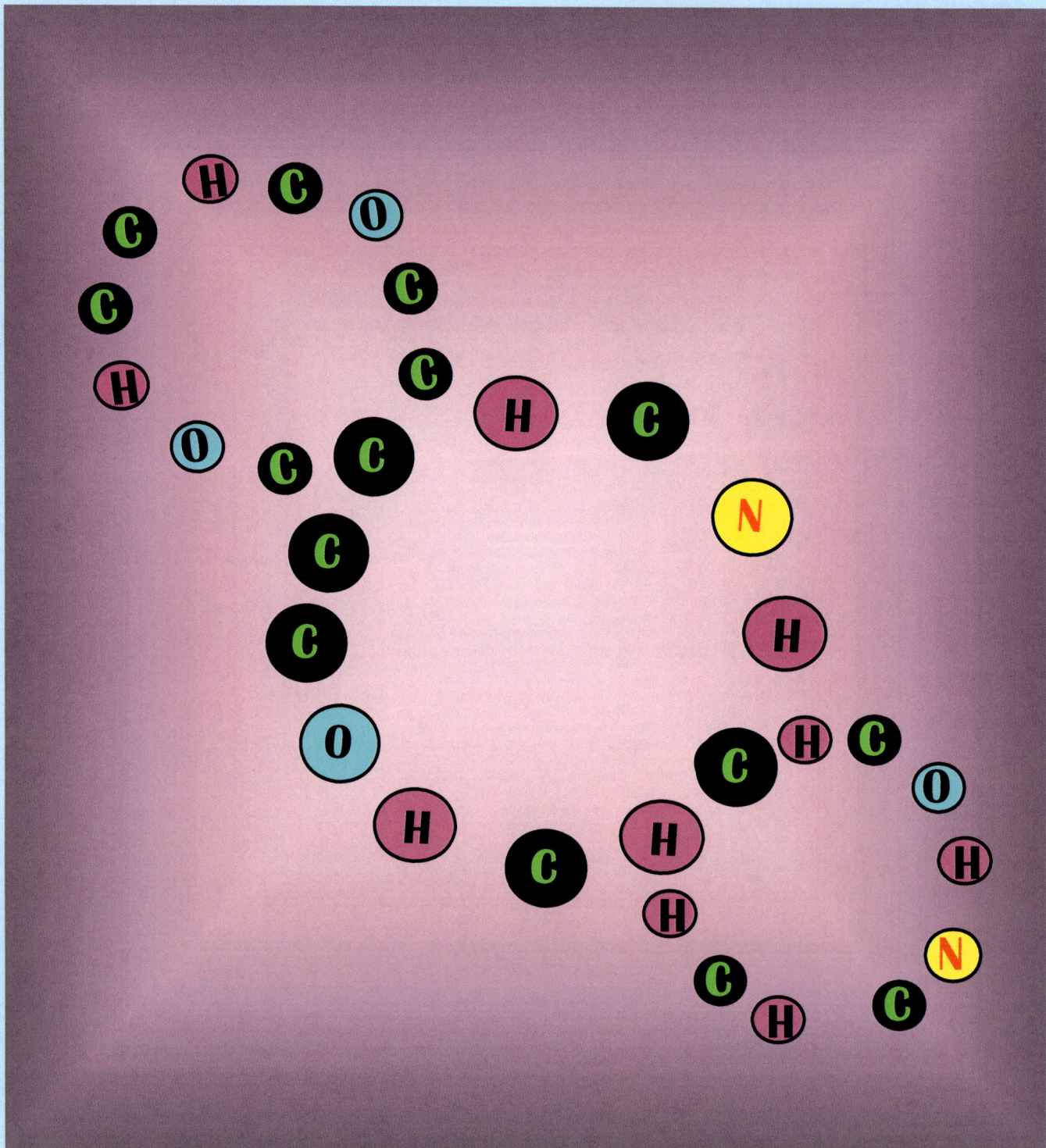

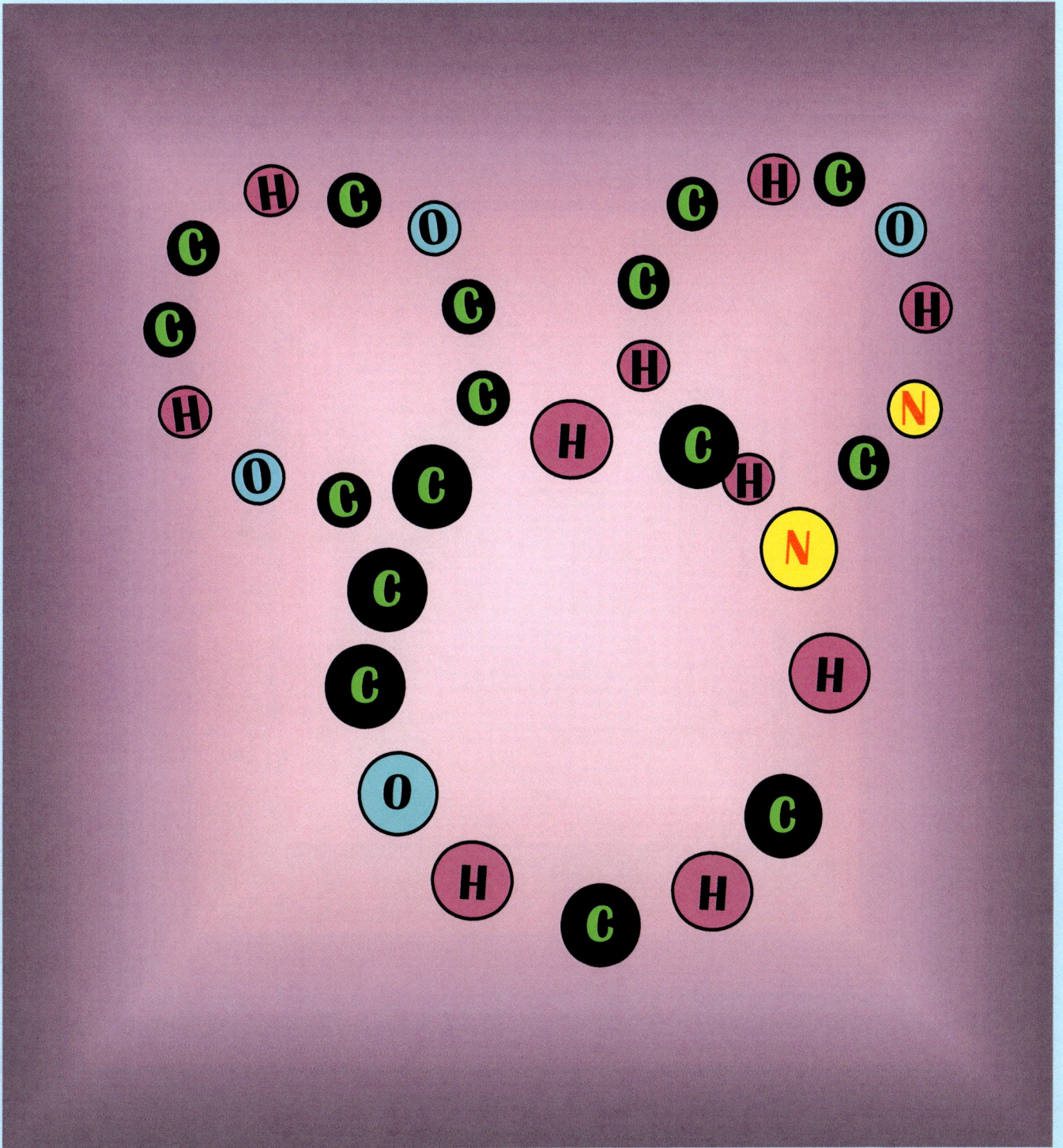

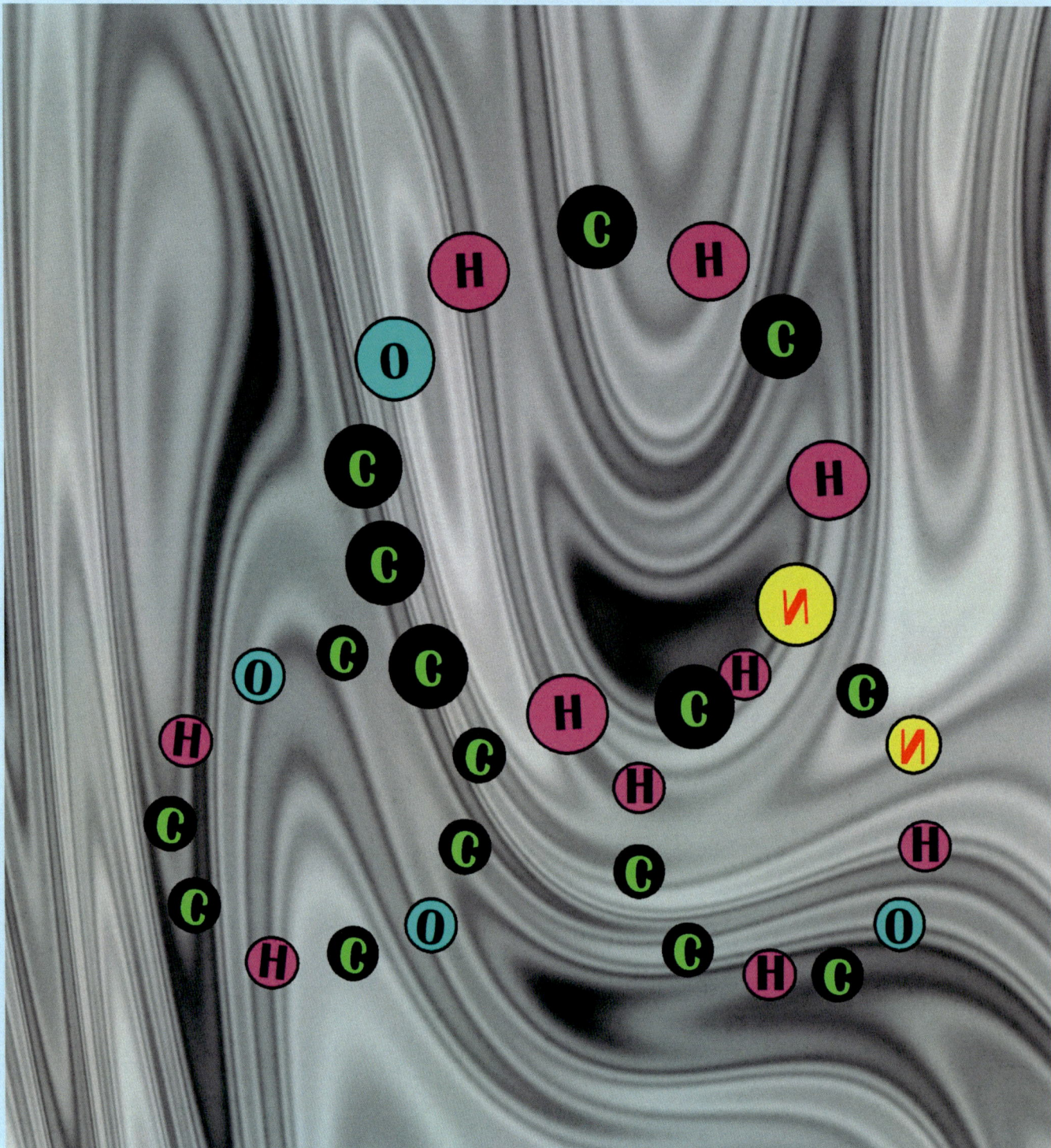

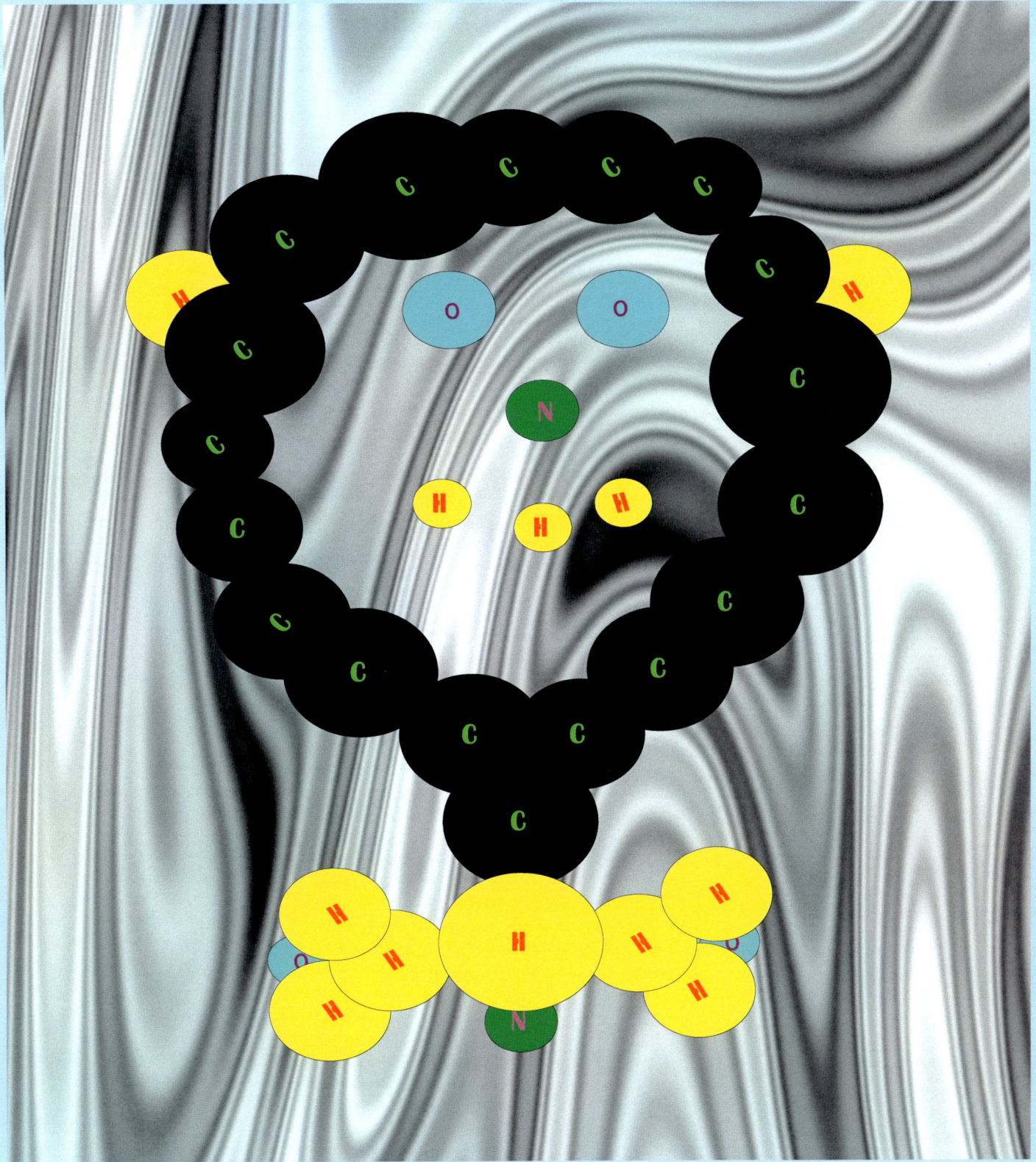

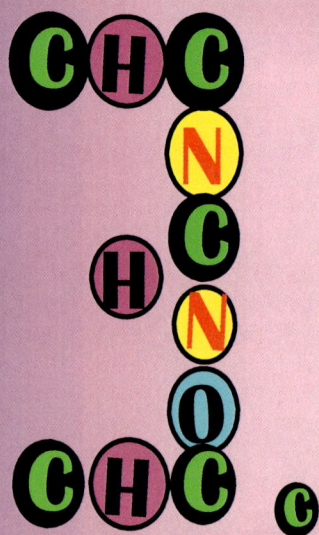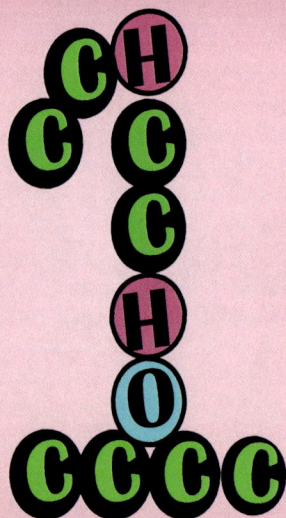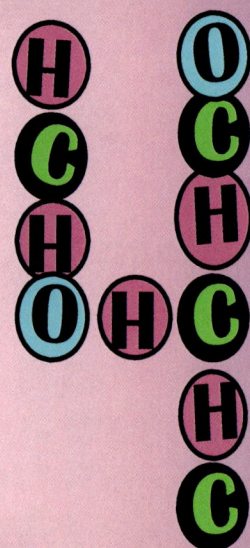

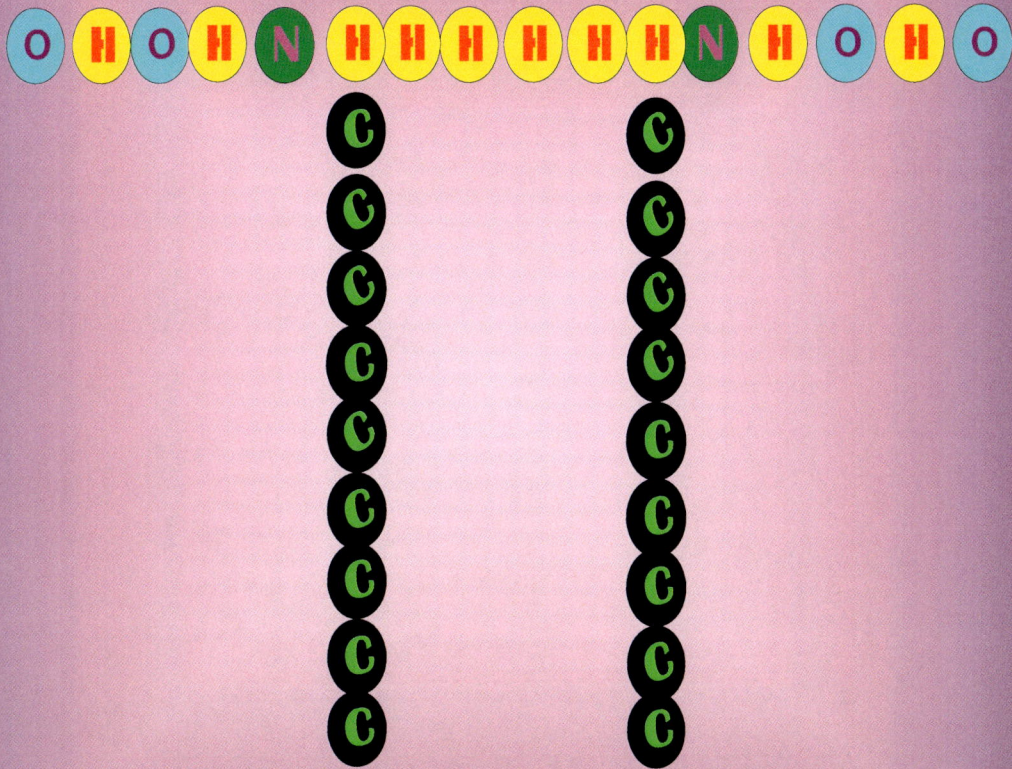

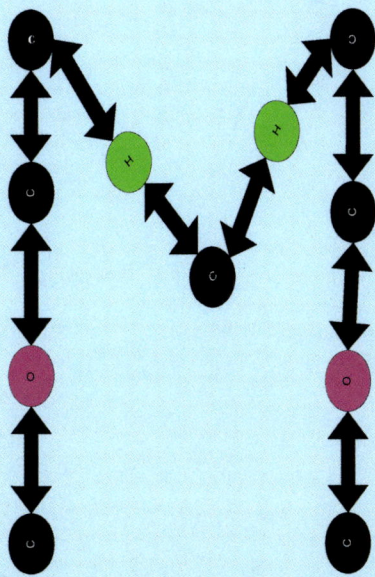
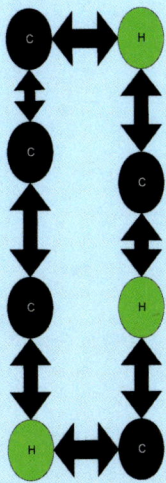
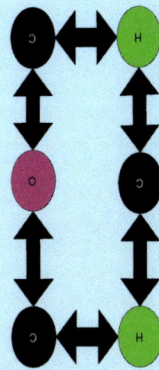
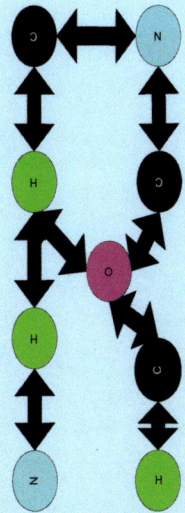

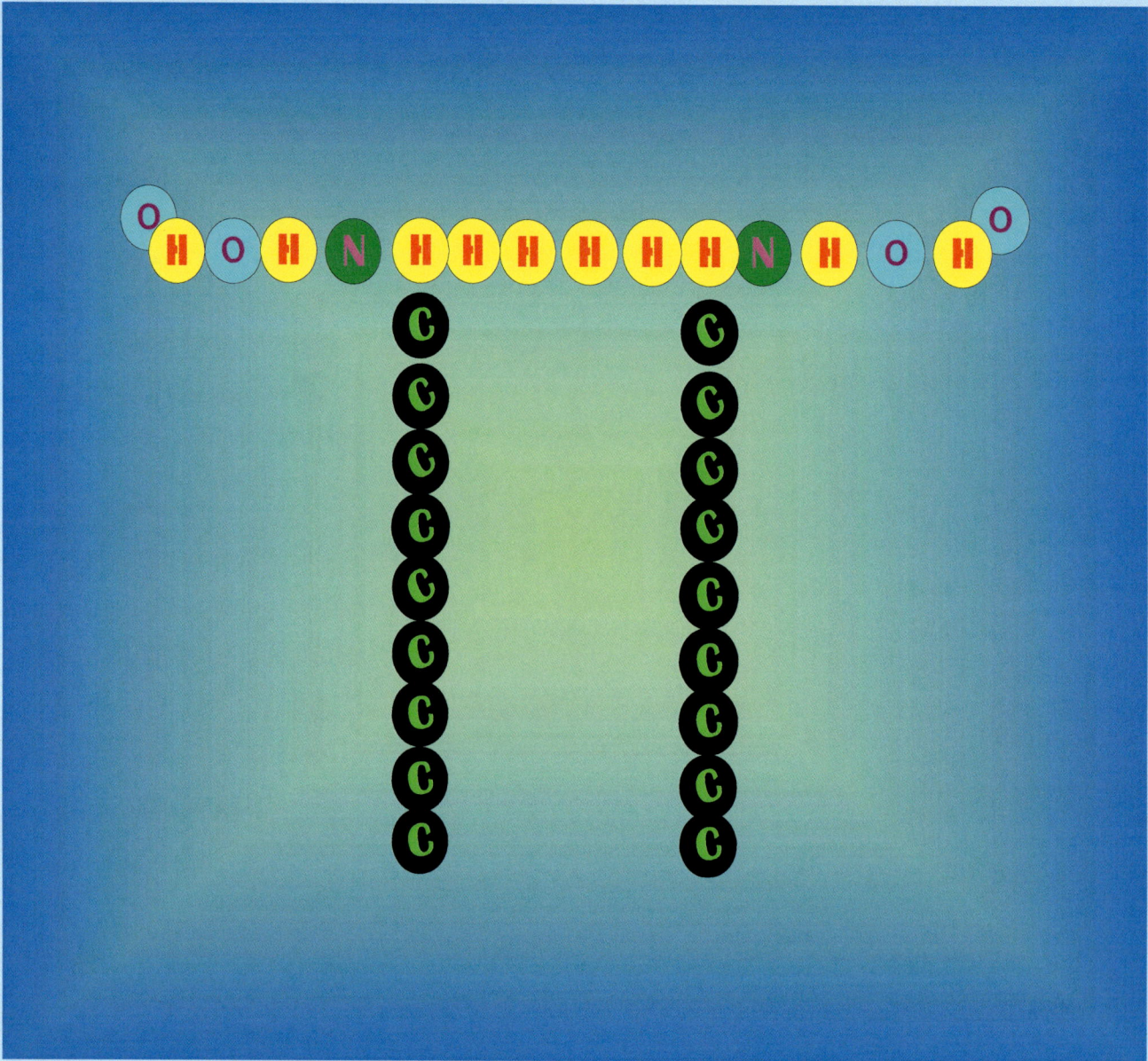

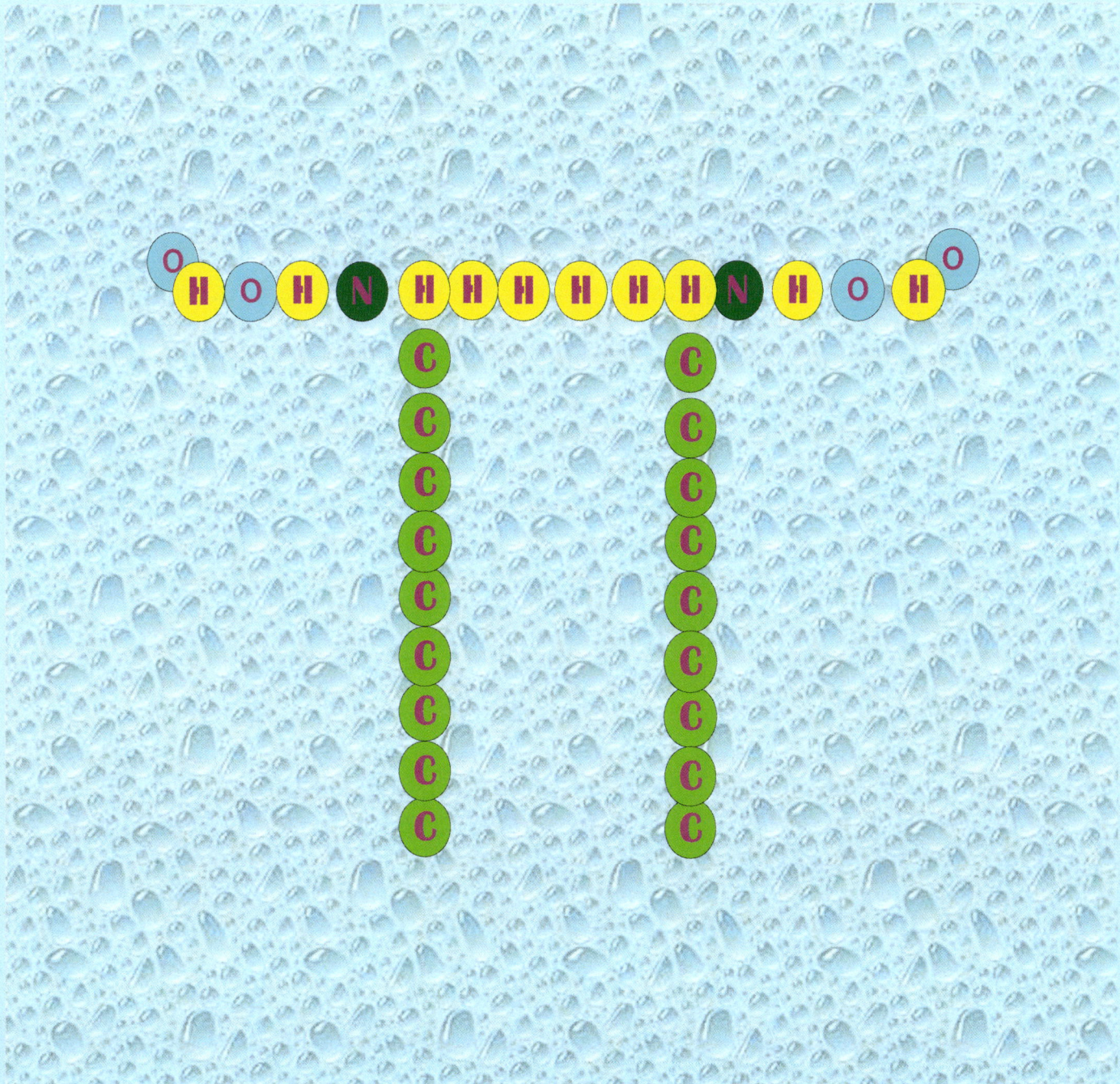

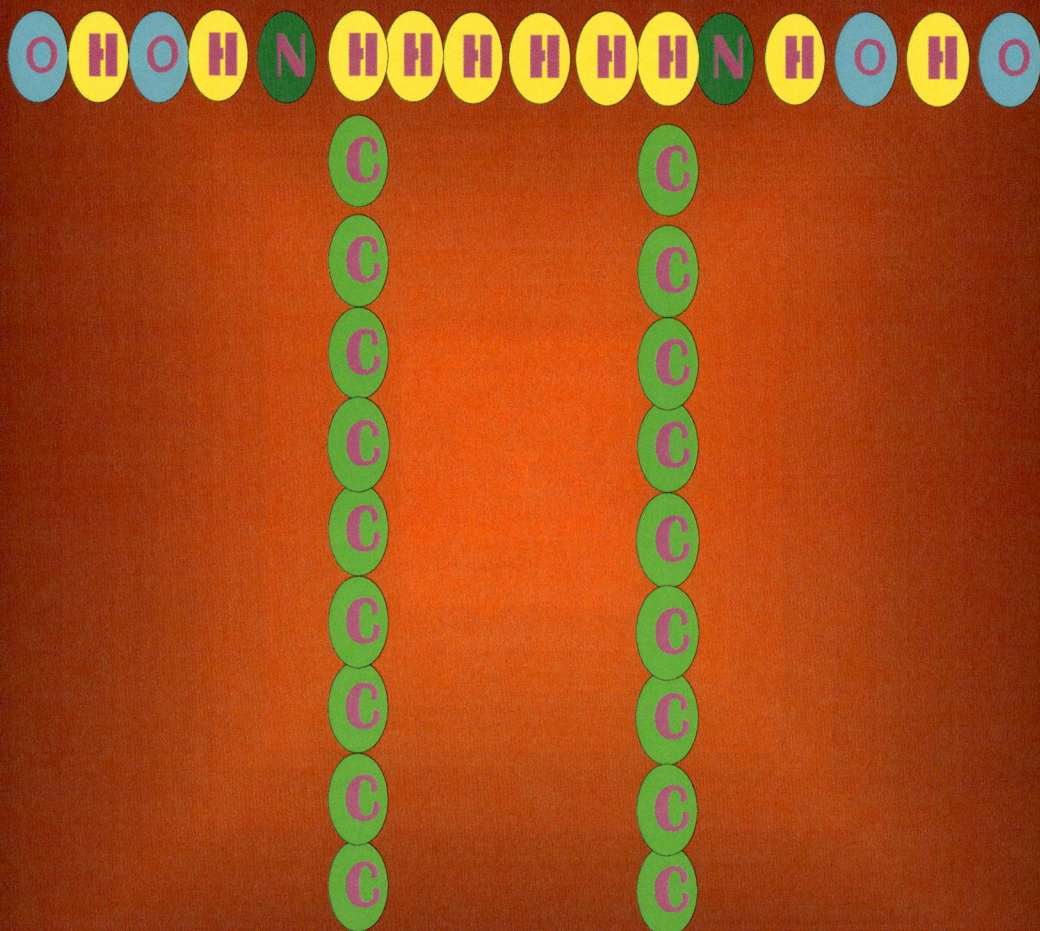

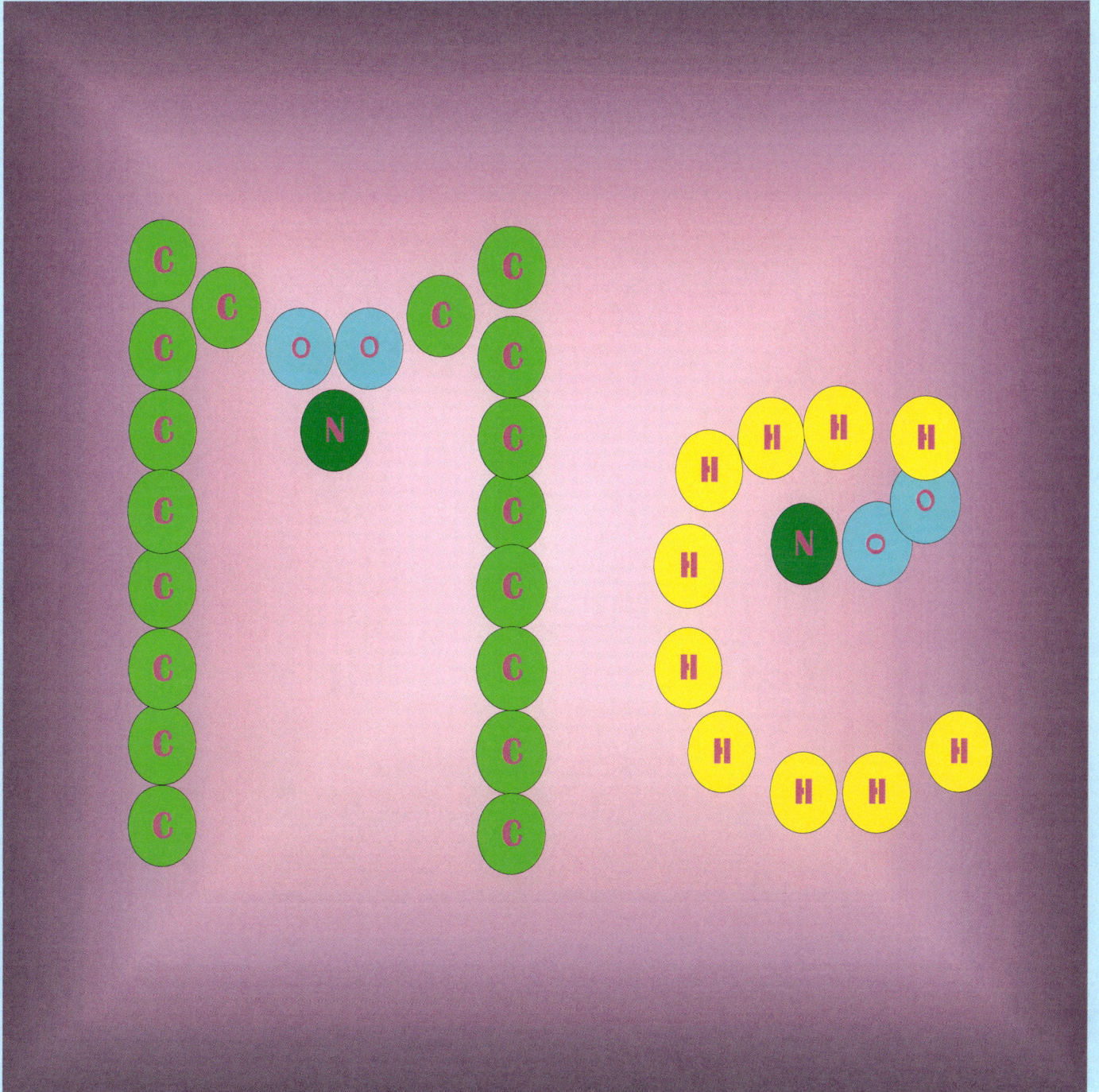

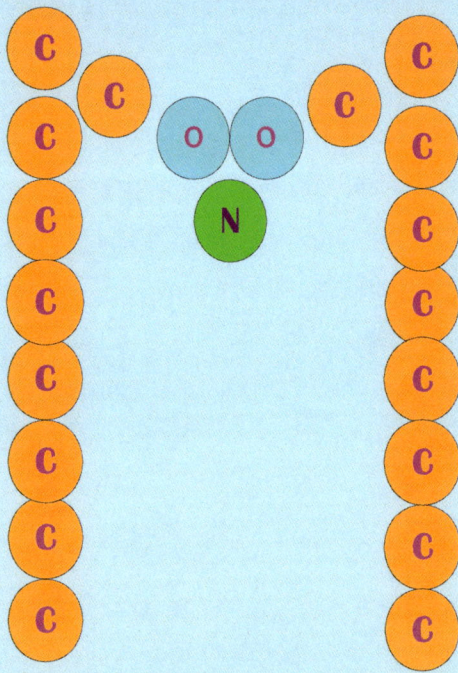
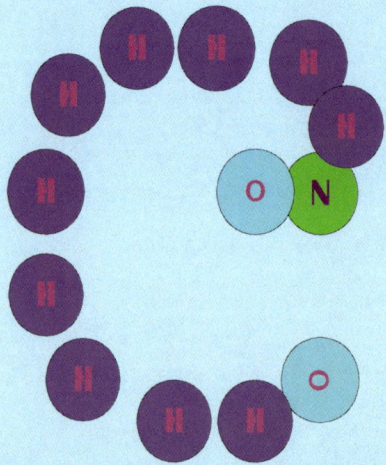

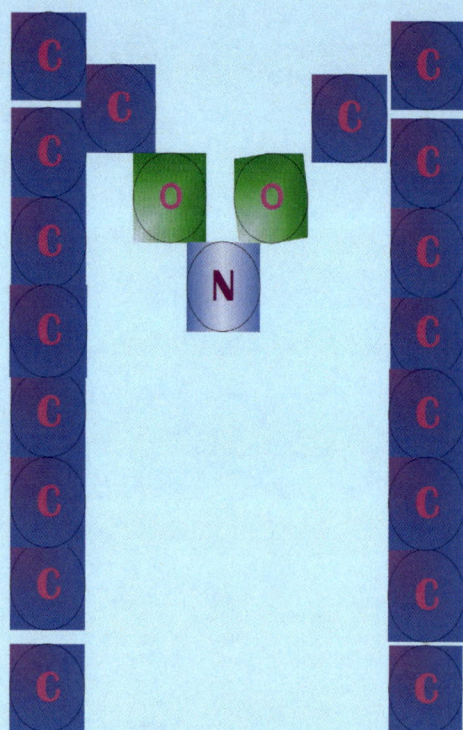

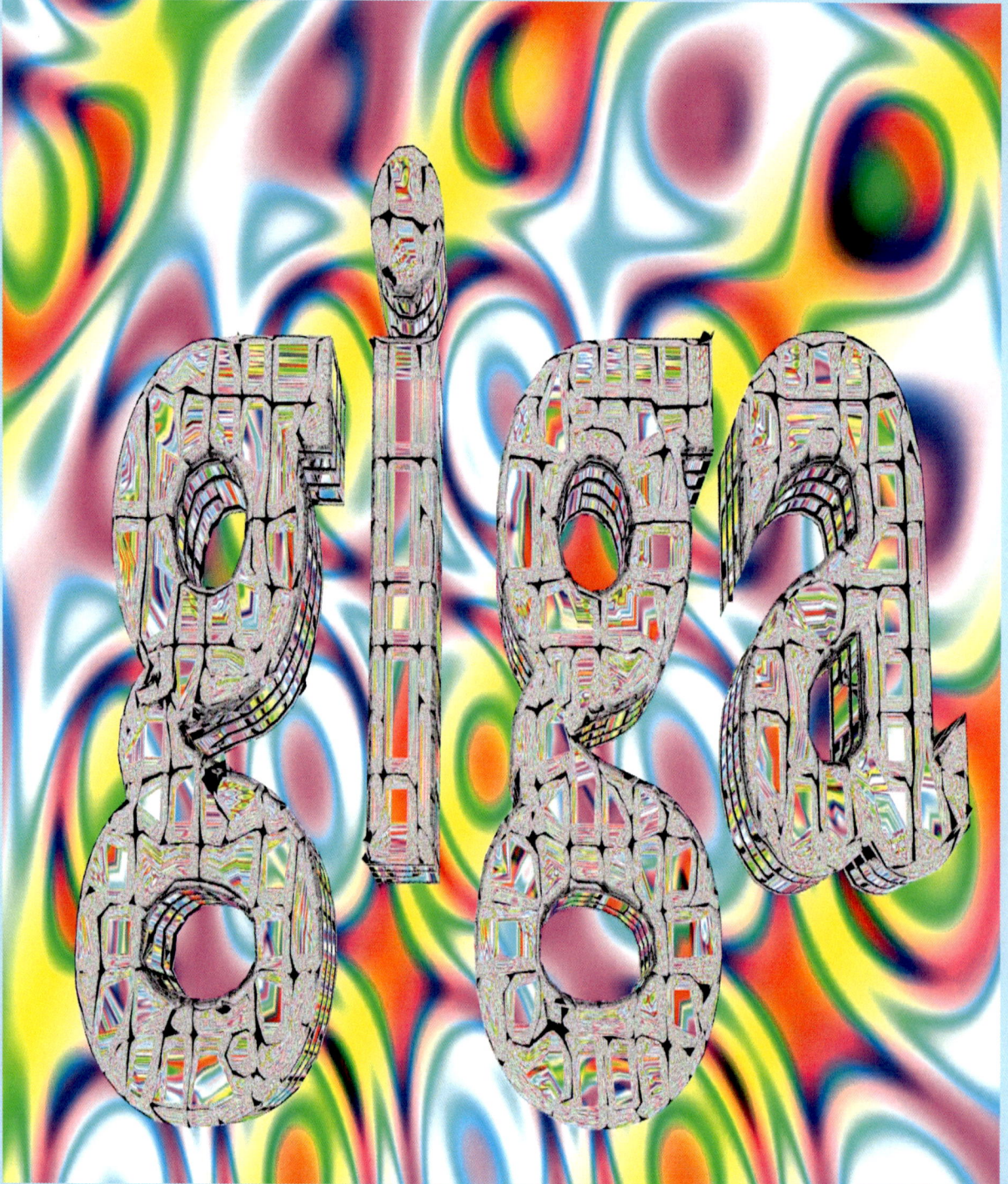

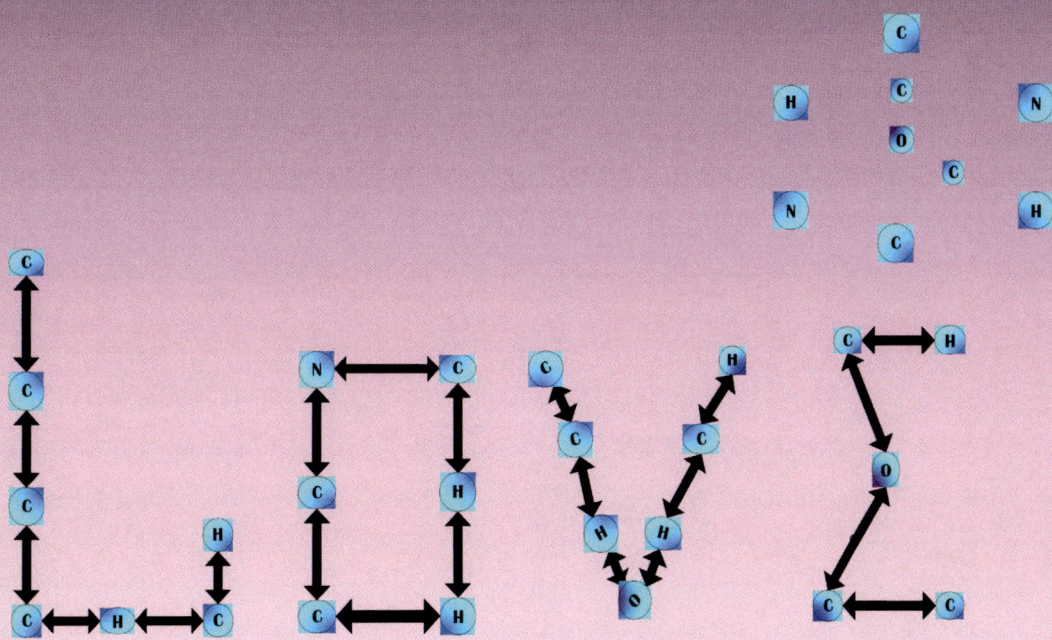

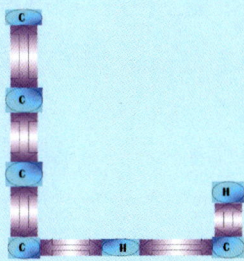
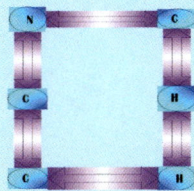
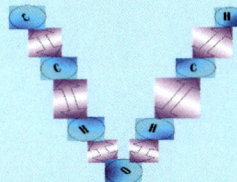
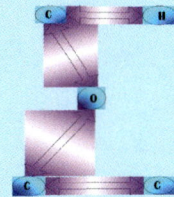
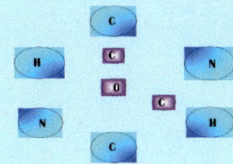

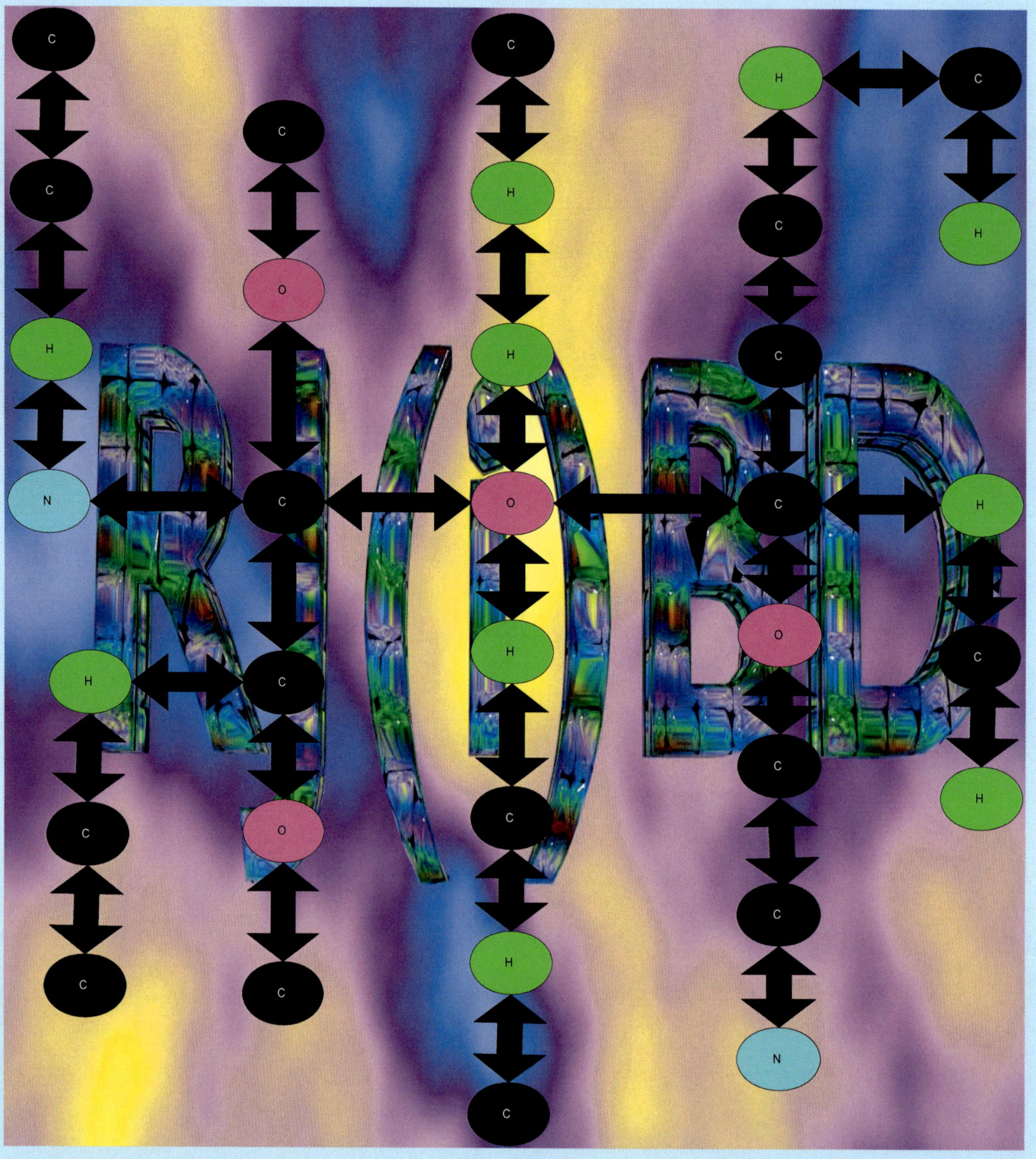

RIB

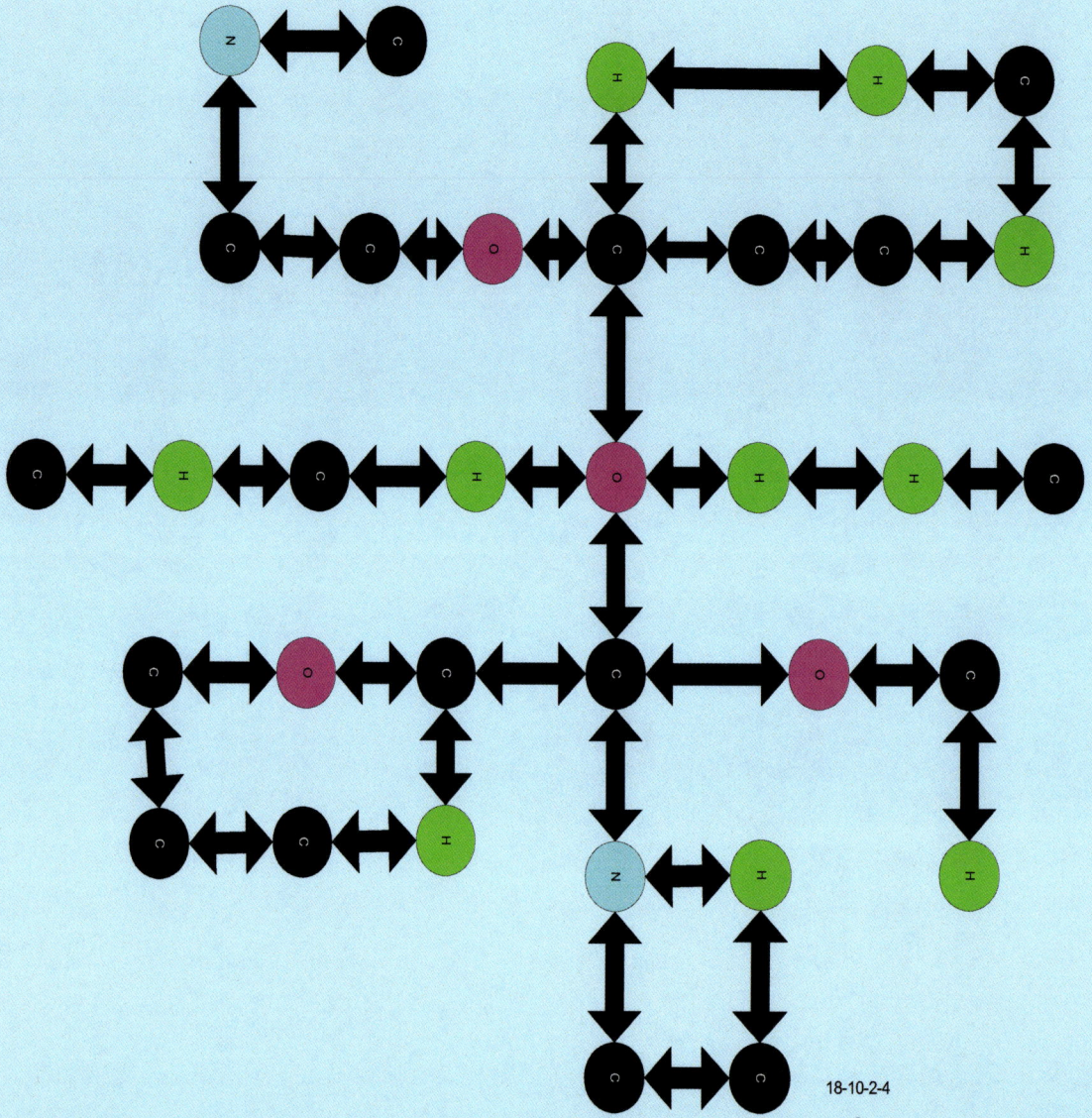

18-10-2-4
©

C18H10N2O4

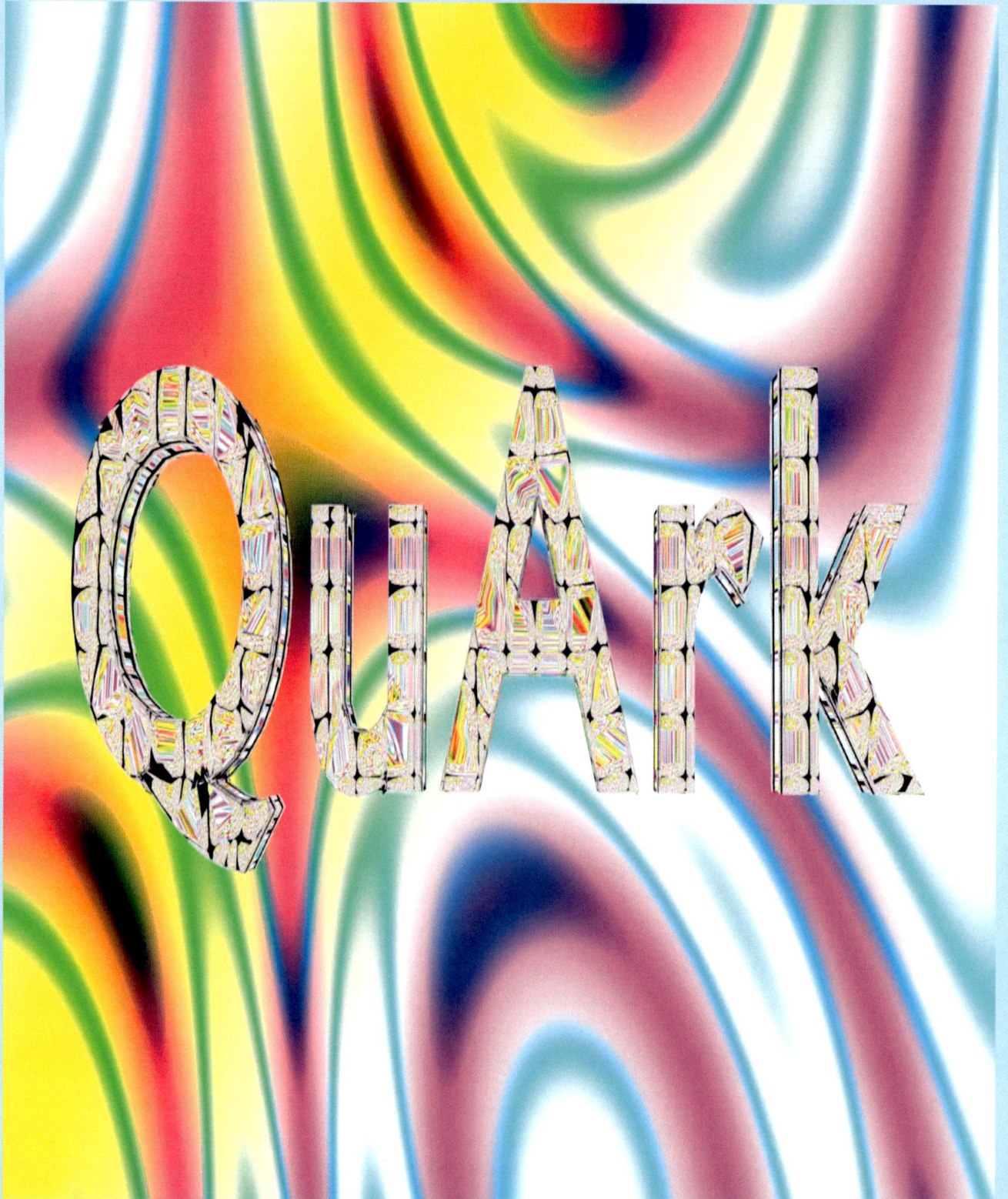